CARADON & LOOE
THE CANAL, RAILWAYS AND MINES

R. Derek Sach

CARADON & LOOE
THE CANAL, RAILWAYS AND MINES

BY
MICHAEL MESSENGER

TWELVEHEADS PRESS

TRURO 2015

CONTENTS

Introduction 5
Chapter 1   Beginnings 9
Chapter 2   The Canal 15
Chapter 3   Horses and Gravity 25
Chapter 4   The Steam Railways 36
Chapter 5   Hopes and Despair 53
Chapter 6   Change of Direction 66
Chapter 7   The Great Western and After 82
Chapter 8   From the Sea to the Moor 94
Chapter 9   Locomotives and Rolling Stock 122
Chapter 10 Men and Machines 141
Chapter 11 The Future 153
                Sources and acknowledgements 154
                Bibliography 155
                References 156
Appendices:
1   Chronology 158
2   Traffic figures and accounts 159
3   Copper and tin production of the Caradon District 161
4   Locomotive and Rolling Stock details 162
5   Early Byelaws and Regulations 163
6   Borlase Childs' memories 164
7   Mines around Caradon Hill 165
Index 167

Units of measurement and money used in this book are those which were concurrent with events described. They may be converted as follows:
Money: £1 =   20 shillings (s) = 100 pence (p)
                  1 guinea = 21 shillings
                  1 shilling = 12 pence (d)
Length: 1 mile = 8 furlongs = 80 chains = 1,760 yards = 1.6093 kilometres
                  1 yard = 3 feet = 36 inches = 0.9144 metres
                  1 fathom = 6 feet
Weight   1 ton = 20 hundredweight (cwt) = 1.016 tonnes

All rights reserved. No part of this publication may be reproduced or transmitted in any form
or by any means without the prior permission of the publisher.
© Michael Messenger 2015.

TWELVEHEADS PRESS

First published 1978 by Twelveheads Press.
Second edition 2001 by Twelveheads Press
Third edition 2015 by Twelveheads Press
2 Woodside Cottages, Chacewater, Truro, Cornwall TR4 8LP.
ISBN 978 0 906294 82 6
British Library Cataloguing-in-Publication Data.
A catalogue record for this book is available from the British Library.
Printed by Short Run Press Ltd, Exeter

INTRODUCTION

This is a local story; a story of a local canal serving local farmers and two local railways serving local mines and industries. All were created and run, more or less, by Cornish people using their own capital and resources. Why then should such enterprises generate an interest that extends well beyond parish boundaries?

The canal came first, engineered by a surveyor and a clockmaker to successfully meet agricultural needs and was a rare feature in the Cornish landscape. Then came the wealth of Caradon Hill and a pressing need to transport hundreds of thousands of tons of copper ore and granite to the sea. So the surveyor skilfully engineered a railway – a gravity railway – to meet the canal and in due course, as the canal became overwhelmed with traffic, another railway replaced it. Allied to these developments the harbour at Looe was being expanded to cater for the self-same traffic in copper and granite, and other industries – explosives and foundries – were establishing themselves.

Like all local enterprises these ventures had their idiosyncrasies and very individual characters. The 'free' passenger service to Caradon, although it lasted but a dozen years, has caught the public imagination and always makes a good yarn. The technologies of both canal and railways were behind the times when

CARADON & LOOE – THE CANAL, RAILWAYS AND MINES

The port of Looe came into being because of the mineral wealth brought down by canal and railway from Caradon Hill. Although this had ceased when this photograph was taken about 1902 there was still much commercial traffic. The MARY OF GLASGOW was a regular visitor to Looe at that time and the wagons, at the far south of the quay lines, are laden with imported coal. They are Caradon six-ton wagons with end screw brakes but now lettered 'L. & L'. No 62 is nearest the camera while the furthest appears to be No 67.
ROYAL INSTITUTION OF CORNWALL

new and always remained so, but they worked and the transport system – rail or water – serviced its community. The independent minds of the directors of the two lines also manifest themselves in various ways, whether by ignoring or evading Parliament's strictures when it suited or by fighting their own corners despite the close links and interdependence. The romance of the riches of the Caradon mines has also contributed to the indefinable aura that surrounds the railways that served them.

When one endeavours to consider the achievements of the railways and the canal in relation to the local communities and industries one is faced with a chicken and egg situation for the railways and canal, mines and quarries and, indeed, Looe Harbour were all reliant on each other and would not have existed alone. A good half million tons of copper ore were carried to Looe and more than a hundred thousand tons of granite. How much coal went the opposite way to be burned in the boilers of the mines on Bodmin Moor can only be guessed at.

Both the railways came into being solely because of the mineral wealth of Caradon Hill; they were instigated to serve the copper mines and granite quarries and serve them they did, but when the death knell sounded for the mines

INTRODUCTION

and quarries it sounded for the railways also. However, they struggled on to survive into the twentieth century and to be connected with the national network. Financial problems meant both railway companies became swallowed up by the vast Great Western Railway and thus became part of the fame of that empire.

In some ways the association with the GWR is to be regretted for it has meant that the two railways have often been thought of as mere offshoots of that empire and frequently in recent writings they have been regarded as simple branch lines. Whilst the Looe branch might, at first glance today, appear to be simply that, the Looe company was in fact independent for more than twice as long as it was a GWR branch and the Liskeard & Caradon Railway was a GWR branch for but seven and a half years of its seventy year working life.

When reading this story the reader must put away notions of how canals and railways appear in the present day. Even the most neglected branch of our current national rail system is a motorway in comparison to the country lanes of the Caradon and Looe lines. Imagine two almost parallel lines of flimsy wrought iron rail running down a dirt track, sometimes standing proud of the ground perched on top of a row of

This view characterises the scene on the branch during much of the twentieth century and as remembered by most people who can recall the days of steam when the line was, essentially, a Great Western Railway branch. In July 1951, 5521 runs around its train at Coombe Junction before heading on down the valley to Looe. But behind 5521 is Lamellion Bridge, as it was built in 1860 and a firm reminder of the line's origins as a mineral railway.
P. W. B. SEMMENS

CARADON & LOOE – THE CANAL, RAILWAYS AND MINES

granite blocks. There are no sweeping curves, more a series of corners, and indeed there are sometimes 'corners' on straight lengths of track. Down this runs a rather agricultural timber wagon, lurching and jumping at the rail joints and curves, and atop this sits a dusty conductor trying to juggle the screw brake to stop it going too fast but not so slow that it stops. If the whole contraption gets to Moorswater without coming off the rails he is grateful.

Similarly the remote, lonely and beautiful moorland setting of Caradon Hill today belies the tremendous industrial activity it saw in the middle of the nineteenth century. Up to 2,000 people could have been working here, above and below ground, and it needs an account such as that of Wilkie Collins, reproduced in part in Chapter 3, to describe adequately the almost unimaginable scene at that time.

The canal too bore little comparison to the neatly manicured lengths of the modern English canal network. We are fortunate now to have some photographs of the canal when it was working and these, with their rugged lock beams crafted from a handy tree trunk, speak volumes. The boatmen also had their problems. Too little water, for example, and they were hauling their craft bodily over the mud. A working canal really did mean work and this is the background to the history of these transport systems.

Specific claims to fame include the Kilmar Railway as the highest railway in Cornwall, being almost entirely over 1,000 feet above sea level throughout its length. The Liskeard & Caradon Railway was a rare example of a nineteenth century railway built for gravity working and the Liskeard & Looe Union Canal Company's railway was one of the few light railways authorised under the Regulation of Railways Act 1868. Something to be less proud of was the use of granite blocks in the permanent way well into the twentieth century, even for passenger trains, albeit a possibly unique survival.

This then is a unique story of a transport system built to meet a specific need: to service the bonanza of Caradon copper, a mining discovery that germinated, blossomed, withered and died all within fifty years. It is a story of ingenuity and capability, of independence and interdependence, of hope and despair. It could only have happened in Victorian Britain.

A trip to Looe on the branch line even today soon reveals to the observant traveller that this is a railway with a difference, albeit during the twentieth century it changed its character drastically. After the Great War its development and decline, and twenty-first century revival, follows that of so many other railway branch lines throughout the country. Gerry Beale has captured well the atmosphere of the Great Western branch in his *The Liskeard and Looe Branch*. I make no apology, therefore, for placing the emphasis on the earlier independent history when the system was a unique feature of the Cornish landscape. This is, after all, a local story.

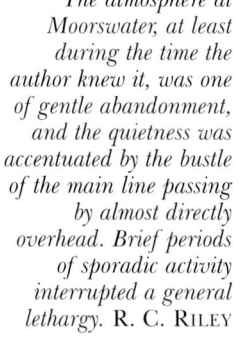

The atmosphere at Moorswater, at least during the time the author knew it, was one of gentle abandonment, and the quietness was accentuated by the bustle of the main line passing by almost directly overhead. Brief periods of sporadic activity interrupted a general lethargy. R. C. RILEY

CHAPTER ONE
BEGINNINGS

The utility and very great benefit that will arise to Liskeard and its neighbourhood, from the adoption of so important an improvement, is clearly understood and we hope the design will be speedily carried into effect.
ROYAL CORNWALL GAZETTE, 1823

At the end of the eighteenth century Liskeard was a prosperous market town with a rich agricultural hinterland. Granted a Charter in 1240 by Prince Richard, Earl of Cornwall and brother to Henry III, the town had returned representatives to Parliament since 1294. Daniel Defoe in 1724 found it 'a fashionable town' and well built, while Marshall in 1796 reported it 'a large populous decent looking place [that] would appear respectable in any part of the Kingdom'. Self sufficient for many manufactured goods, other necessities came through the quay at St Germans, ten miles to the south east, and over the turnpike road from Torpoint that had commenced building in 1770. Although since Elizabeth I's reign Liskeard had been a coinage town, for the payment of dues on tin, no tin had passed through the town for many years and the ancient open workings at the foot of the Cheesewring had contributed nothing to the wealth of the district.[1]

The farms surrounding the town were small but well cultivated, while to the north the downs and moors were reckoned to be some of the most profitable grazing in Cornwall. As in the rest of the county, the acid soil needed liberal dressings of 'manure'. On the north coast sea sand provided the necessary improvement (and was later responsible for the births of the Bude Canal and the Bodmin & Wadebridge Railway) but the south for some years had also made use of the limestone of the Plymouth area and a string of limekilns ran up the East Looe valley. Some four or five tons per acre were spread each year and at the appropriate season the kilns would be burning day and night, a steady stream of packhorses trudging to and fro taking the burnt lime to the fields. It took 14½ tons of limestone to make 100 bushels (double Winchester bushels of 150lbs) of lime. Carts and waggons did not come into general use in Cornwall until early in the nineteenth century (the first to be built in Liskeard was said to be a clumsy device in 1796) and all goods travelled on the backs of horses. It is not surprising that more modern means of transport were considered.

In 1774 Edmund Leach, of Stoke Climsland, had made a survey of the Tamar Valley for a canal and in the summer of 1777 he was asked by an unknown Liskeard 'gentleman' to do the same for the Looe River. Leach was a proponent of contour canals [2] and suggested a line starting at Banka Mill, a mile and three-quarters north west of Liskeard, and following the 300 feet contour. After passing close to Liskeard town 'a machine' would return the level to that of the river to save excessive meanderings around side valleys and it then continued close to the 100

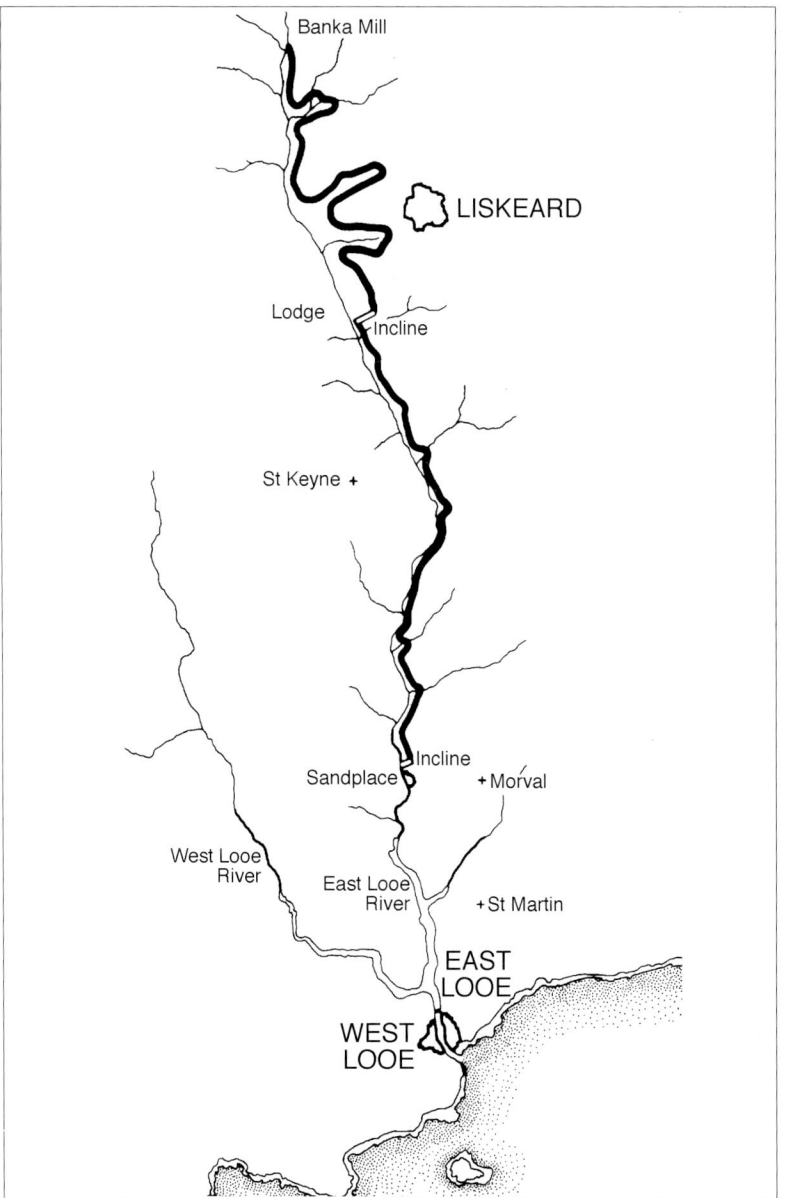

Edmund Leach's proposal of 1777 was for a contour canal, with two level sections linked by an incline plane. A further incline would have taken boats to and from the river at Sandplace.

> **PROMISES** of Support having been lately made, towards the completion of an Object which has long been contemplated as desirable, by many of the Inhabitants of LOOE, LISKEARD, and the neighbouring Parishes, (viz.) *The Improvement of the Communication between these two Towns;* either by A TURNPIKE ROAD, A RAIL ROAD, OR CANAL, FROM LOOE, BY SAND-PLACE, TO LOOE MILLS: IT is hereby requested, that such Gentlemen as may approve of either of the proposed undertakings, will meet at the *Town Hall in Liskeard,* on TUESDAY the 5th Day of AUGUST next, at 11 o'Clock in the Forenoon, *to take into consideration the merits of the respective Plans;* ESTIMATES of which, will be then submitted.
>
> *PETER GLUBB.*
>
> LISKEARD, 10th. July, 1823.   [BOASE, Printer, Liskeard.]

Peter Glubb's notice calling a meeting of interested parties on 5 August 1823. In the event, the meeting was held on Saturday 2 August.

feet contour. Another inclined plane at Sandplace would have lowered the boats and their cargoes to the river, which here was tidal and navigable. Although by river it was only about eight miles between Banka Mill and Sandplace, Leach's canal would have wound along some fifteen miles of hillside, thus bringing the benefits of cheaply transported lime to some ninety six square miles of potentially good land.

He estimated the cost at £17,495, including £1,000 for each of the two 'machines' or inclined planes, but he thought this could be reduced somewhat by using convict labour. The inclined planes would be worked by water wheels or by the convicts in 'walking wheels'. Leach also suggested a canal to Tideford, near St Germans, but his gentleman must have lost enthusiasm for the idea of a canal to Liskeard as nothing was done.

The next recorded scheme was surveyed under the patronage of Lord Eliot by George Bentley and Thomas Bolton who were then, in 1795, working on several west country canals. Their line was to run from the end of Market Street, Liskeard, to Lodge Barton and thence down the valley to Steps, below Sandplace, but the large number of locks required between Liskeard and Lodge ruled it out, although the survey was to come in useful some years later.[3]

On 10 July 1823 Peter Glubb, a Liskeard solicitor, issued a notice calling a meeting at the Town Hall, Liskeard, to consider 'the improvement of the Communication between these two Towns; either by a Turnpike Road, a Rail Road, or Canal, from Looe, by Sandplace, to Looe Mills'. The meeting was duly held on 2 August – not the fifth as stated in the notice – attended by Sir Edward Buller, the two Mayors of Looe and 'many other gentlemen of the neighbourhood' and, after agreement as to the general benefit, a committee was appointed 'to sit and make progress'.[4] A week later a similar meeting at East Looe also gave its blessing to the plan. The committee made progress and wrote to James Green who made even greater progress by giving his report twelve days later on 30 August.

James Green was engaged in the enlargement of the Exeter Canal at this time and a few years earlier had been engineer to the Bude Canal. He had been assistant to John Rennie before becoming County Bridge Surveyor in Devon in 1808, a position he discharged with notable distinction. He therefore had much experience to draw on. His report[5] was based on a previous survey, undoubtedly Bentley and Bolton's, with much additional information from a Liskeard land-surveyor, Robert Coad, hence its rapid appearance. Green reported as requested on the possibilities of a turnpike, railroad and canal but had little experience or liking of railroads. The road would have been the cheapest to construct but the main traffic envisaged, lime, would be free of toll and the income from other traffic, £150, would not have been worthwhile. The canal would cost under £14,000 and, he estimated, have a net income of £906 compared with £10,500 and £467 respectively for the railroad and £6,700 and £150 for the road. If the canal's tolls were increased by one-third the net income would be £1,325. 23,481 tons of estimated traffic would travel up the canal but only 1,500 tons down and the transport costs saved by canal users would amount to £3,598. A tub-boat canal was proposed with four-ton boats travelling in trains and height would be gained by two inclined planes. Green felt there to be too little water for the number of locks required for the rise of 180 feet in 6¼ miles, foreseeing shortage in summer and trouble with the mills of the valley. The lower section was to be wider and deeper to permit the existing stone-barges to reach Sandplace and Causeland.

The committee must have been impressed, for on 10 September Peter Glubb issued a notice of intent to go to Parliament with a Bill for a canal from Moorswater to Terras Pill, fed by a leat from Trekeive Lake, near Redgate, together with powers for harbour improvements at Looe, tramroads to Redgate and a turnpike road to Liskeard. A week later a meeting resolved to employ Green to 'draw a map and apply to Parliament'. The committee appeared well supported, for on 27 September the *Royal Cornwall Gazette* reported nearly three-quarters of the shares had been subscribed for in less than a fortnight. Putting one's name down to subscribe, however, is a different matter to putting the cash down and after the plan of the canal had been deposited with the Clerk of the Peace at the end of September all went quiet. John Buller later reported that not only had there been very strong opposition from Lostwithiel and Fowey but there was a 'weakness of the proprietors in a pecuniary point of view and other insuperable obstacles'.[6]

The following year the scheme was revived again and on 21 December 1824 a meeting at Liskeard, chaired by Lord Eliot, considered reports by James Green, a Mr Hitchins and son, George Bentley (the partner of Bolton) and by Robert Coad and Richard Retallick. The meeting resolved

> that the Plan of a Canal by Locks from the Tideway at Tarras Hill [*sic*] near Looe to Moorswater near Liskeard, a distance of about six miles with a Towing Path of sufficient width for Gentlemen's Carriages and for a road to be opened from Looe Mills, near the head of the canal, to Banka Mill, about one mile from Moorswater to Liskeard, is perfectly practicable, and that it will greatly increase the trade of the Three Towns, contribute highly to the improvement of the Land in the several Parishes to the North of the Canal by facilitating the conveyance of Manure, be equally advantageous to the Mines and valuable Moor Stone Quarries in its vicinity, and be of lasting benefit to the Neighbourhood in general.[7]

The cost was estimated at £12,500 and a nineteen-man committee of management was appointed.

The mention of a towpath sufficiently wide for carriages is not without significance. John Buller, Member of Parliament for Exeter, owned a substantial estate at Morval, including the village of Sandplace through which the canal was to run. Buller was opposed to the canal on what are now called environmental grounds – it would destroy the beauty of the valley and his private roads and woods would be subject to continual trespass – but in view of the obvious strong local support for the scheme he had not made his feelings known. Owing to opposition elsewhere, however, his Parliamentary support was needed and the committee obtained this by the promise of a good carriage road into Liskeard. Buller also agreed, verbally, that if the works were completed as planned he would make no charge for his land, provided his tenants were satisfied.

Opposition came from the Corporations of Lostwithiel and Fowey who feared the canal feeder would deplete the waters of the Fowey River. William Rashleigh and Vice Admiral Sir Charles Vinnicombe Penrose, KCB, also petitioned against the Bill[8] but, with the help of John Buller and his friends, it was passed by both Houses and received the Royal Assent on 22 June 1825. Such was the support for the canal that in March, when returning from giving evidence to the Parliamentary Committee, Richard Retallick

> was met about three miles from Liskeard by above 600 persons, who took the horses from the chaise and pulled him in by hand – all the music that could be mustered walking before and playing 'See the conquering hero comes'[9]

and Peter Glubb was afforded a similar reception when the Bill completed its journey through Parliament.

Although similarities remained James Green's report was completely disregarded and the canal was constructed to the plans of Coad and Retallick.

The Act, 6 George IV cap.clxiii, incorporated the Liskeard & Looe Union Canal Company and consisted of 135 clauses covering all aspects of the construction and operation of

The Company Seal of the Liskeard & Looe Union Canal as preserved in the Great Western Railway Museum at Swindon. The Latin motto 'Non nobis solum' can be translated as 'Not for us alone', indicating perhaps the motives of the canal proprietors. In fact no example of the use of this seal has been found by the author and the more common one depicts a typical English narrow boat against a background of a wooded hillside.
AUTHOR'S COLLECTION

the canal. The authorised capital was £13,000 in £25 shares and was to be fully subscribed before work commenced; the Act stated £10,450 was already subscribed. If this proved insufficient £10,000 could be borrowed on mortgage. The canal was to be completed within five years.

Water could be taken from the Looe River and from the Crylla stream, although the latter was strictly controlled to protect the waters of the River Fowey. The water passing under Lostwithiel Bridge was to be measured and no more than one fifty-fourth of this figure could be used in April, May, June, August, September and October. In other months the key of the sluices was to be kept by the Mayor of Lostwithiel. During the months they could be opened the sluices were to be closed within two hours of the reservoir filling and could not be re-opened until it was down to 1,000 cubic yards of water. Two surveyors were to be appointed, one by Lostwithiel Corporation and one by the Canal Company, who were to superintend and enforce these stipulations.

The deposited plans show the canal running on the west side of the Looe River to just below Trussel Bridge where it crosses and runs thence to Moorswater on the east side. The plans deposited with the Clerk of the Peace and with the House of Lords, both drawn by Robert Coad, differ slightly in that feeders running parallel and above the canal are shown on the former. Roads are marked from Moorswater to Banka Mill and to Liskeard.

John Edgcumbe, civil engineer, and Thomas Esterbrook, architect and builder, had estimated to Parliament the total cost to be £12,577 for just under six miles of canal, 26 feet wide at surface, 14 feet at bottom and four feet deep. 134 people, almost all local, had put their names down as subscribers and included the Lord Eliot (£150), Sir William Pringle (£100), Rowland Stephenson (£1,500, the largest), John Buller (£500), Sir Manassah Massa Lopez, Bart (£525), the Hon. John Walpole (£625), Messrs Glubb & Lyne (£500), Davies Gilbert (£125) and Thomas Bond (£75). Most of the remainder were small subscribers for one or two shares only.[10]

Some of the names had changed by the time the Act was printed; one notable omission being John Edgcumbe, who had been involved in various canal schemes elsewhere for many years previous. Neither he nor Thomas Esterbrook receive any subsequent mention in the records of the canal and one wonders if these are two of the 'early friends' obliquely referred to at the first General Meeting as deserting the project.

Within a month of the passing of the Act, on Tuesday 19 July, a party of shareholders complete with band went from Liskeard to Terras Pill where, having met a similar party from East and West Looe, Peter Glubb ceremoniously turned the first turf. The party then returned to the Town Hall, Liskeard, for the first General Meeting, where thanks were given to numerous people including the Earl of St Germans, the Lord Eliot and Davies Gilbert for their support. Peter Glubb, in particular, was thanked for his zeal at all times, mention being made of the 'arduous struggle' and 'powerfully combined opposition'. Richard Retallick was thanked for his devotion to the cause and for 'keeping alive the project when some of its early friends deserted it' and Robert Coad for a 'very scientific report in answer to the report of the opposed engineer'. Regrettably the House of Commons records were badly depleted in a fire in 1834 and fuller details of this opposition do not survive. No doubt they would have given a clue to the strange formula for drawing water from the Crylla stream.

After the meeting

a dinner was served in the Hall to between two and three hundred gentlemen; four hogsheads of cider were given to the multitude, and bread and meat distributed to the poor. The evening was spent in the utmost hilarity, and in joyous anticipation of the benefits that will be derived by the neighbourhood from the projected undertaking.[11]

Robert Coad, the company's engineer, was soon at work, making plans and preparing for the construction. Richard Retallick was appointed Superintendent of the Works and construction commenced on 6 September. The canal was ordered to be started at Lodge, Landlooe and Terras and the first lock was to be at Lodge. The boats were to be of 20 tons capacity and within a month it was decided to buy one to carry stone down part of the canal that was ready; the company were quarrying stone themselves along the route. By November a mile of the canal was excavated and hopes were high that it would be built within the original estimate. In mid-November the first boat was launched at Coombe.

Robert Rean, a shareholder of East Looe, was appointed Surgeon and Apothecary and 6d per month was to be deducted from the wages of each employee to pay for his services. Although unusual in canal practice sick clubs of this nature were common in the mines of west Cornwall. It is not recorded whether Mr Rean's services were often called upon.

The second General Meeting was held in February 1826 and some discord is apparent. A motion that 'a civil engineer properly qualified'

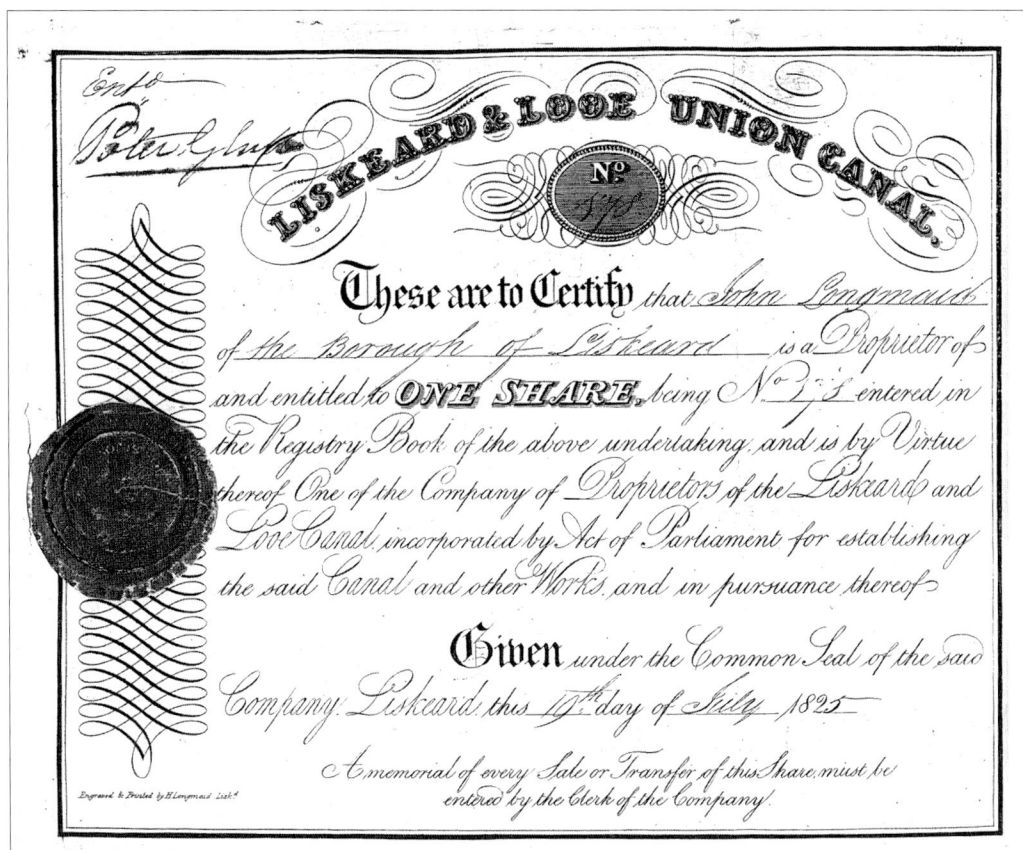

A LLUC share certificate dated 19 July 1825 representing one share of £25. John Longmaid was a director for twelve years from 1826. Peter Glubb has signed the certificate, top left, to show that he had entered it in the register of shareholders.

be called to inspect the works and report on Coad and Retallick was defeated 49 votes to 10 and at the subsequent election four out of the nine members of the Committee of Management changed. Soon after, the Committee became concerned at the rate of expenditure; £8 had been called up on each share but was not coming in too well. Some of the works were to be let by tender and the labourers' contracts were to include all tools, sharpening and repairing, except wheelbarrows and planks, the former to be made by the company's workmen instead of bought.

In June it was observed that only £10,875 was subscribed, although the Act specified all the £13,000 capital was to be subscribed for before work started. To get over this, suitable proprietors were approached to increase their subscriptions and, in September when the Solicitor, Peter Glubb, was suing those proprietors who had not met the calls on their shares, these 'certain gentlemen', who included Glubb, were exempted from meeting calls. A Special General Meeting in May 1827 ratified all previous meetings, when the company should not have been operating, and at another, in June 1828, the shares additionally subscribed for were all forfeit, not a penny having been paid on them.

By June 1826 several locks were completed and to celebrate their re-election as Members of Parliament for Liskeard Lord Eliot and Sir William Pringle visited the canal, accompanied by the inevitable band, and 'in the presence of 1,000 people who lined its banks, passed and repassed the locks in a boat'. After pronouncing themselves pleased with progress, the Members returned to the town and a handsome dinner at Mr Webb's hostelry.[12]

Progress was not all it appeared, however, as some difficulties were being encountered at the other end of the line. A Mr Eliot owned land on the west side of the river, where the canal was intended to be, but was holding out for over-high compensation. John Buller agreed for the line to be on his side of the river, the east, and again agreed to make no charge for any land providing the carriage road was built and his tenants suitably compensated for damage and inconvenience. However, when his promised road showed no signs of materialising he began to be uneasy, for not only this but what towpath there was was so narrow, rough and often flooded he could neither walk nor ride on it. The company pleaded lack of funds but needed Buller's favour as they were even then considering extending the canal down to Looe and would need his support, and land. Land had proved more expensive than anticipated – they had petitioned the Duchy of Cornwall to waive or reduce the costs of land – and money was short. The shareholders were concerned at the number of calls and one landowner at least had been asked if he would accept 4% interest until he could be paid. Buller also demanded, as compensation, bridges at Terras over canal and river as well as improvements to his roads and lands that were damaged as a result of the canal's construction. The Committee willingly agreed, for promises were easy to make, but little was done. Buller realised the road would seriously embarrass the company's funds and did not pursue it too hard although he complained bitterly to his solicitor:

> I feel it however to be a great sacrifice that I am making to them for a good Carriage Road up the Valley would have been the greatest comfort imaginable to me and I still earnestly wish it could be carried into effect.

As the canal proceeded his complaints grew. At Sandplace his limekilns were now cut off from the river bank by the new channel and although he had demanded access as before, in other words free use of the canal as he had used the river, three of his tenants had already agreed to pay 1d per ton toll. The arguments dragged on for some years, Counsel's opinions sought by Buller were not very helpful to him, and eventually he settled, grudgingly, for £600 and a bridge over the canal at Terras. In return the company granted him free use of the canal as far as Plashford for himself and his tenants and free use of the towpath.[13]

At least part of the canal was brought into use on 27 August 1827 for the carriage of coals, bringing a sharp drop in the price of that commodity in Liskeard, and shortly after Drakewalls Tin-Smelting Company began exporting through Looe, although this latter traffic appears short-lived. The following March the *Royal Cornwall Gazette* reported that the canal was in full use but in June the lock at Terras was still not complete. The rates of toll set in June were rescinded in September and replaced with a simplified, slightly cheaper, list which excluded wharfage. They were, per ton per mile:

Limestone, culm or coals therefor,
   building stone, road stone and clay 1½d
Sand and manure..2d
Burnt lime 3d
Grain, flour and potatoes, coals,
   culm, salt, timber deals, brick, tiles,
   and junk 6d
Metallic ores and smelted metals..................4d
All other goods, wares and
   merchandise, hay, straw, cattle,
   calves, sheep and swine, farm stock 8d
Exclusive of wharfage and cellarage.

Later that month a special meeting of the Committee of Management agreed a set of ten Byelaws for the regulation of traffic. Several were concerned with saving water or protecting the property and works of the company; No 7 forbade horses to browse on the fences [*sic*] of the towpath. Others restricted the hours the canal could be used and directed that the owner's name and number should be painted on each side of the stern of his boat. Fines varied from ten shillings to five pounds. See Appendix 5 for the full set of Byelaws.

Although apparently in full use the canal was not altogether complete. Buller had complained of the slovenly and unfinished state of the works and the Minute Books bear this out. Quite a few major repairs were necessary as soon as May 1829 and the reservoir at Moorswater and the feeder from the Crylla were not completed until 1830.

So it was that Liskeard and Looe were connected by canal. Not a very great canal by English standards but important to the local community and economy. As canals go it was late upon the scene, although not the last Cornish canal, and it was really intruding into the Railway Age. However, a canal had been mooted for some fifty years, the eminent James Green had shown a marked preference for a waterway and the local men who built it undoubtedly felt more capable of building an established means of conveyance than a new-fangled railway. Only the Portreath Tramroad, a plateway, was in use in the county and Cornwall's first edge-railway, the Redruth & Chasewater, was still under construction at the time. Across the border the Plymouth & Dartmoor Railway had been operating since 1821 but had not proved a singular success. The Bude Canal was opened only a few years before and the next railway in the county, the Pentewan, was still in the planning stage, so the Liskeard & Looe Union Canal spanned the two ages, Canal and Railway, in Cornwall.

CHAPTER TWO
THE CANAL

Another of those beneficial schemes projected in modern times.
JOHN ALLEN, 1856

Having built its canal the Committee of Management got down to running it and to building roads to act as feeders. For the next few years the Committee's Minute Books are almost the only source of information on the canal but fortunately they reflect the mood and worries of the Committee well.

The road from Moorswater up into Liskeard at Dean Well was constructed during 1829, the estimated cost being £878 although Allen gives the final cost as £1,200.[1] The Minutes suggest this sum was raised by public subscription but it is not clear if it was or if by mortgage. The road rose steadily at gradients of between 1 in 19 and 1 in 29 and, as soon as it was open, traffic diverted to it from the steep turnpike. The Canal Company promptly demanded a subscription of £16 per annum from the Turnpike Trustees towards the maintenance and at the same time let out the collection of the tolls to John Short who had tendered £19 to do so. The road was always a bone of contention with the Liskeard Turnpike Trustees with whom it competed. In 1839 they complained of people evading their tolls by using the canal road and were permitted to erect a gate at Moorswater for people not on canal business. Nothing came of a proposal of 1851 to take over the road, nor of a complaint that the £16 repair charge was illegal. In fact two years later the Canal Company upped the charge to £21 and a somewhat empty gesture was made in 1881 when it was agreed that the Trustees could take over the road, for their powers were to expire in November that year. Liskeard Borough Council took control and, after some quibbling, the company made an annual grant of £15 towards its maintenance until 1888 when the payment was discontinued. The road continues to be the main approach from the west into Liskeard, although for through traffic it is now superseded by the by-pass.

In the spring of 1830 Coad surveyed a road from Looe Mills to Banka Mill and concluded the expense could not be justified. The 47 chains (1034 yards) to Highwood would cost £270 and the 57 chains (1254 yards) thence to Banka Mill another £350. He later amended these figures to £195 and £132 respectively on slightly different routes and considered this expense worthwhile if public subscriptions could be raised to build connecting roads to Lampretton, Trekeive Ford or even on to Palmers Bridge, east of Bolventor on the present A30. In the event only a length of road to Highwood appears to have been made in about 1835.

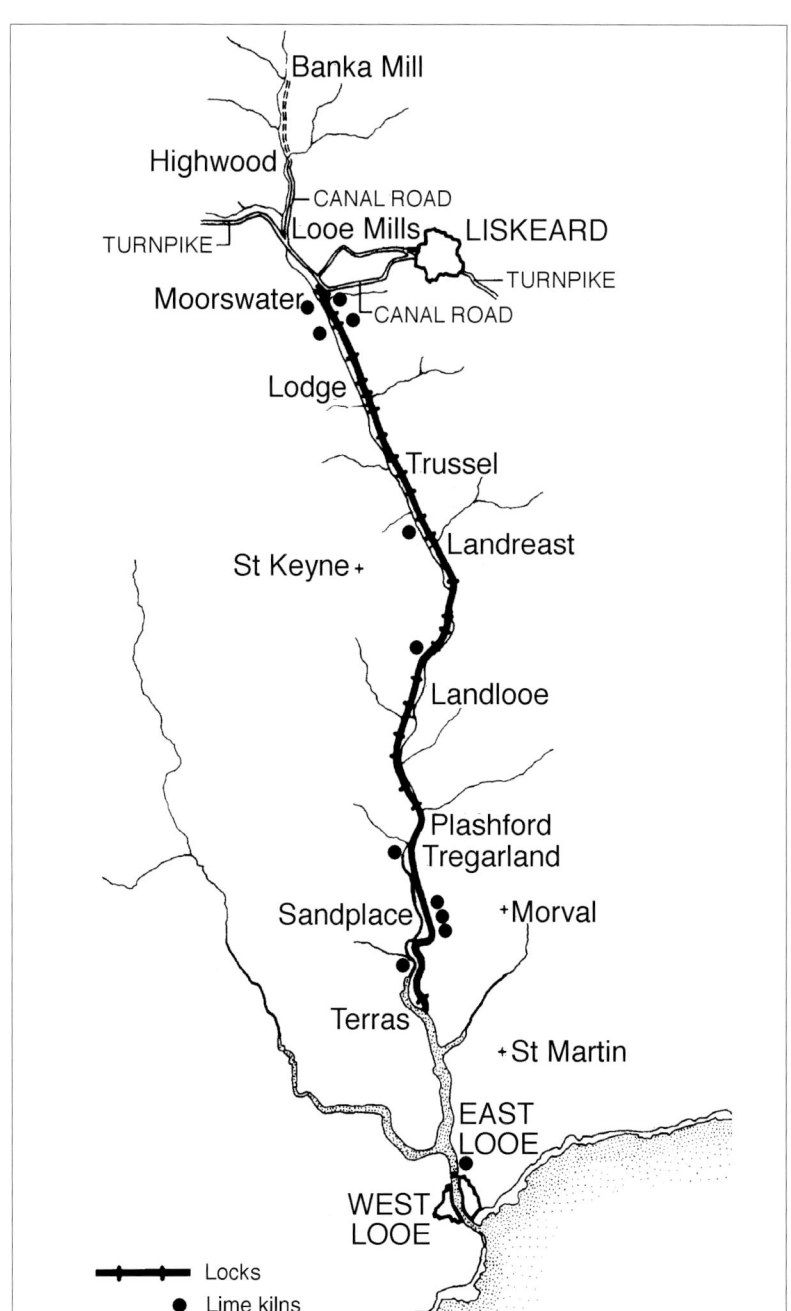

The Liskeard & Looe Union Canal, as built. Also shown are the canal roads to Liskeard and to Highwood and the proposed extension to Banka Mill.

15

A detail of a larger view across Moorswater, taken in the 1920s, showing Hodge's limekiln and the plateway ramp, still in place but not in use. Also visible are some of the earlier cottages and the sheds for storing and transshipping goods. LISKEARD OLD CORNWALL SOCIETY

Drawing of Hodge's limekiln at Moorswater showing the position of the water wheel and plateway turntable and ramp. William Hodge consulted with Robert Coad on the design and based it on one at Tavistock, which was similarly equipped. FROM A DRAWING BY MARTIN WATTS

The plateway turntable on the top of Hodge's kiln. It has been pushed up out of its seating by a sapling. Beyond can be seen another limekiln and the start of the Liskeard By-pass work. September 1974. M. J. MESSENGER

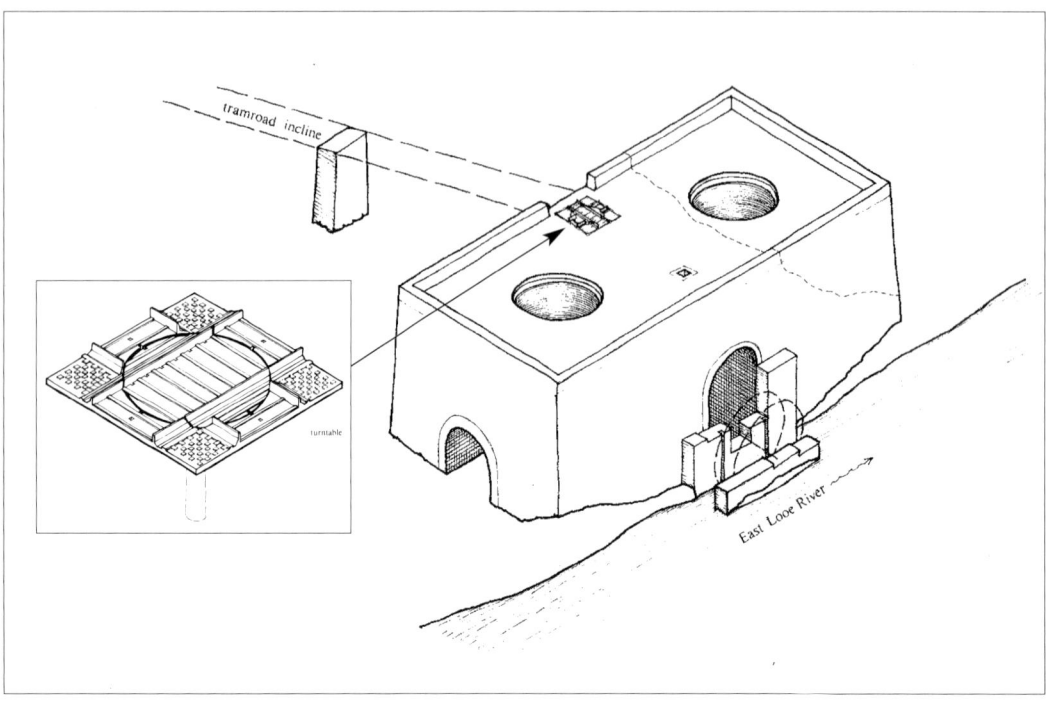

The purpose of the roads was to facilitate the distribution of lime and sea-sand from the head of the canal and thus, by making these manures available to a wider area, increase the traffic on the canal. The drop in price of coal when the waterway was opened has already been noted and the same happened to lime and sand. Sand dredged up from Talland and Lantivet bays in considerable quantities was formerly taken to Sandplace, hence the name of that village, at the head of navigation of the river. Now the head of navigation was transferred to Moorswater to the loss of Sandplace. Several limekilns were also built at Moorswater and elsewhere along the line, again to the detriment of Sandplace, and added to Buller's list of grievances. He complained that four out of seven kilns were now useless either because the trade had been transferred up the valley or the canal had cut them off from the river bank.

The loss of trade was inevitable, for farmers from the Liskeard and Dobwalls areas, for example, were not going to Sandplace for lime when they could get it at Moorswater. The ease with which it could be obtained now so far inland had increased demand considerably and the barges that brought the limestone from the Plymouth quarries were doing a roaring trade. Space at Looe on which to store the stone pending transfer to canal boats was somewhat restricted and in addition to seizing all the beaches the bargemen had taken control of a shingle bank that then existed in the harbour. By gaining the monopoly of supply they were able to charge 14d per ton to convey the stone instead of 12d as before. A petition to William IV was prepared asking that the Canal Company be permitted to lease the bank but little was done.[2] The lime boom proved shortlived and the shingle remained to be dredged in 1864.

Most of the traffic was up the canal and consisted mainly of limestone and sand, house coal and culm (small hard coal for burning the limestone), the Liskeard coal trade having transferred to Moorswater from St Germans. Some granite traffic had been hoped for from the east part of St Neot parish and an extension of the canal had been considered but found too expensive.[3] A little traffic found its way down the canal, tin blocks from Drakewalls and copper ore from St Neot, probably Wheal Mary, but it was small. A dividend of twenty five shillings – five per cent – was first paid in 1830, for the previous year, but income both before and after this date was used for capital expenditure.[4] A mortgage for £1,200 was given to William Glencross of Devonport in 1830 to be replaced two years later with another for £3,000 and, amongst other things, the latter enabled them to pay Buller's £600. Money was short and a close watch was kept on finances for some years. At first the company's books were in a 'confused state' and Mr Philp, later Treasurer, was paid £5 to examine and correct them, but not until 1843 was it ordered that all accounts should be in books, not on sheets of paper. Some anomalies in the toll collections were suspected and it was found that the toll clerks and collectors had not been 'so regular as they could have wished yet as more attention has been promised the Committee are satisfied'.

The company owned no boats itself, leaving this to the carriers and merchants who employed the boatmen, so the company had very few direct employees. The boatmen were drawn, not as one might expect, from the coastal sea-faring community, but from agricultural labourers.[5] Each 'Captain' obtained from the company's clerk at Looe, a Mr Tregenna, a 'check' which was handed in on entering the canal at Terras. The check showed what his cargo was so that the appropriate toll could be levied but evasion is evident for it became necessary for the lock at Tregarland, the first above Terras, to be padlocked to ensure a check was handed in. Accounts were rendered quarterly but were paid so dilatorily that it became necessary to call for security from the traders if credit was required. In 1834 the system was changed and payment was made on entering the canal, if credit was not arranged, and Tregenna was promptly discharged. Dividends were often held up until dues were paid. The boats held sixteen tons, although the byelaws specified eighteen tons as the minimum above Sandplace, and hauled by horses they took eight hours to navigate the canal.[6]

A good deal of time in the early 1830s was given to erecting cellars and wharves at Moorswater for the increasing trade. In 1832 a quay 130 feet long and 26 feet wide was laid for the lime trade of John Bowden & Co and a 'railroad' laid down on it. Tramways also connected the quays with the limekilns of William Hodge and John Lyne on the west and east sides of the canal head respectively. Waterwheels hauled wagons up inclines to the tops of the kilns; Hodge's tramway was a plateway of 30 inches gauge.

A section of the company's Act gave them powers to haul before the Magistrates anyone found swimming in the canal, with a maximum penalty of £2 or one month's hard labour. Alas, poor young Butters drowned whilst drunk and trying to float on some timber in the water in June 1833[6] but the Committee of Management solemnly resolved to take legal action against the next person found swimming in the canal.[7]

At the twelfth Annual General Meeting in February 1836 the shareholders were told of an increase in all traffic, except lime owing to the 'unprecedented agricultural distress'. The boom that followed the finish of the Napoleonic Wars was past its peak and the dividend was cut to £1 per share (4%) from the usual 5%. However, it was also reported

> that the neighbouring mines being about to be prosecuted with spirit and capital sufficient to ensure their success in which case there is every probability that the produce of the said mines will be shipped at Looe thereby affording back carriage to the boats employed on the canal which have now scarcely any back carriage.[8]

In the lee of Stow's Hill, north of Caradon Hill, Cornwall Great United Mines were preparing to search for tin but it was another venture that was to fulfil the Committee's hopes. In the meantime, though, the canal itself was occupying their attention.

Richard Retallick had been Superintendent from the start and took over as Clerk also from Peter Glubb in 1829 when his salary, including that of his assistant, was £80 a year. From Christmas 1831 he tendered to take charge of all repairs of the canal for £160 per year. This was accepted but his salary was cut to £15. Four years later the repairs were not proving all they should have been, if they had been done at all, although how much can be attributed to the shoddy workmanship Buller complained of can only be guessed at.

A long report showed every lock to be in urgent need of major repair with gates needing repairing and walls rebuilding. A set of gates was in a 'shattered condition', one lock was so muddy and weedy as to stop the passage of boats, while another was a 'very dangerous place owing to lack of foundations'. The necessary work was ordered to be put in hand but Retallick was eventually relieved of his contract, although he stayed as Clerk until 1854. Samuel Bone was given the contract, at £145 per year, but he proved little better and gave up the job in 1852, some years after he had asked to be released from it. After this the company seems to have done its own maintenance. The report of 1836, incidentally, confirms that only 24 locks were built whereas 25 were initially planned.

The boatmen operated most locks themselves but Terras had a succession of lock keepers whose duties included collecting cash tolls as boats entered the canal. John Howard held this position in 1851 when he was promoted to be 'lock keeper and policeman of the whole line', with a weekly wage of 16s plus a new suit annually. It would have been Howard who reported three boatmen in November 1856 for disobeying byelaws concerning the use of locks and water wastage.

On the west flank of Caradon Hill the Clymo party's perseverance was being rewarded by increasingly massive finds of copper (see Chapter 3) and the ores were soon finding their way to the quays at Moorswater. Apart from building more ore yards this increased downwards traffic did not seem to cause any

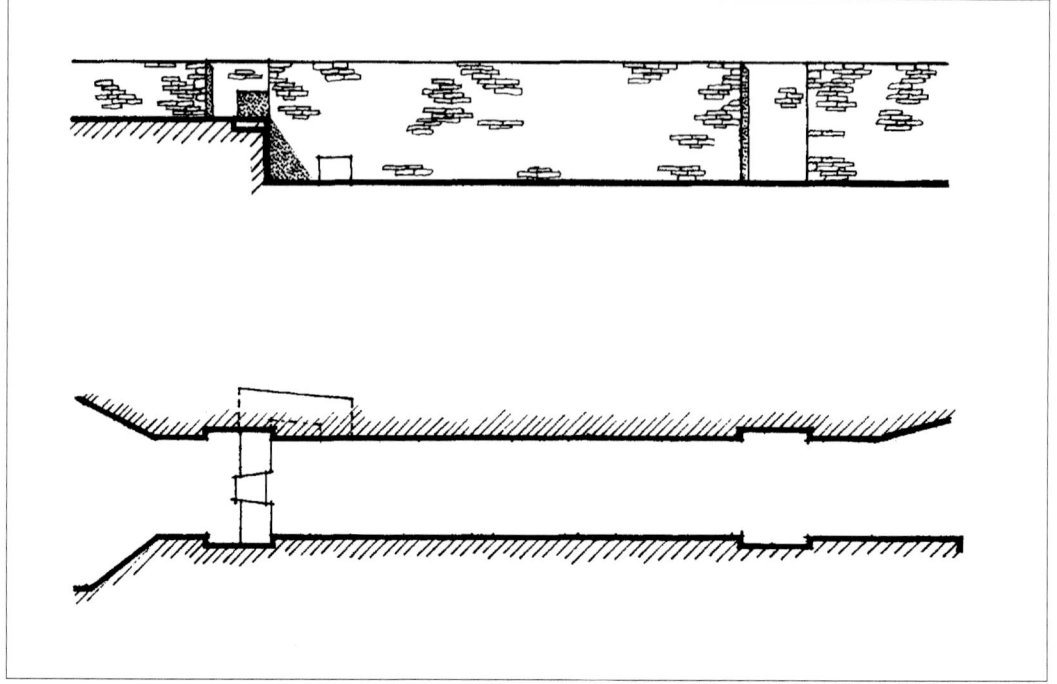

Plan and section of a typical canal lock. [Based on a survey by Peter Stanier.]

problems, although a shortage of water was anticipated. At this early stage the quantities involved were still less than the upward traffic and usefully filled otherwise empty boats.

Tolls on the canal had been collected by the company direct but for 1840 they were let, as in turnpike practice and as the Canal Road tolls had been since 1831, but the dividend the following year was held up as a result of the contractors being 'not yet ready with their moneys' and the practice was not repeated. The net profit each year was about £300 or £400 at this time, although in 1842 the £400 announced at the Annual General Meeting was reduced the following month to £28 when the company's solicitor had presented his bill, which included the purchase price of the lease of Lamellion Mills bought four years earlier. Little differentiation was made at this time between capital and operating expenditure. The Committee was rather concerned with a further fall off in the lime trade – the post-Napoleonic War boom that gave much strength to the canal in its early days was drawing to a close – and the Minutes include a long report on the subject. Apart from mentioning what a benefit to Liskeard the canal had been and how much more expensive coal and lime would be without it, the report states that St Germans and Lerryn were the chief places of competition. Charges on the canal for limestone were 3d per ton mile for boat hire and 1d per ton mile toll (reduced from 1½d). With lime costing 15d a bushel (on credit – 14½d ready money) at the kiln mouth, canal transport alone formed a substantial portion of the lime merchants' costs although tolls, the Canal Company's share, were a small enough figure. The report advocated low prices to keep trade at Moorswater and suggested a company be formed to 'organise' the trade. No traffic figures are available for this period so it is not possible to see just how bad the decline was, although in 1849, the first figures extant, only a little over 7,000 tons of limestone were carried,[9] as was a similar quantity in 1854. The canal would have been in a serious position were it not for the ores from Caradon.

The toll on copper ore for the journey down the canal had been reduced from 1s 6d (six miles at 3d) to 1s 3d and was further reduced to 1s per ton at the 1842 AGM. Granite tolls were also lowered to the same level and the next year tolls on coal were dropped from 3s per ton (i.e. 6d per ton mile) to 2s because traders at Looe and St Germans were able to undercut the Liskeard merchants. Drawback was to be allowed on coal already in the cellars at Moorswater and, in July, no less than 400 tons was thus allowed for.

Several railways were now coming on to the scene; some a cause for concern. The Cornwall Railway and the Cornwall & Devon Central Railway were involved in an intense battle for the privilege of constructing the main line into Cornwall and the Liskeard & Looe Union Canal Company resolved to oppose both, as did the young Liskeard & Caradon Railway. The Cornwall Railway had proposed a branch to Looe but the Canal Company's opposition obtained deletion of the clause from the Bill and the substitution of one authorising the purchase or lease of both the LLUC and LCR. In the event the Central line did not receive the approval of Parliament and the Cornwall Company exhausted its funds building its switchback main line. The authorised branch at Moorswater to connect with the Caradon line was abandoned.

The ever increasing copper traffic had given birth to the Liskeard & Caradon Railway, as related in Chapter 3, and whose rails had eventually reached Moorswater in 1846. The LCR was short of cash from the outset and the LLUC, along with South and West Caradon Mines, took up twenty five forfeited shares to assist the railway. John Bowden, an old friend of the canal, lent the necessary £625 and he was repaid with interest six months later – such was the prosperous state of the canal at that time – although no dividend could be paid that year (1845) as a result. The canal had made room at Moorswater for the railway terminus, demolishing a cottage in the process, but it was not until 1850 that the railway finally agreed to pay rent, £6 per year, for the site.

Rapid prosperity was brought to the canal by the Caradon line for, with now easy transport, many more mines were opening up and copper and tin ores that had formerly gone to other quays and wharves to the east were now despatched to Looe. Coal and iron flowed up

Moorswater Viaduct in 1856, before the Cornwall Railway opened, and showing in the foreground the canal and Lamellion Mills and bridge. Beyond the bridge a branch of the canal turns left to serve a lime kiln whilst the main line of the canal veers to the right, behind the mill, to follow the east side of the valley to Moorswater, beyond the viaduct.
AUTHOR'S COLLECTION

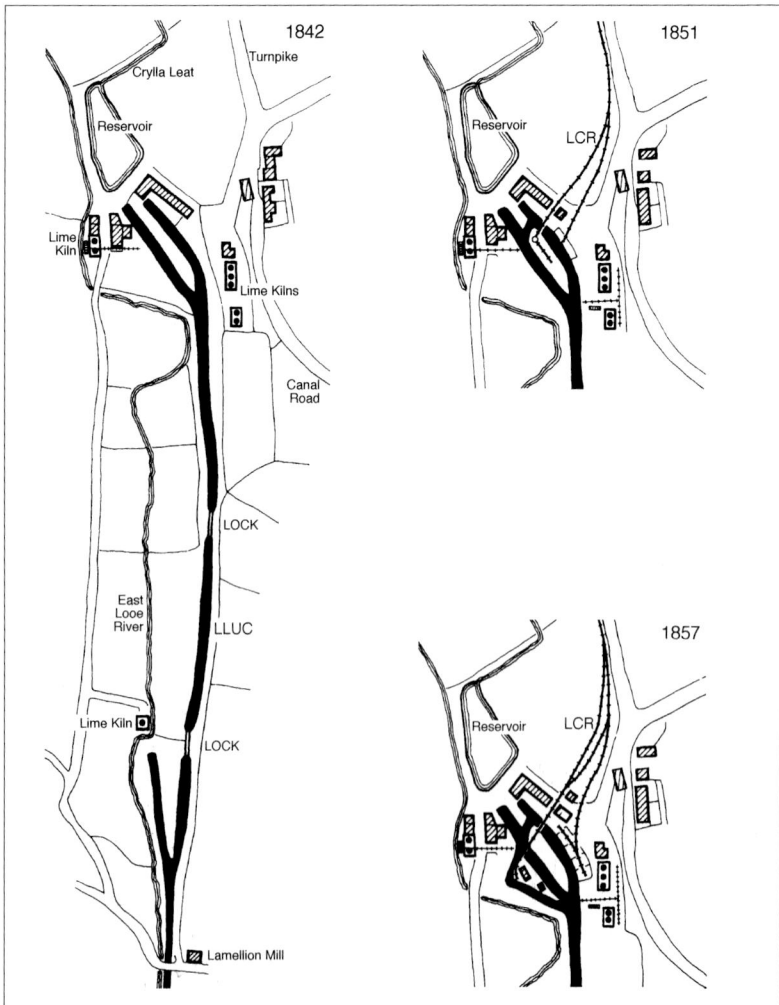

This series of plans of Moorswater shows how the canal head expanded to meet the growth in traffic. [Sources: 1842 CRO QS/PDR 10/1, 1851 CRO Bor/Lisk 393, 1857 CRO/QS PDR 10/2, QS/PDR 10/7.]

the canal (metaphorically speaking) to satisfy the mines' voracious appetites and, as soon as the Looe Harbour Commissioners had made something of a respectable port at Looe, they wrested the timber trade from Lostwithiel. The net profits were now into four figures each year and the Committee began to systematically repay the mortgagees. What had been an adequate water supply for agricultural purposes was now proving insufficient for the heavy mineral traffic and more attention was given to the Crylla leat. The millers north of Moorswater attempted to tap the leat and the company was put to considerable expense preventing this. In the Looe valley the millers were complaining loudly but Retallick claimed that their water supply had actually improved since the opening of the canal.[10] George Taylor accused the canal of stealing the water of Lamellion Mills (sub-let to him by the company) for, by laying in wait, he had caught a man red-handed at the sluice and was proceeding to prosecute.[11] These complaints, accusations and counter-accusations were to continue unabated while such heavy demands were made by the canal on the waters of the Looe valley.

To cope with the still increasing traffic extra wharves were built, more land was purchased and a new cut made at the head of the canal. Coal was even being landed on the towpath because of growing congestion. As one means of easing this Edward Geach suggested extending the canal south from Terras to Shutta Point (near the later site of Looe station) to cope with the 'daily increasing traffic'. Some action was taken but the idea was soon dropped. Richard Retallick resigned the post of Clerk in February 1854, a job he had held since 1829, and Thomas Milton took the position until his death in 1883. As a sure sign of prosperity not only did the Treasurer buy, in 1854, a 'Milner iron safe' but a bank account was opened with Messrs Robins, Foster & Company, the East Cornwall Bank. The same year Evan Hopkins, a lime and coal merchant and a shareholder, served a Bill of Chancery on the company charging them with mismanagement. The details are not known but the company appear to have acted *ultra vires*, for a Special Meeting decided that the offending acts had beneficial results and ratified them. The Vice Chancellor dismissed Hopkins' suit, with costs against him, but meanwhile he abortively attempted to sell one of the company's coal stores and, when he later tried to dispose of his shares, the Clerk refused to accept the transfer as he had not settled the costs.

Despite the heavy traffic time appears to have been found each year to drain the canal for a day for maintenance and the Committee of Management took this opportunity for a little pleasure. As the waters receded men went in with two-handed nets of regulation mesh to catch the salmon peel, but as many were small enough to pass through the legal mesh, another man went behind with a shrimping net. Thus, illegally, it was ensured there was sufficient for the Committee's lunch at the Bullers Arms Hotel at Sandplace.[12]

Annual accounts for the last few years of the canal's life have survived and these show how the traffic had grown. In 1849 (the first available) 21,713 tons were carried including 7,546 tons of copper and 6,175 tons of coal.[13] Ten years later the total was 48,193 tons, well over double, to which the two commodities contributed 17,361 tons and 15,712 tons respectively and in addition 8,297 tons of granite were included. The net profit each year was almost £2,000. The capacity of the canal (1857) was 160 tons per day and, taking a six day working week, this gives an annual capacity of little more than 48,000 tons. Each boat carried 16 tons and in 1849 there were but thirteen boats. Eight hours were taken for the seven mile journey to Looe harbour, including the negotiation of the twenty four locks.[14] A little simple arithmetic shows that the canal's resources at this time were, indeed, stretched to their limit. As early as the mid-forties a report stated transhipment to be a waste and that ore was often washed away while stacked on the quays at Moorswater.[15] How much worse it must have been ten years later when transhipment was costing from 4d to 6d per ton, in spite of the LCR using ore wagons that could be run over a barge on a trestle or gantry and the contents dropped straight in through bottom doors. James Jenkin Trathan, of the partnership of Jenkin & Trathan, had been appointed Superintendent, Surveyor and Engineer in 1854 (his partner Silvanus Jenkin was Engineer to the LCR) and in June 1857 the partners were asked to prepare an estimate of the cost of a railway from Moorswater to Looe. Their report was dated 30 September. A railway could carry, with a locomotive making three trips, 300 tons a day at 1s 3d per ton less than the canal and, they said, the capacity could be doubled by simply doubling the amount of rolling stock. The estimated cost was £11,000. They were concerned about competition from the Cornwall Railway, then constructing, and that because of congestion the canal was already losing trade to Calstock and St Germans. The report was accepted and a Special General Meeting of shareholders called on 13 October. Jenkin & Trathan's further report to that body pointed out that a railway was not a speculation but a necessity and could be in addition to the canal, although it is hard to believe they seriously expected the canal to continue alongside the railway. The meeting approved the proposals and it was left to the Committee to obtain the necessary Parliamentary approval.

John Buller was dead by now and it was the turn of his son, John Francis Buller, to oppose the railway. His lands were needed, however, and agreement was reached to purchase these for £483, and to provide a couple of sidings for his use. The Admiralty also opposed the plans – their interest was in the navigation of the river – but the Duchy of Cornwall intervened on the company's behalf. Some landowners objected at first but the Bill had an unopposed passage through both Houses, receiving the Royal Assent on 11 May 1858.

The canal lock near Lodge with another beyond and Moorswater Viaduct in the distance. The state of the stonework, the timber beams of the gates and the leaking gates at the upper end of the lock give an indication of the state of repair of the canal after some 35 years' work. This view is from a stereo card published by W. Spreat, of Exeter, about 1858/9. The caption reads 'The canal, which conveys the produce of the Caradon Mines and Cheesewring Granite Quarries to Looe, is carried through a beautiful valley which is spanned by the celebrated Moorswater Viaduct. There are a great many small locks on the Canal, to provide for the continuous fall, which are very picturesque, and the walk on the towing path is altogether one of great beauty.' COLLECTION STEPHEN ROWSON.

The close proximity of canal, railway and river at Terras can be clearly seen in this 1959 view. Terras lock is immediately before the bridge and the bridge into the river just above it, in the middle of the S-bend of the railway. The gatekeepers cottage is to the left of the lock. For holiday-makers on their way to Looe, the journey down the East Looe Valley made a wonderful introduction to Cornwall. 4585 with a Saturday special at Terras.
PETER W. GRAY

The Liskeard & Looe Railway Act 1858 (21 Victoria cap.xi) was quite short, only 48 sections in all, but contained the necessary and usual authorities for the construction of the railway. The new capital, in addition to the old, was £13,000 in £25 shares and the borrowing powers £4,000. Powers were given to make agreements with the LCR and the Looe Harbour Commissioners and to form a Joint Committee with the former. Locomotive power was authorised, at a toll of 1d per mile or per ton mile, but was not to cross the end of Looe Bridge to Buller Quay on the level. Only two sections of the Canal Act of 1825 were repealed, notably that providing penalties for the 'destruction of the canal'.

500 tons of rails were ordered from the Rhymney Iron Company, in south Wales, and granite blocks from Cheesewring Quarry. Construction of the line went to tender; John Brown and William Williams got the contract for the section from Moorswater to Terras Pill, Messrs Bone & Firks that from Terras to Shutta Point and the separate contract for the bridges went to Messrs Bone, Firks and Sargent. Some land had to be bought as the line was to be built alongside the canal but work began in 1859 as soon as was possible. Parliamentary Returns at 30 June 1859 showed that out of 82 employees on the railway 76 were labourers and artificers, so either the company was providing labour itself or it included the contractors' employees in the returns. The use of granite blocks at so late a date seems strange but they were, presumably, serving the LCR well and were cheaply available locally. The engineers' limited experience in railway matters may have been relevant, as may have been their involvement in the Cheesewring Granite Quarry, but in January 1860 they suggested laying the rails on wood through the Looe estuary. Longitudinal timber sleepers were used, therefore, from Tregarland to Looe Bridge, as in broad gauge practice and as used on the Cornwall Railway, then newly built through the county.

The construction appears to have been incident free, although a contractor's horses slipped off the embankment near Terras at high tide and were drowned. Also near Terras, in September, some human remains in a chest were unearthed.

In July Jenkin & Trathan reported the formation complete to Shutta Point and rails laid south as far as Tregarland. Work had been held up by the wet weather but the line was expected to be ready by summer. £6,750 had been borrowed by February, quite in excess of the Act's authority, but in May it was found another £5,000 was needed to complete the line. The engineer was instructed to complete the permanent way works only, leaving the accommodation works, and the solicitor was to acquire the necessary money. This came from the company's bankers plus a further £1,000 from Peter Clymo (making £3,000 from this latter source alone). Having no money for rolling stock an arrangement was made with the LCR for that company to provide the wagons and the LLUC an engine. James Murphy of Newport, Monmouthshire, offered to supply and work a locomotive at £3 per day; the company providing water and a shed. This was accepted and a four-coupled tank locomotive duly arrived via the Cornwall Railway on the 18 December 1860. The opening was fixed for Thursday 27 December and the *Royal Cornwall Gazette* described the event thus:

> The proceedings of Thursday were very successful. The opening train consisted of a locomotive engine (constructed at Newport [*sic*]) and twelve open trucks, started at Moorswater, amidst the cheers of the numerous spectators, shortly after half past 10 a.m. It contained the directors, several gentlemen of the neighbourhood, the band of the Liskeard Rifle Corps, and many of the members, besides a host of other persons. At every little village and hamlet through which the train passed, the cottagers came out and cheered lustily, and in one or two places triumphal arches of more or less beauty were erected, under which the train had to pass. A few minutes after 11 it arrived at the terminus in West Looe [*sic* – it should read East Looe], which at present is on the extensive quay running by the side of the harbour, commencing from the bridge. At Looe everyone turned out and did his best to welcome the train. The streets were gaily decorated, and arches of evergreens, erected in great variety, with all kinds of appropriate mottoes.[16]

A public dinner was held in the afternoon and in the evening there was tea and a concert in aid of the Looe Artillery Volunteers. The railway had cost £21,000, that is £3,000 per mile, but this low figure was a result of the company already owning much of the land.

Despite now owning a railway the constitution laid down in the 1825 Act still held good; the company was still the Liskeard & Looe Union Canal Company controlled by a Committee of Management, not a Board of Directors.

As when the canal was built, the workmanship of the railway was not all it should have been. Bone and Firks claimed extra over their contract and the arbitrator, William Pease of St Blazey, awarded them £406.[17] When the line was constructing the Waywardens of Morval (Waywardens were in charge of parish roads) had complained of the state of their roads and when completed John Francis Buller complained it was not screened from the road. A sixteen feet high screen was called for – later reduced to eight – 'every other board should be higher than the one it adjoins, being more ornamental'.[18] When the fence was erected Buller complained he could not get to the waterside and wanted a gap put in it. A tart minute directed the officers to meet him and 'establish precisely what he wants'.

Even before the canal was superseded by the railway the recently formed Liskeard Water Company had been casting covetous eyes at the LLUC's water supply and in May 1861 the Committee agreed it should have use of the Crylla leat and its water. A subsequent agreement gave it perpetual use for £5 per annum, the Water Company taking responsibility for maintenance. The section of canal that remained in use, from Sandplace down, was supplied with water through a culvert under the railway.

The canal was also concerning Mr Buller. 374 yards of his quays at Sandplace and quays at New Bridge and Steps had either been cut off or destroyed by the railway and the canal needed clearing. Between 1862 and 1867 £179 was spent on repairs to the canal but it is unlikely that any of these were above Sandplace. Probably it was only used for agricultural traffic by the tenants of the Morval estate who had free use and one suspects there was positive discouragement. Although in 1867 the tenants and inhabitants of Duloe parish complained 'since the railway was made the canal is useless'[19] Buller took no action until 1877.

The railway crossed the canal in five places, three below Sandplace by bridges which should have had a headroom of four feet. However, like Coad's locks, their foundations were poor or lacking and the bridges were sinking. In 1865 the lock gates at Terras were lowered, and hence the water level, to increase the headroom but conversely this decreased the depth. An arch was put in to replace the timber beam of the bridge below Terras because the walls were falling together and this too did not help the navigation. With little or no maintenance in later years the canal became silted and

An 1890 view of Sandplace shows the middle kiln of the three in the village. In the foreground is the truncated remains of the canal and its quay while on the left is the railway that supplanted it and the small goods shed erected alongside the siding.
ROYAL INSTITUTION OF CORNWALL;
REF: MORVAL 4

weedgrown, the banks overgrown and giving way, and Buller's complaints began, although to little result. Matters came to a head on 4 November 1884 when representatives of all parties met at Terras to witness a boat enter the waterway. It was loaded with 14 tons 2 cwt of sand, less than the usual 16 tons, and passed beneath the railway bridge with but one inch clear above the gunwale. Had the load been any less it would not have cleared but had it been heavier the barge would probably have grounded. Only two or three of the original boats now survived; they could only be used at low tide and most use was made of small boats taking one to one and a half tons. Buller's men had taken the experiment as proving their point but to the railway and canal people it showed the canal was perfectly navigable and another lengthy correspondence ensued. A comment by Buller's solicitor gives a good impression of the state of the canal at the time as well as the attitude of his client:

> The employment of any number of men or horses would not improve the facility of entrance or exit whilst as to the canal itself it is sufficient to say that there is no towpath available for horses and that it ought not to be expected of Mr Buller that he should employ sufficient hauling power to drag a barge over the mud banks which the company ought to remove.[20]

John Francis Buller sought Counsel's opinion and, like his father, received little comfort; 'The case is one of very considerable difficulty and nicety'. He was told his best course was arbitration but in a little over a year the LCR, who now worked the LLR and had responsibility for the canal, was in the hands of a Receiver.

In 1901 Mrs Tremayne had succeeded to the Morval estates and her tenants were taking 150 to 200 boat loads a year of sand or seaweed (for manure) up the canal. Mostly this was in 1½-ton boats and a 3d toll was levied, although the two surviving 16-ton boats had to pay 1s 9d on their occasional visits to Sandplace. The tolls were collected by a platelayer but under what authority or agreement the tolls were levied and paid is not known. The waterway itself was a sorry state. The culvert at Sandplace that maintained the water supply under the railway was blocked and no water flowed down the canal. What got in at Terras at high tide through the lock gates that needed replacing flowed out again through the many leaks and breaks in the banks. A small sum was spent dredging and repairing gates in 1901 but less than £5 a year was spent on maintenance in the following years. Dues averaged 35s per annum from 1901 to 1909, collected latterly by Richard Moore of the track gang, in his late 70s, walking miles with his daughter to collect from the consignees. No record was kept of boats using the canal and, after the GWR took over, there is no other record of the canal. Undoubtedly the traffic dwindled as the canal declined in navigability and the issue of a licence in 1911 at a cost of a guinea a year to Admiral Charles Cross, of Polrean, Sandplace, for him to keep a rowing boat in the canal may have been the last 'commercial' business on the Liskeard & Looe Union Canal.[21]

Sandplace, with the canal on the right, the railway curving to the left and the river in between. In the centre is Polrean, one-time home of Admiral Cross, who kept a rowing boat in the canal in 1911. This commercial postcard was probably taken at the latter end of the nineteenth century.
AUTHOR'S COLLECTION

CHAPTER THREE
HORSES AND GRAVITY

Very great Advantages must result to the Landed, Mining, and Commercial Interests in the Neighbourhood, in which the Labouring Population will also largely participate.
LISKEARD & CARADON RAILWAY PROSPECTUS, 1842

Throughout much of Cornwall for very many centuries her rocks and minerals have provided at best wealth and at worst a living for her people. The ancient civilizations knew of her mineral wealth and from earliest times Cornwall has provided much of the world's supply of tin. However, when our story begins at the start of the nineteenth century, Fowey-more, as Bodmin Moor was then known, was making little contribution to the county. Some quarrying of the abundant moorstone that lay scattered around the surface of the ground below Stow's Hill and the Cheesewring had gone on at least during the eighteenth century. Indeed, that most famous inhabitant of the moor, the mathematician Daniel Gumb, was a stone-cutter by trade before he turned to Euclid. Similarly the 'old men', who combined farming with tin-streaming, had excavated the 'backs' of the tin lodes where they outcropped to surface around Stow's Hill to quite considerable depths, fourteen fathoms in places, and for a mile in length but this desultory activity could hardly parallel the commercial enterprises of the west of the county. No tin had been coined at Liskeard, the Stannary Town for the area, for nearly a century and it was a widely held belief that no minerals of any consequence would ever be found east of Truro.

In the west it was copper that had placed Cornwall in the forefront of world mining and it was this mineral that was to bring sudden fame and riches to Caradon Hill, a mile or so to the south of Stow's Hill, although not as a result of any large commercial venture. Exactly how copper ore was discovered on Caradon Hill is now lost in anecdote and rumour. It has been claimed that specks of mineral in molehills gave the first clue to Caradon's wealth but, be that as it may, an adit was started by a miner called Ennor, or so his son later claimed, working for a group of Plymouth and Devonport adventurers. Alas, they took notice of 'one of the knowing ones from the West' who condemned the venture and they gave in. It is known that the Clymo and Kittow families were involved in the 1836 Cornwall Great United Mining Association, an attempt by London adventurers to reopen the old open workings on Stow's Hill for tin, so they were in a position to become familiar with Caradon Hill. Certainly James Clymo and Thomas Kittow took a lease of the South Caradon sett and they searched until copper was struck in 1836.

On the strength of the first specimens James Clymo went to London to raise capital to exploit the discovery but had no success. Finding himself when returning westwards by coach in the company of a prominent west Cornish mine adventurer he offered him half the mine's 64 shares for £5 a share – half face value – but was again refused. Undaunted the miners continued the search and in a few months struck the main ore body, when the shares reached a price of £2,000 each.[1] In 1837 130 tons of ore were raised, fetching £1,198 to pay off the partners' debts, and from then on South Caradon Mine equipped itself solely from the proceeds of copper ore. The original capital of £640, perhaps the equivalent of £50,000 in present day (2015) values, remained unaltered. This is perhaps the most romantic of all the tales of Cornish mining, where a group of miners 'struck it rich' and remained to exploit their discovery and make their fortunes. Hundreds of thousands of pounds-worth of copper ore were to be raised in the next fifty years and a vast sum paid out in dividends.

The good fortune of this discovery did not go unnoticed. In 1837 a search was made on the opposite side of the Seaton Valley for the westwards continuation of the South Caradon lodes and two 'kindly lodes' were cut. Work was suspended until a lease was obtained from the mineral lord in 1839 and the following year West Caradon Mine was founded, with Quakers prominent among the adventurers. Crouch's shaft was sunk and only 17 fathoms down very rich ore was struck, so rich that it looked for a while as though South Caradon's riches would be eclipsed by the West. The first ore, 38 tons, was sold in 1841 for £233 after an outlay of £5,140 and the first dividend was paid in 1844. By 1850 500 were employed of which 260 were underground.[2] Also about 1840 a Mr Crouch was searching to the east for the same lodes at Tokenbury Mine but he had little success and similarly neither did an adit driven on what was to become the site of East Caradon Mine.[3]

On Stow's Hill itself, in 1839 a 50-year old stone mason, John Trethewey, obtained a grant from the Duchy of Cornwall to quarry the

CHEESE WRING.

Taken from the 1842 Prospectus for the LCR, this map shows a slightly less contorted route than that actually built.

granite under the Cheesewring, as opposed to merely cutting up the loose blocks strewn across the moor. Thus by the early 1840s the produce of the moor, although a fraction of what was to come, was creating traffic far in excess of what the parish roads of the district were capable of accommodating. Road transport was expensive anyway; copper ore was costing 4s 6d a ton[4] to get to the head of the canal at Moorswater while Trethewey's granite cost 8s[5] to transport. Nothing seems to have survived of the discussions that led to the decision to build a railway but it was evidently reached by the mine owners with the active encouragement of the Reverend George Poole Norris, the mineral lord of South Caradon Mine[6], and a committee was formed.

Robert Coad, the LLUC engineer, presented his report and survey of a line 'between the Liskeard Canal and the Caradon Mines, Cheesewring and Tokenbury' to a meeting at Liskeard on 25 June 1842. He estimated the cost at £14,500 which did not include £1,500 for the Tokenbury branch as this was not to be constructed until the mines there became productive. The traffic was foreseen as 5,000 tons of copper ore a year from South Caradon Mine, 2,000 tons from West Caradon, 8,000 tons of granite from the Cheesewring and a back carriage up the line of 1,600 tons of coal, iron and timber, giving an annual income of £1,850. From this would be taken £100 for a clerk's salary and £150 for maintenance, leaving £1,600 to give shareholders an 11% return. Evidently the railway was not intended to act as a carrier but merely a toll collector. It is clear that the line was intended to be worked by gravity and laid down accordingly, for the report states 'that Carriages will move down with facility, without the aid of any Power, and be taken back with easy Locomotive or Horse Power'. Coad was assisted by a Mr Brown, Civil Engineer, and he closes his report by congratulating the committee on the comparatively small outlay of Capital required to accomplish so desirable an object, which is mainly to be attributed to the nature of the Country over which the Railroad will pass, rendering, as it does, a Surface line quite practicable, without the expense and laborious assistance of any one Incline Plane.[7]

His plans were welcomed and prospectuses were printed and sent out. It was suggested that the treasurer of the canal and the pursers of the mines should offer railway shares to their respective shareholders, later trying landowners and 'other capitalists'. The initial committee consisted of thirteen men, not all of whom later became directors. These included Thomas and Richard Kittow, E. A. Crouch, John Clogg and Henry Borrow. Surprisingly, Peter Clymo was not on the committee.

On 2 December Captain W. S. Moorsom, who was then engineer to the projected Cornwall Railway (he was later supplanted by Brunel), inspected the proposed line and was glowing in his praise.

> It is rarely that any portion of country for seven miles continuously will admit of a uniform inclination being given to any kind of Road without considerable cuttings and embankments. But in this instance Mr Coad has succeeded with very little cutting or embankment and without any curves that involve serious objection, in laying out a good practical Road for traffic both up and down which I am quite satisfied will work well and economically.

He recommended horse power and that the line be open to carriers, subject to byelaws. The cost he estimated at a little under £16,000 and with an estimated income of £1,285 thought a return of 9% possible. Captain Moorsom could find them a contractor who would build the railway for £12,000 taking 20% in shares, but he thought it might be cheaper if they built the line themselves.[8]

The planned route from Moorswater to South Caradon was much as subsequently built but the Cheesewring and Tokenbury branches were proposed on quite different alignments with no incline to the former. The gradients from Moorswater to Polwrath were to be 1 in 61, on to South Caradon 1 in 128, the Tokenbury branch 1 in 58 and the Cheesewring branch 1 in 34¾. Two tunnels were initially planned, under the two turnpikes encountered, one of 82 yards at Moorswater and another short one of 44 yards at Tremabe,[9] although only the latter was discussed by the Parliamentary Committee that considered the proposals. Coad's estimate to that Committee of the cost was £11,959 10s 6d and it was told £9,350 of the £12,000 capital was already subscribed for, £1,070 10s in deposits paid and 38 of the 57 subscribers had a local interest in the line.[10] Although fourteen roads, including two turnpikes, were to be crossed on the level this was accepted as the line was to be horse drawn.

The Committee's report stated that the pre-railway means of transport was insufficient for agriculture and mining purposes, then about 13,500 tons a year. It commented on the large amount of granite that was expected but that little was expected from passenger traffic. The engineers were stated to be Captain Moorsom and Robert Coad, although the former was presumably in an advisory capacity only. Richard Retallick was also involved and the newly-qualified Silvanus Jenkin had joined Coad in 1842.

The report being favourable and there being no opposition, Parliament's sanction was forthcoming and the Royal Assent was given to the Liskeard & Caradon Railway Act, 6-7 Victoria cap.xliii, on 26 June 1843. The first eight directors, and their initial shareholdings, of the Liskeard & Caradon Railway Company were to be:

George Poole Norris	(Mineral lord – South Caradon Mine)	£1,000
Peter Clymo	(South Caradon Mine)	£375
Edward Geach	Liskeard & Looe Union Canal)	£250
Samuel Abbott	(Liskeard & Looe Union Canal)	£150
James Clymo	(South Caradon Mine)	£375
John Allen	(West Caradon Mine)	£250
Robert Taylor	(St Cleer)	£100
Benjamin Hart Lyne	(Solicitor of Liskeard)	£1,200

The capital was £12,000 in £25 shares with borrowing powers of £4,000 and the line was to be completed within five years. Section 264 (there were 355 sections in all, plus ten

The Company Seal of the Liskeard & Caradon Railway.
AUTHOR'S COLLECTION

LISKEARD AND CARADON RAILWAY.

REGULATIONS

To be observed for the use of the Railway.

1. THAT no Carriage used on the Railway shall pass over the Line at a greater *average rate* than Eight miles an hour; nor shall, on any portion of the Line, exceed the rate of Twelve miles an hour; nor shall any Carriage when crossing any Public Carriage Way, exceed the rate of Six miles an hour. And that every Conductor of any Carriage which shall pass over any portion of the Line contrary to the above Regulations, shall for every such offence forfeit any sum not exceeding *Five Pounds*, unless the permission in writing of the Directors or their duly authorized Agent for that purpose be first obtained.

2. That every Conductor, when approaching any Highway, Turn Out, Curve, or Station, shall give such signals as the Directors may from time to time order to be given; and every Conductor offending against any such Order shall, for every such offence, forfeit any sum not exceeding *Forty Shillings*.

3. That no person shall be allowed to act as the Conductor of any Carriage, unless he has previously received the approbation of the Directors; and every such Conductor shall carry with him a certificate of such approbation, and shall wear such Badge of his office as the Directors shall from time to time order to be worn. And every such Conductor shall show forth to either of the Directors or to any of their authorized Agents, when required so to do, such Certificate of approbation; and if any Conductor shall refuse so to do, or shall be found conducting a Carriage on the Line without wearing the Badge of his appointment in manner required by the Directors, he shall forfeit for every such offence any sum not exceeding *Forty Shillings*.

4. That all Carriages passing over the Line shall be subject to such Regulations, and for the times of arrival at or departure from any Station, and for the use of the Turn Outs, as the Company shall from time to time issue; such Regulations to be printed and affixed on some conspicuous part of each Station. And every Conductor who shall offend against such Regulations shall, for every such offence, forfeit any sum not exceeding *Forty Shillings*.

5. That not more than *Five Tons* weight shall be carried by any one Carriage over any portion of the Line without the express permission in writing of the Directors or their duly authorized agents first having been obtained; and that every Conductor who shall offend against this Regulation shall, for every such offence, forfeit and pay any sum not exceeding *Forty Shillings*.

6. That no Carriage shall be on, or pass over, the Main Line at any time between one hour after Sunset and one hour before Sunrise; but Carriages delayed on the Line may be left in a Turn Out, and must join the Main Line at the earliest possible time, not interfering with the Company's Regulations for the times of arrival at and departure from any Station. And if any Conductor of any Carriage shall allow it to remain on the Main Line contrary to such Regulations, he shall forfeit and pay for every such offence any sum not exceeding *Forty Shillings*.

BY ORDER OF THE DIRECTORS,

CHRISTR. CHILDS, Secretary.

Dated, 18th day of December, 1844.

R. ESTERBROOK, Jun., PRINTER, STATIONER, BOOKSELLER, &c. LISKEARD.

The first known regulations of the LCR were issued soon after the temporary opening in 1844. They are reproduced in full in Appendix 5.
LISKEARD TOWN MUSEUM

Cheesewring branch would have been too steep to be workable. Also the line would have passed through the centre of West Caradon Mine at surface and doubtless they opposed such disruption.

Little is known of the actual organisation of the construction; some work may have been subcontracted but most was probably done by direct labour under Coad's supervision for there was a pool of unemployed men at the time. Robert Coad was assisted by Silvanus Jenkin and by Henry Rice, the latter to become Surveyor of the Liskeard Turnpike and a prominent Liskeard architect. James Jenkin Trathan also joined Coad's team at this time. Construction started at the Cheesewring early in 1844, this being the source of the granite blocks the rails were to be laid on, and progress was rapid. By March half a mile was completed and fenced and it was hoped to open to Tremabe by midsummer but below Tremabe no progress had been made and problems were arising.[11]

The Duchy of Cornwall was a major landowner in the area, owning all the open moors north of what is now Minions village as well as farms further south. In particular the Duchy possessed High Wood, a coppice to the north of Looe Mills and through which the railway was to go. While they were agreeable to the railway being started on the unenclosed land at the Cheesewring before a price had been agreed for the land, they would not do so at High Wood. Christopher Childs, the LCR secretary, wrote pleading letters offering even to pay for the moorland, although other landowners had given 'waste' land, if it would prevent them having to stop work on the line, but the Duchy were adamant and stated they were not permitted to give land anyway.[12] Thus stalemate arose as the railway had proved more expensive than anticipated and could proceed no further until funds were raised to pay the Duchy's price for High Wood. The directors claimed the Duchy was grossly overcharging for the land but had little option but to pay.

In September, when 70 shares had been forfeit by non-payment of calls, the secretary wrote to the LLUC and the South and West Caradon mines pointing out that the railway could not be completed without these shares being taken, and paid for, and suggested the three enterprises took up the shares themselves. The canal took 25 and the mines split the remainder between them but this was still not sufficient and loans had to be raised from elsewhere.

In the meantime, perhaps in order to make the most of what they did have, it was decided to open the railway as far as possible and on

schedules) stated that powers to cross roads on the level had only been granted on the condition that horse power was used, and should they cross turnpike roads or 'public carriage roads', that is, parish roads, with steam a penalty of £50 applied for each offence. This was to prove significant in later years. The maximum tolls were 4d per ton per mile for metals, minerals, timber and the like, 2d for lime, sand, stone, etc, and 6d for grain, beasts, etc. The tolls were to be exhibited and milestones were to be erected at quarter mile intervals. The railway was to be subject to the Regulation of Railways Act 1840 (3&4V.c.97) and Regulation of Railways Act 1842 (5&6V.c.55). Surprisingly the Act did not specify the gauge but the line was to be built to the standard 4ft 8½ in.

Wasting no time, on 12 July a printed circular advised that Coad was marking out the line and that the directors were 'now in a position to avail themselves of the Act.' The Duchy's officers soon noted there was some deviation from the original plan and this is hardly surprising for, if one looks at the authorised route on a modern contour map, Coad's surveying would seem to have gone a little awry around Polwrath where the

Thursday 28 November 1844 it was opened down to Tremabe, meeting the turnpike road from Liskeard.

> A long train started from the upper terminus and arrived safely at the present completion of the line, where the party was entertained by partaking of a *dejeuner*, the workmen employed were also regaled with roast beef and strong beer ... The greatly improved town of Liskeard was exceedingly gay in consequence of the proceedings, the undertaking being one of great importance to this place.[13]

Whether it was worth the effort of transhipping ores after but a three mile trip down the railway into carts for another three miles to the canal is doubtful. For such a short journey it was inevitable that the ores should continue to be taken from the mines by horse and cart. Possibly it may have been more viable for the quarry to use the railway but there is no evidence for this and Trethewey's output was very low. That some traffic was offering is evidenced by a poster issued on 18 December 1844 setting out the regulations for the use of the railway. The aspects covered illustrate the early concerns of the directors and, perhaps, the lessons learned hastily in the first few weeks of operating.

Speed was the subject of the first regulation; a maximum speed of 12 miles per hour was stipulated with an average of no more than eight. Six miles per hour was the limit on road crossings. Quite how speed was to be measured is not known. The 'carriages', or wagons, were each under the control of a 'Conductor' who was instructed to give a signal at each hazard; road crossing, curve or station. The nature of the signal is not specified, alas, but in later years was a whistle or horn.

Only people approved by the directors could act as conductors and they had to carry a certificate of 'approbation' and wear a badge of office. This could imply that conductors were not employees of the company but there is no suggestion that rolling stock was not owned by the LCR. The only reference in the regulations to the wagons themselves was that no more than five tons were to be carried. There is, for example, no regulation requiring the number and owner's name to be painted on the wagon such as the canal company required of boat owners. Unlike the canal, the railway was its own carrier, with the possible exception of Trethewey's granite traffic. All the regulations were backed up with threats of fines of forty shillings (£2) or five pounds.

The line eventually opened through to Moorswater, probably on Monday 8 March 1846 although the evidence for this date is not specific.

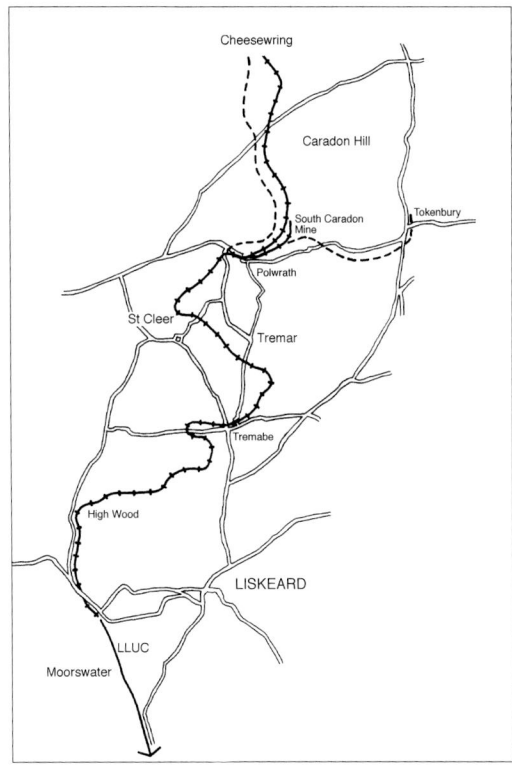

The Liskeard & Caradon Railway as built in 1846. The Tokenbury branch, as authorised by the 1843 Act, remained unbuilt whilst the Cheesewring branch was built on quite a different line to that authorised.

A meeting was held on that day to celebrate the full opening of the line but the report did not actually say that it had been opened then.

The Liskeard & Caradon Railway was by no means Cornwall's first railway, having been preceded by several substantial railways *, some locomotive powered. However it was unique in being built specifically to be operated by gravity. The Pentewan Railway used gravity for part of the run south from St Austell, where the gradient permitted, and several of the other earlier lines appear to have made use of it either occasionally or unofficially. But Robert Coad took the step of adopting it as the principal motive power, ensuring that the gradients and curves would permit free running. Although the route was sinuous it is a tribute to his surveying ability and engineering knowledge that he was able to arrange a steady downhill grade below South Caradon Mine so that traffic could run economically all the way to Moorswater.

The railway as built included no tunnels, ordinary road over-bridges and cuttings having replaced them. The Tokenbury branch was not built, there was neither cash nor traffic for it,

---

*Cornwall's railways, other than internal mine and quarry tramways, that preceded the Liskeard & Caradon Railway were:

	OPENING	GAUGE	POWER
Portreath Tramroad	1811/12	plateway	horse
Redruth & Chasewater Railway	1825	4 feet	horse
Pentewan Railway	1829	about 4 feet	horse
Bodmin & Wadebridge Railway	1834	standard	steam
Hayle Railway	1837	standard	steam

An outstanding early view of Moorswater taken in late 1858 or early 1859, after the Cornwall Railway viaduct was built but before the canal was supplanted by the railway to Looe. At left a chaldron wagon is on a raised siding over the canal, permitting its contents to be discharged into a waiting boat and another wagon is on the right. Behind the siding is a stone yard with an overhead gantry crane.
COLLECTION STEPHEN ROWSON.

and the Cheesewring branch was on quite a different line with the rope-worked Gonamena incline at its lower end to gain height.

Both figures of £12,000 (by Coad) and £16,000 (by Moorsom) had been gross underestimates of the cost of the enterprise. Eight shares had not been taken up but otherwise the authorised capital had been fully expended as had the authorised borrowing powers of £4,000. In addition £5,700 had been borrowed from the East Cornwall Bank, nearly £4,500 from the shareholders and £850 was estimated to be still owing for land. The shareholders had advanced £15 on each share over and above the nominal value of £25, an indication of their strong interest – often vested – in the line. The railway had cost £27,000, which at about £3,200 a mile was very modest, but this was of little comfort to the directors as £11,000 of the expenditure was completely beyond Parliamentary authority. Within a few months of opening its line the LCR was facing its first financial crisis. A further Act of Parliament was necessary and on 25 June 1847 the Liskeard & Caradon Railway Amendment Act 1847 (10-11 Victoria cap.lxii) was passed authorising a further capital of £10,500 and borrowing powers of £3,500. In addition the tolls were increased by 1d per ton per mile and rates now given for passengers; 1st, 2nd and 3rd classes at 3d, 2d and 1d per mile respectively. The new capital was divided into one-third shares of £8 6s 8d each but only 861 were distributed raising £7,175 and no direct advantage was taken of the borrowing powers.

In March 1846 the shareholders considered an application by the Cornwall Railway to purchase the line. A premium of £10,000 was agreed upon but the Cornwall Railway was to be as short of funds as the LCR and no more was done.[14]

Most traffic, despite earlier proposals and recommendations, was carried by the company who acted as carrier as well as toll-collector. In later years it is known that it was the practice for the downward traffic to run in the late afternoon and evening, the wagons running down individually each under the control of a brakesman.[15] The following morning the empty wagons were returned in train by horses and this pattern was undoubtedly laid down in the early days of the line. The railway could ill afford to buy horses so hired them, like the canal company, doing so throughout the company's life. Unlike many early (and not so early) horse-drawn railways the LCR did not need or have passing loops at frequent intervals since the traffic was only in one direction at a time.

In 1848 the railway had 17 employees. Apart from the secretary, treasurer, superintendent and engineer there were 13 'labourers'. Two years later the labourers had become seven guards, or brakesmen, two platelayers, three labourers and a policeman. The last named controlled traffic on the line and from at least 1851 to 1878 was John Kellow. The number of guards fell in 1851 to four but steadily increased until 1859 when there were 14 out of a total workforce of 27, reflecting the gravity method of working.[16] About the time the line finally opened Silvanus Jenkin superseded Robert Coad as engineer and James Trathan became superintendent, or traffic manager.

The line was profitable from the start with traffic increasing daily. In 1849 more than 10,000 tons were carried and this was to treble in the next decade. The net profit that year was £364 and a dividend of 5% was paid on the new shares, but thereafter the profits were applied to reducing the company's debts. The main traffic in the early years was, of course, copper ore, about 7,000 tons a year finding their way to Moorswater. A little under 3,000 tons of coal was usual and a few hundred tons of granite, timber, sand and lime, iron and sundries made up the rest. At South Caradon the line ran almost onto the mine dressing floors and West Caradon had built an inclined plane, at 1 in 6, from the Cheesewring branch to their mine.

At the Cheesewring the railway ran right into the quarry and connected with Trethewey's own tramways but traffic from the quarry was something of a disappointment to the directors who, as Coad's report had shown, had initially placed great hopes in the quarry and its granite. When the railway was proposed B. H. Lyne and others intended to develop the granite trade[17] but Lyne died and John Trethewey retained control, taking out a fresh lease from 1845 with John Clogg and James Symons as partners. John Clogg was described as a gentleman of West Looe and may well have been a coal merchant, supplying local mines and foundries. James Symons was an innkeeper in East Looe. They were using the name Cheesewring Granite Company and a thirty-foot high granite column was exhibited at the Great Exhibition in 1851 in this name. Despite the new partners, Trethewey did not realise the potential of Stow's Hill.

The receipts for granite, the only traffic on the Cheesewring branch (apart from West Caradon's at the bottom end), were very low; a mere 210 tons were carried in 1852, yielding but 2d per ton mile. This figure would appear to be toll only and Trethewey must have been providing his own carriage, for in 1853 when Tregelles and Crouch took over the granite sett the accounts heading changed to read 'Tolls and Carriage' and the rate rose to 4d per ton mile. The tonnage also rose dramatically, 3,364 tons in 1854 and then not less than 4,000 tons a year for some time.

The change in 1853 was the result of the formation of a cost book company, also named the Cheesewring Granite Company, by E. A. Crouch of Liskeard and Nathaniel Tregelles of London who bought out Trethewey's lease. This form of company was common in Cornish mining. Of the twenty shareholders holding the 32 shares, of a nominal £300 each, half were from London and the few from Cornwall included Silvanus Jenkin. Neither Trethewey nor his partners were involved in the new company.

In the meantime early in 1854, seeking fresh traffic for the railway, the directors planned a branch to Phoenix Mine which had recently become productive. This was planned to be about seven-eighths of a mile long, running from near Pontius Piece at the head of the Gonamena incline, but for no apparent reason was not built and instead the mine adventurers laid a narrow gauge line of their own to connect with the Cheesewring branch north of Minions.[18]

To the north of Caradon Hill several old tin mines were showing signs of life. Marke Valley had started about 1830 and with a 50 feet diameter water-wheel for pumping had sunk a shaft to 26 fathoms but with little success. A fresh company took over in 1840 but it was not until 1846 or 1847 that its first dividend, on tin, was paid and 1850 before dividends became a regular feature. The old open workings south and south-east of Stow's Hill had been the attraction for the 1836 Cornwall Great United Mining Association but, after spending £50,000 on development of the sett looking for tin, work was abandoned. One of the adventurers, Captain Samuel Seccombe, however, had sufficient faith in the mine to take up a lease of a smaller part, renaming it Phoenix in 1843 and nine years later he was rewarded when rich copper was struck.[19]

One reason the district was unexploited for so long was its remoteness and difficulty of

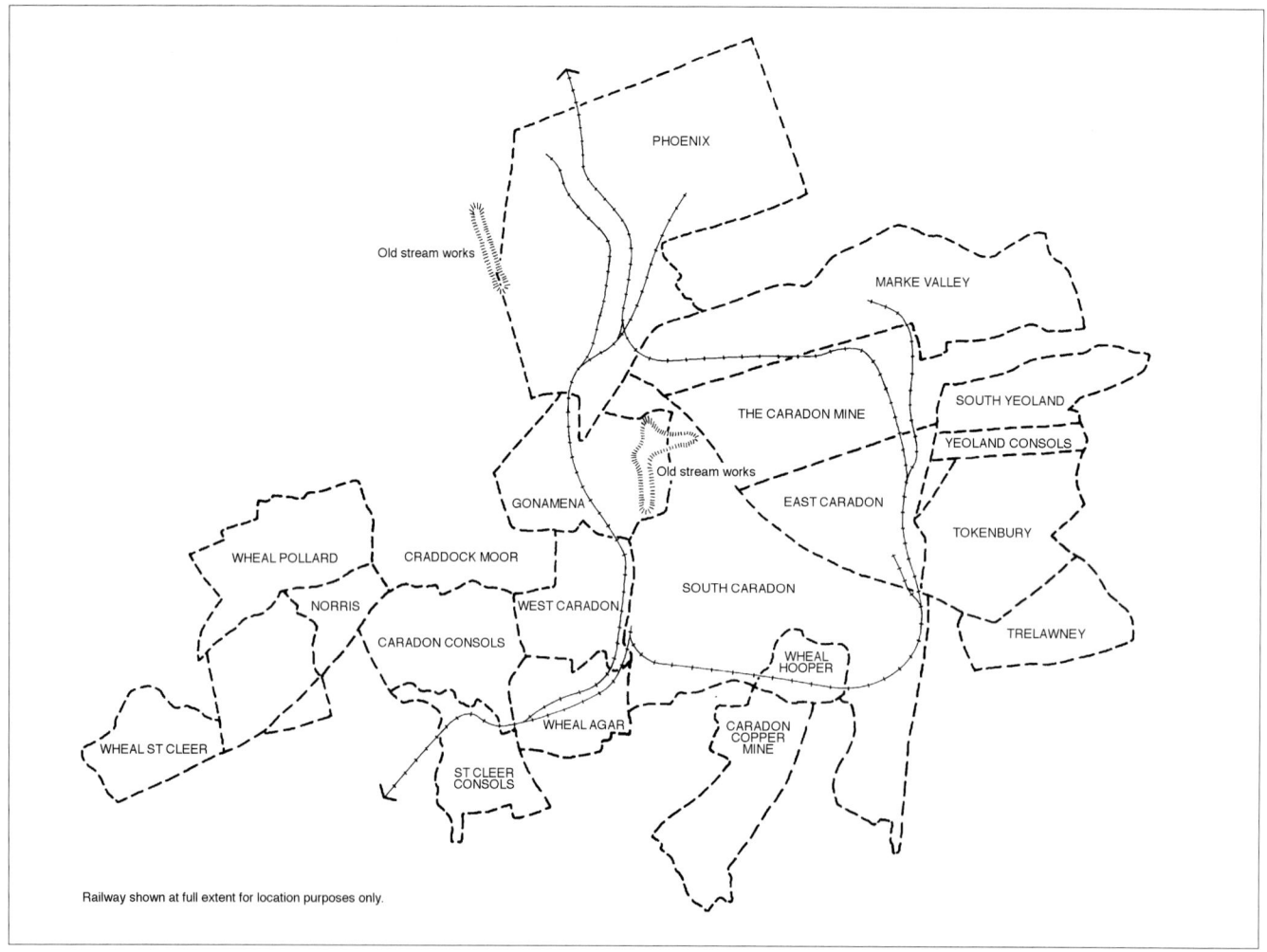

Nicholas Whitley's map showing the Caradon mine setts in 1856 is, in the main, representative of the position throughout the mines' working lives. It predates Glasgow Caradon Consols which took the Tokenbury and Yeoland setts. The railway routes are shown at their fullest extent, despite post-dating the map, to help location.

access but with the opening of the LCR these problems were dispelled and any inhibitions mine promoters and adventurers may have had soon disappeared. Craddock Moor, East Wheal Agar and West Rosedown mines materialised close to the hill and the first-named was profitable for a time. Further out Caradon Consols, Caradon Vale, Caradon United, Great Caradon and several others came on the scene, all hoping the magic name of Caradon would attract both investors and copper. Whilst they may have managed the former they were not so lucky with the latter, for the choice setts containing the major copper lodes were already taken. Furthermore the first mines, in the beginning at least, were sufficiently shallow not to require pumping, water draining out by adit, but these later mines had to seek hard and deep for their copper and needed expensive pumping engines to keep them dry. As well as taking away what copper they produced, the railway also brought their coal. Some of these attempts to emulate the two great Caradon mines struggled on for quite some time but most, with Wheal Norris, Wheal Pollard, Liskeard Consols, Wheal St Cleer and yet more, sank with little trace bar a hole or two in the ground.[20]

Such sudden expansion and development wrought great changes in the hitherto small agricultural communities. The population of St Cleer parish, that most affected, rose dramatically from 982 in 1831 to 1,412 in 1841 and 2,343 in 1851. Whilst nearly a quarter of the miners in 1851 were local men, recruited from the parish, more than 40% came from west of Truro, with a good contingent from St Agnes. Many had made an intermediate stop in mid-Cornwall before moving further eastwards. Another large proportion came from the St Austell district but men were drawn to work in the Caradon mines from all parts of Cornwall, and beyond. By 1861 St Cleer parish reached a population peak of no less than 3,931.[21]

The existing communities at Tremar, St Cleer, Hendra and Crows Nest expanded considerably while virtually new villages arose at Tremarcombe, Darite, Railway Terrace and

Cheesewring Railway (now called Minions). Until housing caught up with the influx overcrowding, and the evils associated with it, was rife and the scene has been compared with that of the mining camps of Colorado and the far west of America.[22] An early riot at Liskeard was on a Saturday payday in 1842 when several hundred miners were busy consuming their pay, in liquid form. It is not without significance that one of the earliest police stations erected by the new County police force, established in 1857, was at St Cleer in 1859 and that it was equipped with shutters for protection.[23] A more civilising influence was the spread of non-conformist chapels, of various denominations, all heartily supported by the miners. Sunday schools, libraries, institutions and brass bands all did their bit to bring civilisation to the area.

Thus, whilst the population figures soared, so did the mortality rate, although death was not so frequently a result of injury and disease at the mines as the squalid conditions at the self-built hovels the miners and their families called home. Malnutrition, poverty and plain dirt engendered typhoid, smallpox and diphtheria and the average life expectancy of those who survived the infant years dropped to as little as 22.[24] Whilst the typical miner's take home pay of a little more than fifty shillings a month was high for the time, he certainly earned it.

As for the scene at the mines themselves back in 1844 the Mining Journal had eulogised:

> The change which the hand of science has effected here is a subject of great congratulation; the moors in the parish of St Cleer, barren and desolate in the extreme, on which nothing useful to the purposes of man was found, but huge masses of granite or scanty sheep pasture, and which were as silent as they were desolate, have assumed a cheerfulness and activity, the result of noisy and busy labour.[25]

A few years later Wilkie Collins, the Victorian novelist, gave the following description of South Caradon Mine, as seen from the Cheesewring branch of the LCR, along which he was walking:

> Soon the scene presented another abrupt and extraordinary change. We had been walking hitherto amid almost invariable silence and solitude; but now with each succeeding minute strange, mingled, unintermitting noises began to grow louder and louder around us. We followed a sharp curve in the tramway, and immediately found ourselves saluted by an entirely new prospect, and surrounded by an utterly bewildering noise. All about us monstrous wheels were turning slowly; machinery was clanking and groaning in the hoarsest discords; invisible waters were pouring onwards with a rushing sound; high above our heads, on skeleton platforms, iron chains clattered fast and fiercely over iron pulleys, and huge steam pumps puffed and gasped, and slowly raised and depressed their heavy black beams of wood. Far beneath the embankment on which we stood, men, women, and children were breaking and washing ore in a perfect marsh of copper-coloured mud and copper-coloured water. We had penetrated to the very centre of the noise, the bustle, and the population on the surface of a great mine.[26]

In 1863 there were 4,000 men, women and children employed at 35 mines and probably a full one-fifth of them were at the South and West Caradons.[27]

In the same way as the mines were the *raison d'etre* of the railway and the saviour of the canal other industries either benefited or grew up to serve them. Foundries at St Blazey, Charlestown, Menheniot and Tavistock gained by the trade and Liskeard, the nearest town, became the commercial centre, expanding its population by 50% in twenty years. Many of Liskeard's fine buildings were built with 'copper' money. A vital commodity for the miners was explosive and in 1846 the East Cornwall Gunpowder Company was established in a quiet valley near Herodsfoot, south west of Liskeard.

The twin towns of East and West Looe once formed a substantial seaport but had remained acutely depressed from the time the Napoleonic Wars had deprived them of their export trade in pilchards. Even after the canal opened they remained two squalid fishing villages. When the canal began bringing copper ore down in

A view of the Caradon mines from Trethevy Quoit about 1856. On the left can be seen the line of the Liskeard & Caradon Railway running below West Caradon Mine, with South Caradon on the hillside opposite. This is the route Wilkie Collins had walked a few years earlier.
AUTHOR'S COLLECTION

Freeman's stone yard has plenty of granite to load whilst on Downgate Quay stands a line of loaded wagons, laden presumably with coal. Looe, probably 1890s.
NEIL PARKHOUSE COLLECTION

An extreme enlargement of a detail of the 1858/9 photograph of Moorswater (page 30) showing one of the early chaldron type ore wagons.
COLLECTION STEPHEN ROWSON.

quantity, diverted by the LCR from Halton and Calstock quays on the River Tamar, the wretched state of the harbour and the dilapidated quays were quite unable to cope. The very existence of the town of East Looe was threatened in October 1846 by a 60 feet breach in the sea wall, caused partly by two ill-conceived wharves on the narrow tidal approach to the harbour.[28] An Act to establish the Looe Harbour Commissioners was obtained in 1848 and soon work commenced to build a breakwater and improved quays. Although the Act provided the appropriate powers and thirteen commissioners, of whom the canal treasurer had to be one, it did not provide funds and money was something of a problem. It was the philanthropy of John Buller that kept the Commissioners going while a stream of letters, some of which can only be described as begging, went to the Admiralty and the Public Works Loan Board. Some money was eventually forthcoming from the Paymaster General and the rapidly increasing trade soon put the Commissioners on a sounder footing. More quays were added but for many years there was inadequate wharfage.

On the railway the traffic was increasing in leaps and bounds, reaching 28,650 tons in 1858 and yielding a net profit of £2,317; copper ores accounted for almost 16,000 tons, coals 5,600 tons and granite 6,572 tons, all of which came or went via the canal. The last of the construction debts had been paid off in 1855 and from the 1856 annual general meeting a regular dividend of five per cent was paid on both old and new shares.

The Cheesewring Granite Company was expanding as fast as it could and in 1856 Tregelles took a lease of the Kilmar granite sett from the Duchy. Kilmar Tor, remote, lonely and beautiful, and the third highest point in Cornwall, was a mile and a half north of the Cheesewring and a mile from any road but was surrounded by a wealth of loose, tumbled granite, easily quarried moorstone. A railway was proposed by the granite company to reach the tor and it was agreed that it would build the line and the LCR would work it. The Kilmar Railway was constructed during the summer of 1858, the rails, carried free on the canal and railway, being laid on granite blocks. On 26 August 1858

the opening of the extended line from Cheesewring to Kilmar Rocks took place with considerable eclat. About 10.30 p.m. [*sic*] a

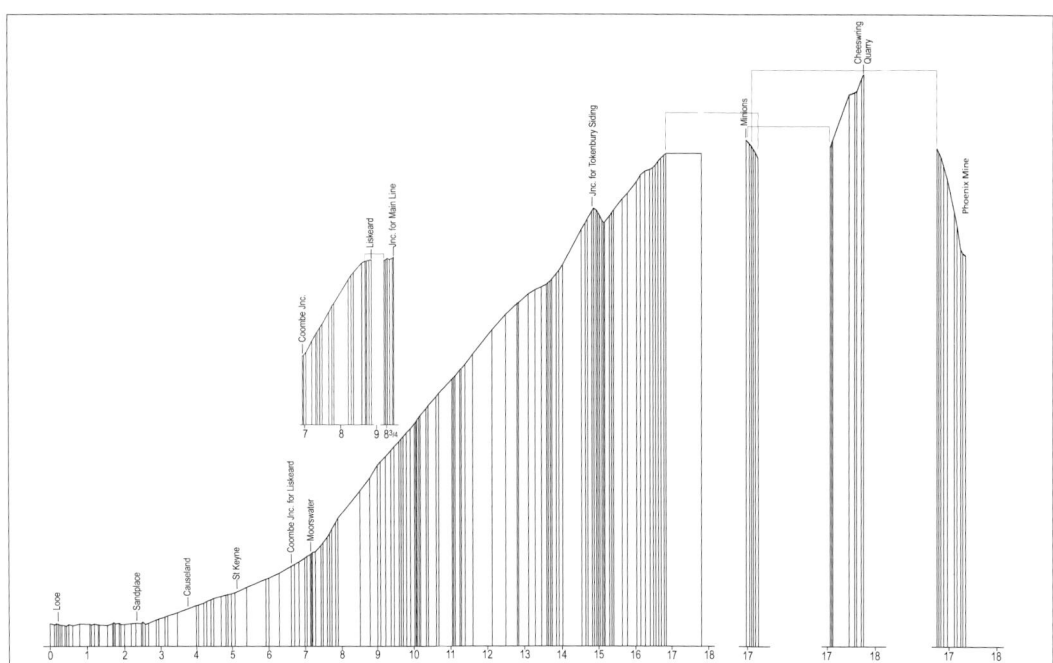

The gradient diagram illustrates how the gradients from Caradon Hill had been engineered to achieve a steady run for gravity traffic. This diagram is based on official GWR profiles of 1917 and the exaggerated vertical scale is 66 times the horizontal.

number of the waggons decorated with flags and evergreens started from the Moorswater terminus conveying the directors and shareholders with many of their friends, and arrived at Kilmar about 2 o'clock, where a collation was spread in a tent, to which they did ample justice. There was also a spread out of doors for the workmen and others. After dinner a number of toasts were given and responded to. A tea was also provided for the persons employed at the granite works at the Cheesewring, after which the train started for Moorswater, and arrived there without any accident about 7 o'clock, all being much pleased with the day's excursion.[29]

The Kilmar Railway left the Cheesewring branch at Minions and, it must be presumed, crossed the Phoenix Mine tramway on the level. In 1859 over 10,000 tons of granite, at 2s 9d per ton toll, went down the line, contributing usefully to the LCR's traffic. It was later to have a major part to play in subsequent plans of the LCR although this was not envisaged at this time.

South Caradon's production continued to increase and West Caradon's, after a booming start, was beginning to fall rapidly but at last the mines near Tokenbury Corner were showing promise and the need for the Tokenbury branch was becoming evident. South Caradon was developing its lodes eastwards and both East Caradon and Glasgow Caradon Consols were on these same lodes. An adit had been commenced in the early 1840s at East Caradon but no other development was done. In 1851 a 21 year lease was obtained from the mineral lords, the same as at Marke Valley, but although the mine showed promise it was not until 1860 that it became profitable. An attempt had been made about 1850 to continue Tokenbury Mine with little success but in 1860 a fresh company, Glasgow Caradon Consols, named after the city of residence of many of its shareholders, took over and this was eventually to join the select few profitable Caradon mines. Marke Valley, too, was bringing up large quantities of copper ore and was soon to join the leaders in terms of tonnage.

Beneath the dumps of West Caradon Mine this is the original route of the LCR looking towards the foot of the Gonamena incline. 1947.
R. S. CARPENTER COLLECTION

CHAPTER FOUR
THE STEAM RAILWAYS

You have the unenvied distinction of having the only railway that can be beaten by one-horse carts.
CHARLES TREGENNA, 1869

The rapidly gathering speed of progress in the nineteenth century was beginning to make itself felt in east Cornwall. On 2 May 1859 the Cornwall Railway had at last opened through from Plymouth to Truro bringing with it greater changes than the county had seen, or was to see, for many years. As a small token of this, Liskeard town on 11 January 1860 adopted 'Greenwich or railway time' by dint of putting the town clock on about sixteen minutes at midday.[1] The influence on the engineers of the two companies, railway and canal, was a little more direct; the Looe company copied the longitudinal sleepers of the main line while the Caradon company seems to have realised, through Silvanus Jenkin, just how primitive a tramway it had. Leifchild's references to a 'real rough tramroad' that only spirits and sprites could travel on[2] was doubtless more literary licence than fact, but nevertheless the LCR was far from being the epitome of a modern railway. Although initially adequate for its purpose the engineering and construction was out of date when it was built and was now even more so. Still relying on horses and gravity, the railway was working to capacity, traffic was still increasing and, as the canal company had found a year or two previously, drastic steps were needed.

Silvanus Jenkin had first mooted steam power in 1854 but, whilst the Regulation of Railways Act 1842 authorised the construction of bridges in place of level crossings without an Act, it was then felt this was too expensive a way to get around Section 264 of the 1843 Act which prohibited steam locomotives crossing public roads on the level and the idea was shelved. This time the directors resolved to go to Parliament for powers to make the line fit for locomotives, to buy the Kilmar Railway and build the Tokenbury branch (powers for which had lapsed). Some local opposition was overcome and the Reverend Norris lent the railway £500 towards Parliamentary expenses.

On 15 May 1860 the Liskeard & Caradon Railway Act 1860 (23 Victoria cap.xx) was passed. It stated the existing issued capital to be £19,825 including £1,000 mortgage debt, authorised new £25 shares up to a total of £12,000 and increased the borrowing powers to £10,000. The two previous Acts were repealed although the continuity and liabilities of the company were maintained, and the later Railways Clauses Consolidation Act 1845 (8&9V.c.20) was incorporated. In addition to authority to buy the Kilmar Railway and build the Tokenbury branch, several deviations were included to ease some of the sharp curves, although none were built, and to avoid the inclined plane at Gonamena on the Cheesewring branch. New rates of toll were fixed with an extra 1d if the company provided

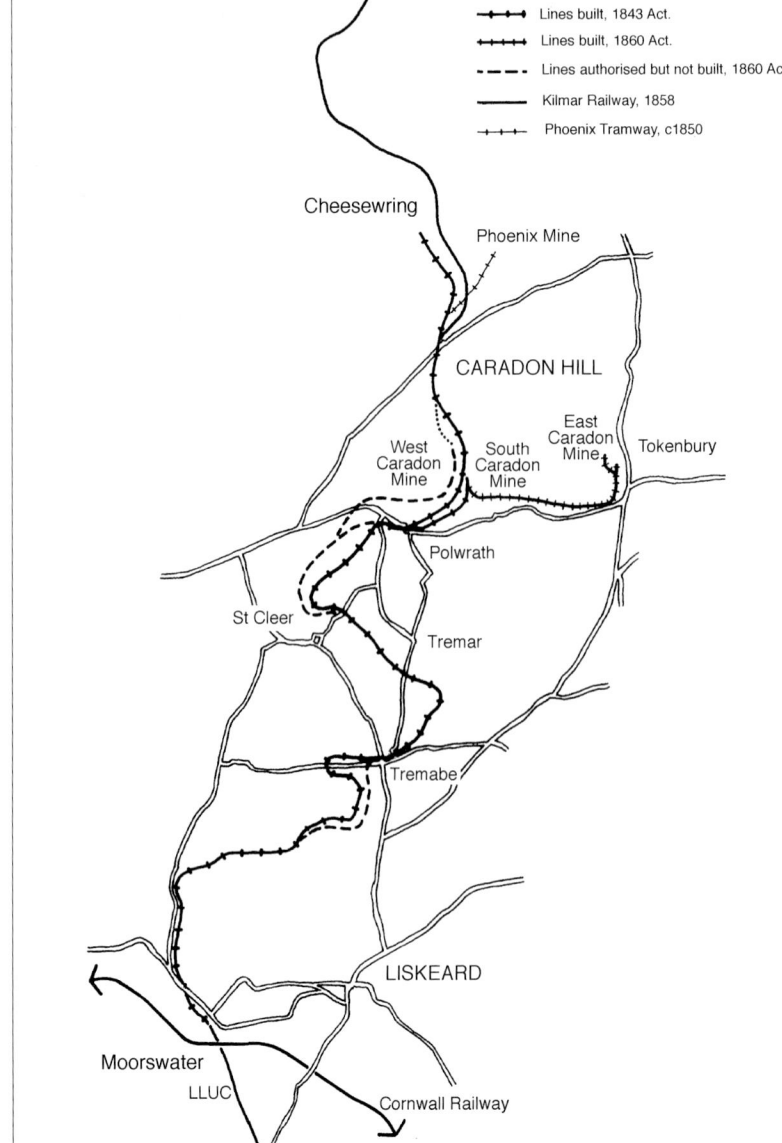

The Liskeard & Caradon Railway in 1861, showing lines built and those that were authorised but not built.

36

carriages and a further 1d toll for propelling power, horse or locomotive engine.

The LLUC railway opened on 27 December 1860 (see Chapter 2) the Looe company hiring a locomotive, *Liskeard*, and the Caradon company providing the wagons, more of which were soon necessary. Construction of the Tokenbury branch commenced and in May 1861 tolls were fixed between Tokenbury Corner and Moorswater. Also that month an extension of the branch onto the East Caradon Mine dressing floors was authorised and it can be assumed the branch was then open. The earthworks of some 550 yards of the new Cheesewring branch were constructed, southwards from Pontius Piece, but were never made use of; possibly West Caradon again objected to it passing through their mine. Part of the earthworks were used about 1865 for the beginnings of a branch into Craddock Moor Mine but this too was never completed. It was on these branches and the alterations to Looe Mills and Foundry bridges to make room for locomotives that much of the £5,000 raised by the LCR in debentures was spent. It also went on additional rolling stock and facilities and, shortly, the LCR's first locomotive. *Liskeard* appeared to be answering its purpose quite well, the LLUC buying it from James Murphy for £600 in September 1861, and an engine shed had been built at Moorswater but in June the LCR had decided to buy their own engine from Gilkes Wilson & Co.

Caradon, a six-coupled saddletank, arrived sometime during 1862, possibly August, but may not have proved too satisfactory at first as a new set of wheels was ordered in December. Certainly horse power was still in use on the LCR main line in August for on the 9th two wagons ran away and killed four horses that were waiting to haul wagons up the line.[3] Another engine, *Cheesewring*, was bought two years later to assist *Caradon*.

In March 1862 a Joint Committee was formed between the two companies for traffic purposes; the LCR being represented by three directors and the LLUC by two members of the Committee of Management. It was agreed the Caradon company should work all traffic, charging 1^1/$_8$d per ton mile for doing so and buying *Liskeard* for £600. Through tolls were fixed from the mines to Looe, which the LCR were to collect and pass 40% to the LLUC. From 31 March the railways were worked as one unit and it is convenient, therefore, to tell their story together although, it is important to remember, the two companies retained their individuality and independence throughout.

At first traffic continued to increase and the enterprise of the two companies appeared justified. Every inch of space on the quays at East Looe was filled, ore was also being taken to

A bustling Looe quays with copper ore neatly stacked in parcels ready for shipping in almost all available space. The stone yard with its gantry crane and derrick is also full of large blocks of Cheesewring granite. Date is unknown but in the absence of Looe Guildhall it is earlier than 1877.
ROYAL INSTITUTION OF CORNWALL;
REF: LOOE H52

The site of Looe station prior to the building of the passenger station in 1879. The track on the river bank is laid with longitudinal sleepers. Note the wharf office and the timber water tank. Bullers Quay is lined with ships loading copper ore and granite. Compare with page 50.
NEIL PARKHOUSE COLLECTION

West Looe, and the LLUC were building extra wharves above Looe Bridge. After less than a year's use the rails laid on the quays by the Looe Harbour Commissioners were showing signs of wear and tear. Late in 1862 it was reported the harbour's trade had increased by 300% in ten years and the harbour dues were now about £1,000 a year. A problem that plagued the harbour for some years was the tardiness of the Swansea smelters in shipping the copper ore from Looe. Often it could not be moved until the weather was suitable for the voyage around Land's End but the smelters also left the ore, often for months, until they needed it or until their own vessels were free to carry it. Coal came from mines also owned by the smelters; a 'package deal' with the copper mines is likely, and a ship bringing coal in would take ore out. But the ships' masters were not keen on this trade, the dead weight and acidity making copper a dangerous cargo, and there was a shortage of vessels because of this.[4]

Copper ore traffic on the railway reached a peak of over 27,000 tons in 1863 but declined after this date although coal continued to increase for a few years, reaching a maximum of 22,000 tons, reflecting the fact that the mines were having to go deeper and pump more water. Limestone and granite remained steady with 4,000 tons and 7,000 tons respectively travelling over the Looe line, while lead ore from Wheal Mary Ann at Menheniot made a small but useful contribution. In view of the increased traffic the salaries of the Superintendent, the Engineer and the Secretary were increased by 50%; to £150 for the first named and £75 each for the other two.

In an attempt to improve facilities at Looe the two companies agreed to scour the harbour and dredge the shingle bank, while it was suggested to the Harbour Commissioners that they build a new pier. Charles Tregenna, the Commissioners' Clerk since 1848, is likely to have been the Tregenna summarily dismissed by the LLUC in 1834 as their Clerk at Looe. He was certainly no friend of the railways for his reply is vitriolic, and worth quoting in full:

My dear Sir,
I have received yours of yesterday and am glad to find that you have not forgotten Looe Harbour.
Nothing would give Looe Harbour Commissioners greater pleasure than the laying of the foundation stone of a new pier but their efforts are paralysed by the following reports. In the first place it is said that the Liskeard & Caradon & Looe Railway Companies cannot compete with the one horse carts and to enable them to do so they beg money from the poor. It is reported that you encourage the competition of other lines by enormous charges – 5d per ton per mile for ores and 3d for granite – preferring high prices

A Fowey-registered vessel enters Looe harbour, while a screw tug manoeuvres near Downgate Quay. On the quay wagons are being unloaded, possibly of china clay.
NEIL PARKHOUSE COLLECTION

and little trade. Another report is rather damaging to the Commissioners for it is said that they give you £180 per year to bring the traffic of two mines to the port.

It is also stated that you are about to sell your lines to the Cornwall Railway Company and that you will stipulate what otherwise they would be disinclined to do – that they shall shut them up.

And lastly it is reported that, preferring the rural to the marine, you are about to make your terminus at St Mabe!! I shall be glad to hear from you that some of these rumours are false for as long as they are current they are not encouraging to an imitation of the Harbour Commissioners of St Ives.

I am, yours faithfully,
Charles Tregenna[5]

How much this extra-ordinary letter accurately reflected local opinion can only be guessed at. Virtually all the mineral traffic offering from the Caradon Hill district travelled down the railway to Looe and had the railway not been there or the charges too high it would have gone eastwards to Calstock and the River Tamar. The two mines referred to were East Caradon and Marke Valley which, in 1862, had negotiated favourable rates for their ore and coal traffic for the following seven years. The low rates of the agreement were later to prove an embarrassment to the railways and no similar agreements were made with other mines. Tregenna's reference to the competition of one-horse carts must have been a favourite phrase of his for he repeats it four years later in another sarcastic letter. There is no substance for his other 'reports' and one doubts this also. Nothing was done for, as Tregenna himself wrote a few months later, 'the Harbour Commissioners are just now hard up for cash' and for some years after the LLUC Engineer reported no progress at Looe.

The west Cornish mines reached their peak of copper production in the 1850s, but the east was a decade behind. Although West Caradon's tonnage was declining, its place had been taken by East Caradon and, to a lesser extent, Craddock Moor. Phoenix and Marke Valley both contributed substantially to the railways' traffic, although the former was soon to commence a rapid decline. The mine had reached a depth of 214 fathoms (1,284 feet) and the copper ores appeared to be running out. The shareholders wanted to abandon it but once again an act of faith saved Phoenix. William West of St Blazey had been the mine's engineer since 1850, having erected engines here and at other Caradon mines, and he was convinced that the mine could be worked more profitably for tin which, unusually, was here found alongside the copper. In 1868 he acquired a controlling interest, re-equipped the mine for tin production and Phoenix once again started a

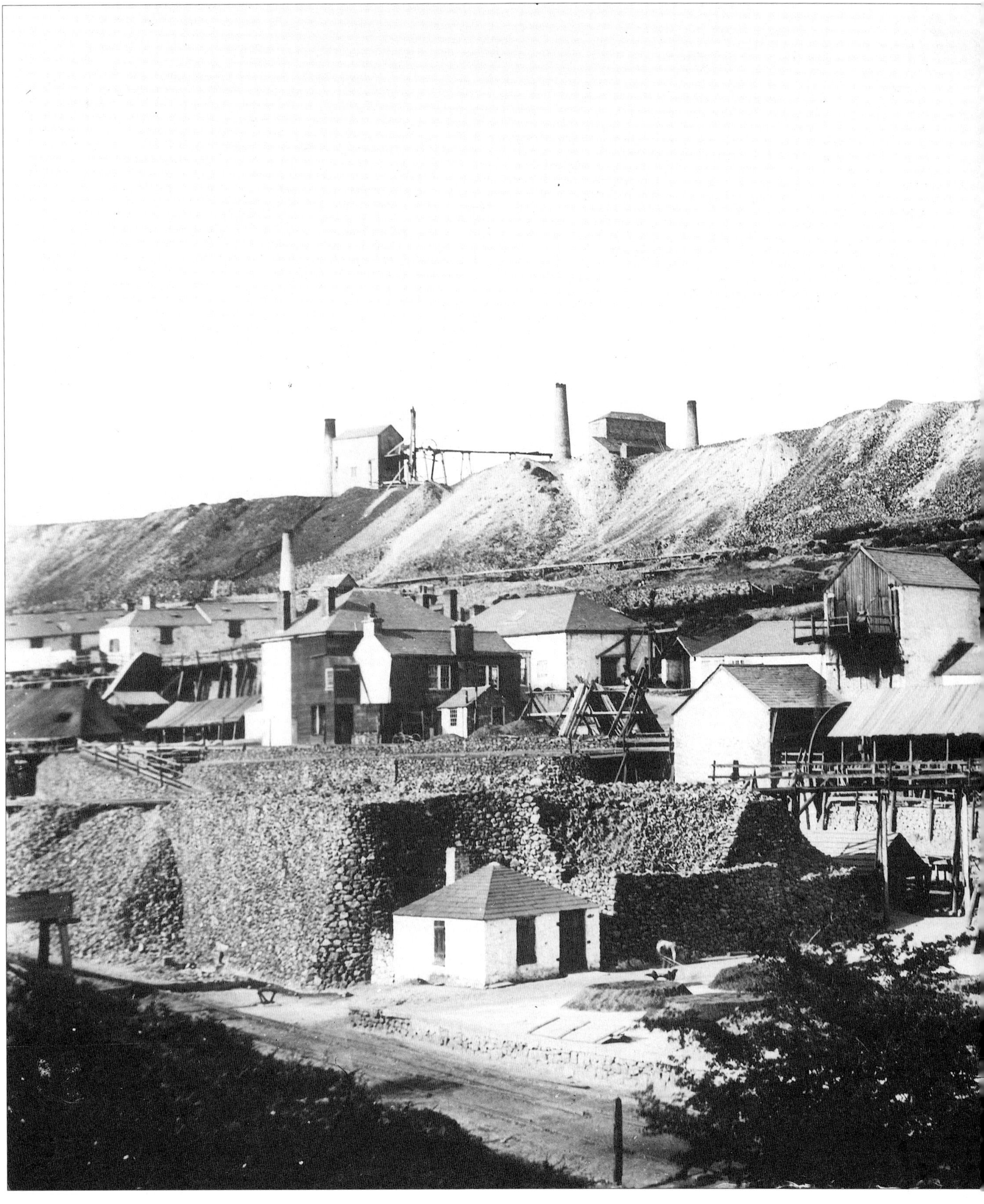

South Caradon Mine prior to its final closure in 1885. In the immediate foreground is the LCR siding with 6-ton wagons 80 and 70. Behind them are the storage floors with neat parcels of copper ore awaiting shipment. The overhead trestle carries two narrow gauge wagons, typical of what was used underground, and one of which is tipping a light coloured material. Between the two wagons is what may be a weighing machine. Central in the picture is the 30-inch stamps engine driving 24 heads of stamps and a crusher. To the left are the count house and offices, and beyond are the group of buildings that housed the miners' dries, blacksmith shops, stores, etc. On the skyline, from left to right, are the pumping and winding engine houses of Engine, or Sump, Shaft and the pumping house of Pearce's Shaft. Below their dumps runs the tramway from Rule's and Kittow's Shaft and also what appears to be a wooden launder.
NEIL PARKHOUSE
COLLECTION

CARADON & LOOE – THE CANAL, RAILWAYS AND MINES

A very similar view to that on the previous pages taken some fifty years later.
L&GRP

fresh life.[6] Marke Valley, along with South Caradon, was to produce substantial quantities of copper for many years yet. The profitable mines still prospered but foreign competition had begun to put the market price of copper ore on a downward slide that was to see the end of all copper mining in Cornwall.

The sums of money involved in the mines even by today's standards were quite large. Although South Caradon had a capital of only £640, being the initial outlay of the founding Clymos and Kittows, others were less fortunate. As a rule the older the mine the less was the initial cost but much depended on how soon the mine became remunerative. West Caradon's outlay by 1862 was only £5,120 but Marke Valley's was £40,725 and at Phoenix £62,425 was spent by Cornwall Great United and Captain Seccombe before that mine became profitable. The riches that could be gained were considerable however. The 512 twenty-five shilling shares of South Caradon were changing hands in 1862 at £400 each, giving the mine a value of more than £200,000, while almost that sum had been paid out in dividends; £386 per 25s share. Since the commencement of the mine £600,000 had been paid out to labourers, miners and merchants and £43,000 to the mineral lord, the Reverend G. P. Norris.[7] By 1886, when the mine closed, £1¾m of ore had been sold and over £½m paid out in dividends.[8]

South Caradon was an exception, however, albeit a golden exception, and although her immediate neighbours were paying propositions, large sums of money were lost in the many smaller mines of the area that raised little but hopes. Although initially expensive Phoenix paid out considerable dividends; at one time £2,000 was distributed on the 12,000 shares every sixteen weeks and by 1860 £150,000 had been paid out, increasing to £200,000 by 1881. Under the cost book system of accounting used by the mines at that time, few reserves were retained and most profits were distributed in each accounting period. Conversely if a mine made a loss, or was needing some expensive equipment, then shareholders were called upon to cover this. Such calls were less well recorded than dividends, of course.

Perhaps the easiest money was made by the mineral lords who owned the rights to the minerals beneath the surface of the land. Their dues amounted to a proportion of the value of the ore raised; in the case of West Caradon it was one-fifteenth and Marke Valley and East Caradon paid one-eighteenth. A sympathetic lord would often reduce the dues, or remit them altogether, when a mine was on hard times, as the Duchy did for Phoenix in 1885. When a lease was due for renewal and the mine still working at a profit a grasping lord could almost literally hold the mine to ransom, for if new terms could not be agreed the mine owners had no option but to abandon the mine. The South Caradon's lord, the Reverend Norris, was of more kindly disposition and when he renewed the mine's lease in May 1862 a substantial piece of plate was presented to him in recognition of his benevolence. He could well afford to be generous – the dues mentioned above were for what was otherwise mere moorland grazing – but it was a dispute with his successor, his son-in-law J. S. Hawker, that was to hasten the eventual closure of the mine.

One of the causes of the heavy expenditure by the mining companies was the need for machinery to pump the mines, to haul up the ores and to crush it when it was got to surface. A Newcomen engine is believed to have worked about 1730 at the old Stows mine, later part of Phoenix United, but the first engine in the district in the nineteenth century was erected at South Caradon in or about 1837. By 1872 William West alone claimed to have erected 100 engines around Caradon Hill, although this sounds something of an exaggeration. Beam engines were used for pumping, winding and stamping and came in all sizes from 14-inch (cylinder diameter) to 70-inch and 80-inch. Horizontal engines powered other machinery, such as saw benches and, latterly, air compressors. When closure eventually came to South Caradon the mine possessed no less than 13 engines of all types. West Caradon in 1863 owned six engines and Phoenix United in 1870 ten. The boilers of these engines, three or four boilers each in the case of the larger engines, were prodigious consumers of coal, much of which found its way up Caradon Hill by means

THE STEAM RAILWAY

Phoenix Mine in the latter half of the nineteenth century, viewed from the west, and probably taken from near Cheesewring Quarry. From left to right can be seen West Phoenix stamps with the dressing floors in front of them, behind are Phoenix stamps, Seccombe's winding and pumping engines are centrally on the skyline, and Sump winding engine is in front of the latter. To the right is the Count House, along with blacksmith's shop and other workshops. On the far right is the horizontal winder for West's Shaft, the shaft itself being in the centre of the photograph beyond the railway track. The latter, running across the centre of the photograph towards the stamps, is the foot of the Phoenix incline. This rare photograph illustrates dramatically the extent and activity of a large nineteenth century Cornish mine. AUTHOR'S COLLECTION

of the railway. Phoenix, for example, in 1872 was using 370 to 400 tons of coal a week, importing it themselves via Looe.

Where water supplies permitted, water wheels did much of the crushing and stamping of ores and were also used for pumping and winding. 30 feet diameter wheels were common and there were a number of 50 feet diameter, while two of 60 feet are recorded.

Elsewhere on surface were blacksmiths' forges, carpenters' shops, miners' dries, gunpowder magazines and all the other attributes of a major mining district. Below ground were many miles of levels, drives and crosscuts, rises and winzes, adits and stopes, extending down to as much as 250 fathoms (1,500 feet – 467m). South Caradon had more than 3,000 fathoms (nearly 3½ miles – 5.5km) of tram rails both underground and at surface.

The Cheesewring and surrounding moor had long been popular for a day's excursion and special trains on the LCR were a regular feature. One of the earliest was in June 1850 when the Liskeard Temperance Society took 300 of their members to the Cheesewring in seven, presumably overcrowded, wagons.[9] The novelty attracted, according to the *West Briton*, thousands of people, which suggests it was one of the first such trips. In May 1869 the railway declined to take 300 children from Liskeard to Looe as they 'could not risk so many children' but the following August the Looe Artillery Volunteers were carried, but at their own risk. The British Association, in August 1877, visited the Caradon and Phoenix mines and it is recorded the engine showered all the eminent company in the ten wagons behind with fine ash.[10]

Casual traffic on the regular mineral trains was always strongly discouraged and the issue of passes strictly controlled, with reprimands being issued to those who disobeyed. Generally local businessmen received passes although a Dr Kerswill was refused. Each year the directors had their own special 'inspection' train, on which invited friends joined them. Such trains were hauled up the line by horses and returned by gravity in the evening, the brakesman having a whistle to blow at each level crossing in the same way as the mineral trains.[11]

To the north of the mining district several competing railways were threatening to link north Cornwall with the rest of the country's railway system and to meet this threat in 1865 the LCR resolved to consider extending northwards itself to connect with the proposed Launceston, Bodmin & Wadebridge Railway, a L&SWR protégé. Consideration was also given to opening the Looe line to passengers and building a link to the Cornwall Railway at Liskeard. Silvanus Jenkin surveyed the latter and estimated the cost at £7,000 but the financial position of the LCR would permit no more.

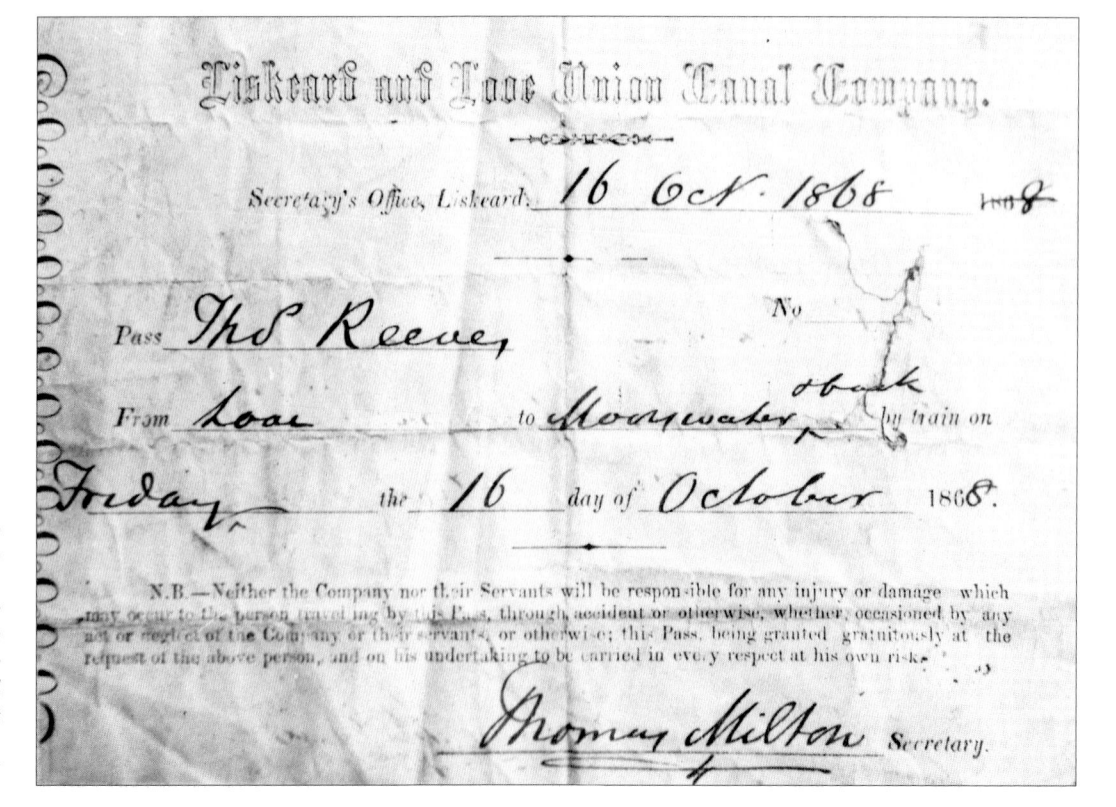

A free pass issued to Thomas Reeves, probably a mason from East Looe, by Thomas Milton, the LLUC's Secretary. As can be seen, passes were issued individually and for specific journeys at this time.
AUTHOR'S COLLECTION

Some new traffic was offered in 1867 in the form of china clay when a storage shed was quoted for at Moorswater and quay space allocated at Looe but it is not certain the traffic materialised. The LCR was improving its line as best it could; stone sleepers being replaced with wood, the level crossing at Woodhill was replaced by a bridge and a third new locomotive, *Kilmar*, was bought in 1869 to join *Caradon* and *Cheesewring*. Complaints had been received from traders at Looe regarding the availability of wagons. The traders, and Tregenna, complained that there were never enough wagons and ships were avoiding Looe because of the time taken to discharge. The mines, Tregenna claimed, all needed wagons at the last minute, just when a fleet held up by storm was likely to come in needing the same wagons.[12] The LCR maintained that there were sufficient wagons for the traffic and the proper remedy was the improvement of the port of Looe. The rails on the quayside were relaid by the Commissioners to permit ships to discharge direct into rail wagons and the complaints ceased, although the declining copper traffic may well have contributed to this.

A sign of this decrease was the first of many requests from the mines and merchants for reductions in the rate of toll but all were refused for some years. The mines' output was declining as reducing world prices made their operations less economic and emigration became a regular occurrence among the mining communities. A dip in traffic in 1866 was attributed to the general commercial crisis, the depression of the metal market and the 'unfortunate and misguided combination of many of the working miners'. Leaner times were encouraging the beginning of trade unionism.

Miners at East Caradon and Marke Valley had gone on strike in 1866 because of the low prices offered for the pitches they were to work. A miners' society had been formed for mutual help and welfare but many mine owners were opposed to it and refused to employ its members. In 1872 some 300 child labourers came out on strike. Girls were paid 6s a week and South Caradon offered an extra penny a day. West Caradon girls, followed by those of other mines, came out on strike and the boys at Phoenix supported them. They were seeking 2d a day and the mines gradually relented.[13]

Both railway companies were borrowing heavily and were having a little difficulty finding new lenders as loans came up for renewal. In 1869 a branch was built into Phoenix Mine, replacing the narrow gauge tramway, and the following year Freeman & Sons, who had taken over Cheesewring Quarry in 1863, requested a new line into the quarry at a lower level. This

This view of Moorswater, taken in the last two decades of the nineteenth century, is full of detail. Hodge's limekiln, on the far left, still has the plateway incline and tracks and limestone is piled alongside the siding opposite it. The stores and buildings dating from canal days are still in use and there appears to be a further building beyond the wagon repair shop, alongside the engine shed. The long open sided sheds for storing minerals are prominent, with semi-circular corrugated iron roofs. Little rolling stock can be seen; a solitary wagon centrally and a Metropolitan carriage can be discerned by the eastern limekiln, on the right.
LISKEARD OLD
CORNWALL SOCIETY

High tide at Looe presents a serene picture sometime prior to 1879. A line of ten 6-ton wagons, carrying ore and granite, wait to go on to the quays for unloading. Lump coal is stacked high in the centre of the picture, with two more wagons nearby. Behind the water tower is the later site of the passenger station.
NEIL PARKHOUSE COLLECTION

was built in 1871. Also in 1870 the engineer, Jenkin, produced a plan to avoid the Gonamena incline by extending the Tokenbury branch through Marke Valley to Phoenix Mine. It was quite beyond their powers but nevertheless an approach was made to the landowners concerned for their opinion. This was favourable and it was agreed, in view of the benefits to the mines and to agriculture, that the land would be granted free. The conditions were that ownership of the land would be transferred, a siding would be provided for the landowners' use and completion of the line would be within seven years, or else the land would be retaken. The landowners appear to be the mineral lords of the East Caradon, Marke Valley and West Rosedown mines. Construction of the branch began in 1872 but soon ceased due to the LCR's lack of funds.

A puzzling feature in the LCR's Statutory Returns of Traffic is a startling leap in total minerals carried from 39,491 tons in 1867 to

The stone yard on Looe quays was in use until about 1932 and this photograph could be of the derrick being dismantled about 1939, with a no doubt helpful row of 'advisers'. Beyond the derrick can be seen the overhead travelling crane that also served the stone yard.
ROBERT TIVENDALE COLLECTION

61,108 tons the following year. There is no positive evidence, but the Minute Books indicate increased activity in the granite trade. Freemans were busy at the Cheesewring and a new quarry, with tramway connecting to the Kilmar Railway, was opened at Bearah,[14] south of Kilmar. This extra tonnage would appear, therefore, to be granite and the 1868 figure represents a peak that was steadily eroded each year thereafter.

Expenses in 1869 were five or six times those of ten years previous when all traffic was horse drawn, but total receipts had only increased by less than three times and, from this time, income began a decline that continued with rare exception unchecked to the end of the century. It was soon realised that the boom years of copper mining had come to an end and other outlets and sources of income were sought. Again the LCR looked to the north and also this time to the east.

Although some years earlier the Cornwall Railway, with Great Western Railway influence, had won the day against the London & South Western Railway's Cornwall & Devon Central Railway for the main route into the county, the L&SWR was still hoping to connect the Bodmin & Wadebridge Railway, which it acquired in 1846, with the rest of its system. Several lines into Cornwall were mooted via Launceston and north of Bodmin Moor and it was to link with one of these that the extension to Altarnun was proposed, the Kilmar Railway being bought by the LCR in 1879 with this in mind. Another company was proposing to build a line from Tavistock to Callington and hoping to extend to Tokenbury Corner with L&SWR backing. The LCR contacted the L&SWR, probably at Silvanus Jenkin's prompting, in 1876 with a view to the L&SWR buying the line. The year before Jenkin had fallen out with his partner, J. J. Trathan, and the partnership was dissolved, their respective duties on the two railways being split. Jenkin was engineer to the LCR and Trathan traffic manager to both lines and engineer to the LLUC. By 1876 they were not on speaking terms and Trathan made his own approach to the GWR, pointing out that if it would suit the L&SWR to buy the LCR it might suit the GWR better. Nothing came of either gentleman's negotiations and the companies' attentions turned back to internal matters.

Construction of the Marke Valley branch and a separate extension around Caradon Hill, called the Kilmar Junction Railway, recommenced in 1876, the former opening by August 1877 and the latter in November. The KJR had cost £3,600 and the Gonamena incline route was dispensed with immediately. It is strange that the Marke Valley branch had not been built before this late date, for the mine had been an important copper producer for almost twenty years and since 1866 second only to South Caradon. By 1877 it was well past its peak, although the drastic fall in production that was soon to follow was not yet obvious. Glasgow Caradon Consols had just passed its peak of 3,069 tons (1874) and Phoenix and East Caradon were not far from becoming

Running between canal and river, the LLR comes down the East Looe valley and past Terras crossing, in the last decades of the nineteenth century. The canal is full although the tide is low so it was still able to hold water. The longitudinal sleepers can be clearly seen and the level crossing is totally unprotected.
NEIL PARKHOUSE COLLECTION

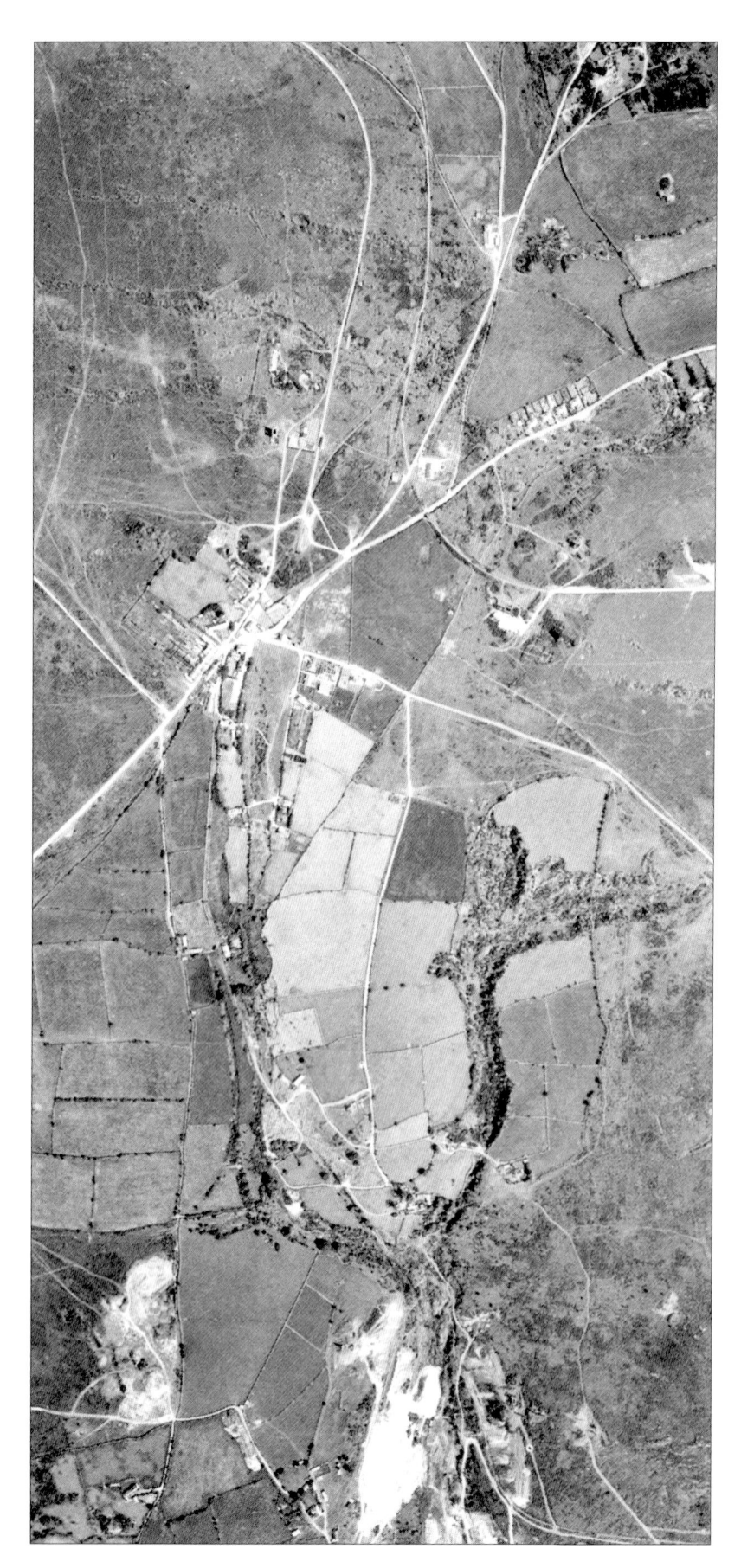

insignificant, tin now being more important to the former. South Caradon seemed to go on as ever with production fluctuating between 5,500 and 6,500 tons each year.

All the mines were clamouring for reductions in carriage charges; despite maintaining production South Caradon had just incurred its first working loss. West Caradon had ceased completely in 1874 and, although South Caradon took over the sett the following year, little work was done. Several significant reductions in tolls had been made but in 1877 a fresh tariff was fixed in which the charge between the mines and Looe varied between 5s per ton and 5s 9d per ton for ore and coal depending on the distance to the mine. The previous range had been from 4s 3d to 6s 10½d.

In July 1877 it was noted that only a verbal agreement existed between the two companies for their working, the interchange of traffic and the apportionment of expenses and receipts. The LCR had been working both lines, charging the LLUC 1¼d per mile (increased from 1⅛d since 1868) and paying 40% of the receipts to the LLUC. The latter maintained their own line from this but now the LCR proposed to formally lease the Looe company's property. The LLUC agreed to this, providing it received a minimum of £1,350 per annum to enable it to pay interest on loans and maintain a dividend. An Act was required to authorise the lease and at the same time powers were sought to make a connection with the Cornwall Railway. The LCR took great pains to assure the LLUC that this latter was not intended as a hostile action although it would undoubtedly cause much loss both to Looe harbour and the LLUC. The Royal *Cornwall Gazette*'s correspondent commented

> People here hardly thought the Liskeard & Caradon Railway Company were rich enough to carry out such an expensive undertaking, but we are glad to find such is the case.

Locally it was felt that mineral exports would be lost to St Germans but there were hardly the same facilities there and it would not have been likely.[15]

Caradon Hill. From south to north, bottom to top, can be seen West and South Caradon mines, with the tramway from the latter running eastwards towards Rule's and Kittow's shafts. The Gonamena incline runs northwest, between fields, and to its left (west) can be seen the abortive branch to Craddock Moor. East of Minions village the Kilmar Junction Railway curves in past Wheal Jenkin and the maze of trackbeds northeast of the village is quite clear. Running off the picture to the north are the Cheesewring branch, Kilmar railway and the Phoenix branch. R. G. SPALDING COLLECTION

However, the Bill was not proceeded with and it was withdrawn, but an agreement was made nevertheless on 29 January 1878 between the two companies for the LCR to lease the entire undertaking of the LLUC. The LCR was to apportion the earnings according to the mileage travelled over each company's line and pay to the LLUC 50% of the gross earnings of the traffic travelling over its railway, less £1,000 and with a minimum payment of £1,350. The agreement was for ten years and the LCR took charge on 27 February 1878.

J. J. Trathan had been ill for some time and unable to attend to his duties on either railway and in June 1878 the LCR sacked him from his post of traffic superintendent with three months salary. In February 1879 the LLUC decided it no longer needed an engineer and traffic manager now the LCR was working the line and dismissed him too, with thanks and a £25 handshake. Smythurst, the station master at Moorswater, was appointed in his place by the LCR at a salary of £100 per annum.

John Francis Buller raised his head again at this time. Apart from complaining about the state of the canal (see Chapter 2) he had been promised a siding at Sandplace when the LLUC railway was building and this had not been provided. After some quibbling over a technical error in the original agreement and as to which company was liable, the LCR built the siding early in 1879.[16]

Complaints also came from Freemans, at Cheesewring Quarry, about the shortage of wagons again but Smythurst arranged to provide them with four daily. Tonnage figures and receipts were steadily declining. Receipts for merchandise and minerals in 1869 totalled £14,213 but ten years later this had fallen to £8,652 and in 1880 45,000 tons were carried, 95% in minerals. Income was sufficient, however, for the LLUC to be paid several hundred pounds over and above the minimum of £1,350 for some years.

An addition to income was provided by the opening of the Looe line to passengers on 11 September 1879. Passenger traffic had been mooted in 1865 and a memorial was received in 1868 on the subject but it was not until 1879 that positive action was taken. Until then passengers had been carried on both lines on mineral trains but only on the express permission of the two companies. In April 1879 Colonel J. H. Rich, of the Board of Trade, made an initial inspection of the Looe line to ascertain what refinements would be needed for a proper passenger service. There were many: permanent way renewals, signals, gradient and mileposts. The platforms were not long enough and the stations needed booking offices, waiting rooms, closets, urinals, clocks and nameboards. Colonel Rich was also concerned at the over-bridges, some of which were a little weak and most were too narrow for normal coaching stock. The proposed station at Moorswater was close to the engine shed and that at Looe nearer to Looe Bridge than eventually built. In order to avoid the expense of providing the 'refinements' called for by Colonel Rich the LCR asked if the line could be worked 'as a light railway' but were informed that the inspection was for a light railway and all

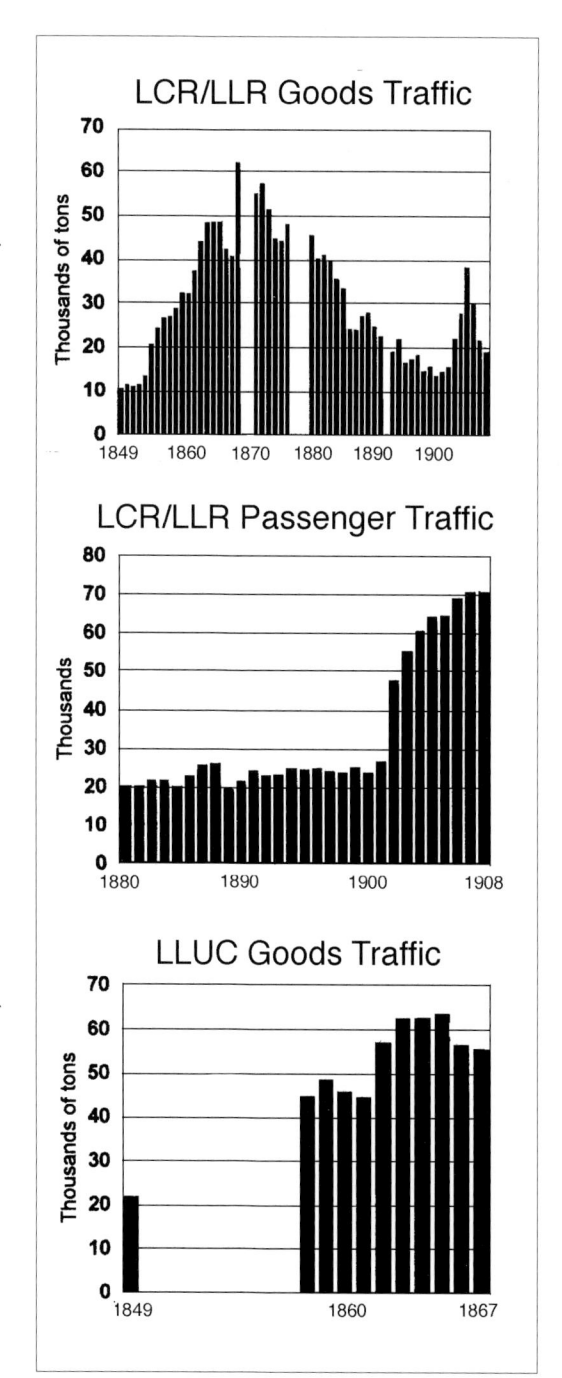

A view southwards towards Looe Bridge from above the station, showing the newly built LLR station, about 1880. Coal and timber are stored opposite the station while the distant quays are full of ore. Comparison with page 38 shows that one rail of the quayside line has been lifted and the siding has become the main line. As a consequence the filler for engines has been moved to the east side of the water tank. The signal is one installed by Stevens & Sons in the summer of 1879.
NEIL PARKHOUSE COLLECTION

the permanent way would require renewing if it was to work as an ordinary line. The LCR pushed on with the work and by August was ready for another inspection. On 7 September 1879 Colonel Rich reported that most of his requirements had been met. Stations had been built at Looe, Causeland and Moorswater, the latter close beneath the viaduct and two short narrow coaches bought. Accordingly he sanctioned the opening as a light railway (under the Regulation of Railways Act 1868 s.29) with a speed limit of 20 m.p.h. The LCR also undertook to work the line with one engine in steam.[17] The station at Sandplace was opened later in 1881.

As the provision of stations and other improvements was done entirely at the LCR's expense they were accordingly to have the benefit of all receipts from this service. The LCR had long hankered after a passenger service over its own line and when Colonel Rich inspected the Looe line he was asked to look at the Caradon also. He 'gave an off-hand opinion that there were many worse lines'[18] and the

At Moorswater station, one of a series of views of CARADON, the three Metropolitan carriages and brake van No 4. On the right is the siding into Freeman's stone yard and beyond is the down starting signal. The upper arm is for passenger trains and the lower for mineral trains. The same applies to the two arms of the home signal seen just south of the viaduct.
JOHN ALSOP COLLECTION

Another view of the same train at Moorswater. This photograph is of interest as it shows the lettering used on the carriages at least in the earlier days of passenger services. Each compartment is lettered and bears the number of the vehicle, thus the four compartments of No.3 carriage are marked A.3 to D.3 and composite carriage No.1, A1 to C1.
JOHN ALSOP COLLECTION

KILMAR outside the shed at Moorswater, some time prior to 1896 as no vacuum brake pipe is fitted. The firebox on the right is interesting but it is not CARADON's.
J. WILLCOCKS

TIMETABLE AUGUST 1882				
Classes	1, 2 & 3	1 & 2 WO	1, 2 & 3	1 & 2 SO
Moorswater	7.30	9.52	4.00	7.15
Sandplace	7.50	10.11	4.20	7.35
Looe	8.00	10.20	4.30	7.45
Looe	8.15	10.53	5.30	8.00
Sandplace	8.25	11.02	5.40	8.10
Moorswater	8.45	11.22	6.00	8.20

'We are glad to see and would call attention to the fact that the time of the afternoon train has been altered and now allows a stay of an hour to be made by the sea at Looe – a pleasant and cheap little trip for our townsfolk.'
Cornish Times 11 March 1882.

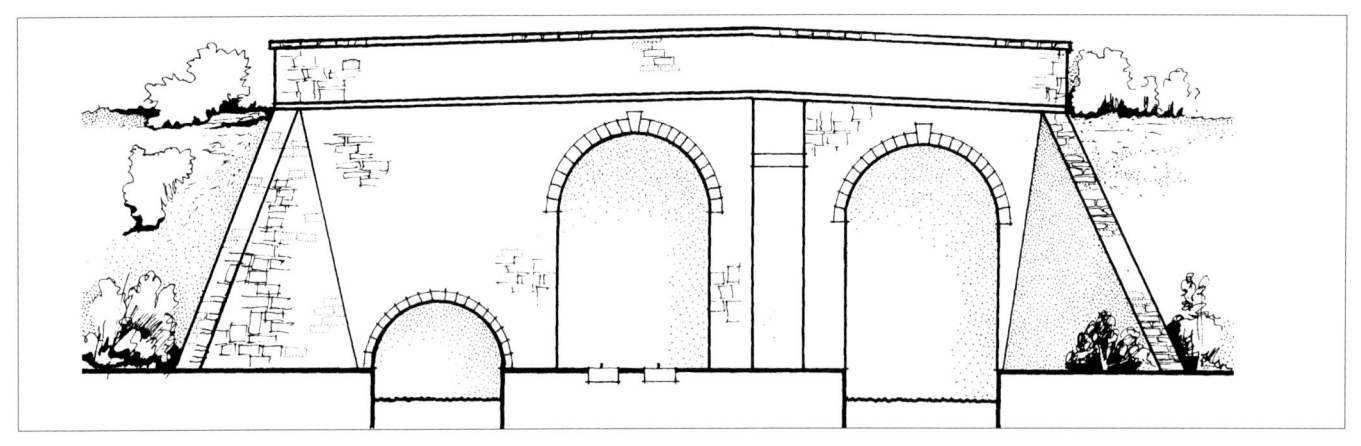

Landlooe Bridge in 1879. The three arches spanned, from left to right, the East Looe River, the Looe railway line and the canal.

Board of Trade was written to to ask if passengers could be carried and charged if they were not hauled by steam. No reply is recorded. The engineer was instructed to report on relaying the many sharp curves on the LCR but little was done, because of the expense. But apart from the curves there was a number of level crossings to be removed or suitably guarded and much of the track needed renewing.

The copper mines at Caradon were now on lean times due to overseas competition and a further blow to the dwindling traffic came in the winter of 1881/82 when the granite works at both the Cheesewring and Kilmar stopped. Back in 1876 it was realised that Freemans had greater interests elsewhere in Cornwall and the Kilmar Railway was seeing very little use at the time of its purchase. Some boost to the granite trade was given by the rebuilding of Moorswater Viaduct but this was short-lived. Foreign competition had begun to make an impact on granite also. Although Marke Valley and Phoenix mines were now concentrating on tin production this mineral was found in much lesser quantities and as it could be refined at the mine, much smaller amounts were available for transport.

Looking for fresh traffic and the possibility of selling the railway to the L&SWR, the LCR proposed to extend to Trewint and offered the LLUC the options of joining with the LCR on the project, selling its railway to the LCR or amalgamating. The LLUC opted for selling its line outright but later decided it had no power to do so and the matter was dropped, leaving the LCR to go ahead with the Trewint extension on its own. Plans were prepared for an Act for this and other planned extensions and to regularise other alterations such as the Kilmar Junction line.

This late nineteenth century postcard view of the north side of Moorswater viaduct also shows the granite yard of Freemans and, on the far left, the LCR signal box.
AUTHOR'S COLLECTION

CHAPTER FIVE

HOPES AND DESPAIR

'This wretched little line.'
MR POPE, 1884

In the west of Cornwall copper mining had been declining since about 1850 due to discoveries in the New World and those mines to the east followed the trend a little later. Unlike many of the western mines few of those around Caradon Hill had deeper deposits of tin to exploit, nor did they have arsenic to supplement their incomes.

South Caradon Mine's dividend had dropped from a peak of £43 in 1864 to thirty shillings fifteen years later. West Caradon had ceased altogether in 1874 and the writing was surely on the wall for the remaining copper mines. With the ailing Devon Great Consols across the River Tamar, the Caradons were the sole survivors of a vast industry and in February 1882, having operated at a loss for some time, it was decided to surrender the lease of South Caradon Mine. A fresh lease of a larger area was to be taken over by a limited company who would continue the work of the existing cost-book company. However, agreement could not be reached to renew the lease on these terms and in May notice was given to abandon the sett. The cause of the disagreement appears to have been political. The Reverend Norris had died in 1870 and his successors, his widow and daughters, were apparently being advised by John S. Hawker, who had married one of the daughters, and they, or he, were said to be not pleased with the outcome of a recent election and the politics of the mine people.[1]

The first impact of this decline was felt by the miners themselves and their families. There were few other metal mining areas to move to in Britain and it was to the ports – Plymouth, Liverpool, London – that they went to seek work around the world. In the coming decades the population figures of the parishes around Caradon Hill tumbled, almost to their pre-mining levels.

Although it is not recorded in the Minute Books the directors of the LCR must have realised that, with little other revenue and

KILMAR at Looe with two LCR carriages and brake van 4, between 1896 and 1901.
ROBERT TIVENDALE COLLECTION

A selection of Liskeard & Caradon Railway card tickets. First class tickets were white, second class buff or pink while third class tickets were green for up travel and blue for down. The free pass return was yellow with a red stripe and may have been for the Caradon line. The Parliamentary ticket was green, and probably gave access to third class. Quite what the circular route from Looe to Moorswater was is not known but the ticket was white. The LCR also issued a variety of excursion and 'Special Pleasure Party' tickets

traffic, their days were numbered too and the need for a link with the outside world was becoming essential. The LLUC Committee of Management's Minute Book at this time shows little concern for anything except the few items regarding the railway that were not the responsibility of the LCR. In sharp contrast the LCR's Minute Books show a flurry of activity that was to last for five or six years.

Yet again, the LCR directors went to Parliament to secure the Liskeard & Caradon Railway Act 1882 which received the Royal Assent on 12 July 1882 after an unopposed passage. This Act (45-6 Victoria cap.cxi) was quite short, having only 34 sections. New capital of £30,800 was sanctioned with borrowing powers of £15,300 and no less than seven 'new' lines were authorised:

Railway No 1: Moorswater to Liskeard, 5½ furlongs (1,210 yards) at 1 in 33
2: Cut off several curves on the mainline between High Wood and South Caradon
3: Tokenbury Corner to Sharptor, as already built
4: Phoenix branch, as already built
5: A 400 yard connection between the Kilmar Railway and the Cheesewring branch at Rillaton
6: A branch to Gold Diggings Quarry of 1¼ miles
7: Sharptor to Trewint, 5½ miles

Railways 3 and 4 were already built and only Railway 5 was to be, although 7 was to be commenced two years later.

Traffic for the Trewint line, or the Northern Extension as it was known, was to come from mines, quarries and china clay deposits that the presence of the railway was to make viable and for which the railway would have the monopoly of transport to Looe and the sea. Some agricultural traffic was expected and no less than 3,250 tons were hoped to be obtained from this lonely stretch of moorland.

The cost of the 5½ miles was estimated at £15,000 and a further extension to Launceston was planned when the North Cornwall Railway was opened by the L&SWR. It was hoped the capital for the line would come from the Altarnun area and much effort was put into touting shares around there, albeit with singular lack of success. The Northern Extension appeared destined to go the way of many of the LCR directors' ideas.[2]

At the end of 1882 an offer to purchase both railways came from Francis Fox, the civil engineer, on behalf of an unnamed syndicate. The bargaining concluded with offers of

A view of the rear of Looe station by Mr Raddy, of Looe, taken before the building was extended in 1901.
ROBERT TIVENDALE COLLECTION

£42,350 for the LLUC and £50,000 for the LCR. The conditions were that both companies should accept the offers and the LCR would complete both the Trewint line and the now planned extension to Camelford, the syndicate providing capital for construction and parliamentary costs. The offers were accepted subject to the respective shareholders giving their approval but Fox, despite apparently having the backing of a 'leading mainline company', had difficulty in raising the necessary £100,000 and within two months he withdrew from the scene. The *Cornish Times* thought the railway's plans were ambitious but selling it a good idea; 'its affairs will then be conducted in a more spirited manner.'[3]

In May 1883 the South Caradon Mining Company had relinquished its lease which was taken over by a completely new and separate limited company, South Caradon Mine Ltd. This was very much London-based, with an office there and directors who lived there, in marked contrast to the old company, although some directors had family connections in Cornwall. The 263 shareholders included J. S. Hawker, Henry Caunter, L. C. Foster and William West (junior), as well as many small shareholders – clerks, farmers, shopkeepers and miners – in Cornwall, London and elsewhere. The new company raised a capital of £50,000, out of which they paid the old company £16,125 for the machinery left on the mine.[4]

Meanwhile plans to continue the Trewint line to Camelford and Boscastle had been prepared and a Bill drawn up. Approaches were made to the L&SWR and its associate, the NCR, to negotiate for a working agreement. An arrangement was made with the latter railway by the LCR but at the cost of withdrawing the Bill which the L&SWR opposed. However

The production of the six principal copper mines from 1845 to 1888-9, plotted to the same scale. The consistent and long lived production of South Caradon Mine shows clearly.

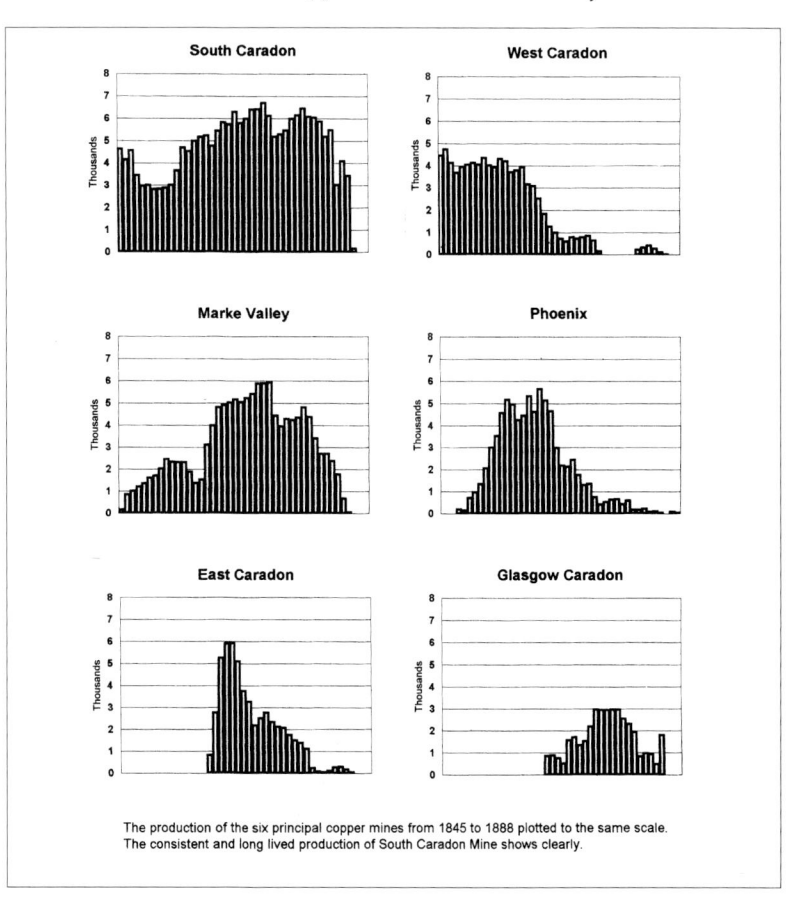

The production of the six principal copper mines from 1845 to 1888 plotted to the same scale. The consistent and long lived production of South Caradon Mine shows clearly.

55

A quiet A38 passes through Moorswater village in the winter afternoon sun in 1963. On the left is the former Commercial Inn, once leased as a home for Smythurst, the LCR Traffic Manager, and centrally is the Forge Cafe. Dropping down to the right, past the photographer's Riley 1.5, is the road to the railway depot. Apart from Moorswater Viaduct, dominating the background, all this was swept away by the Liskeard By-pass just over ten years later.
JOHN L. RAPSON

agreement was reached for a junction between an extension to Launceston and the NCR and a fresh Bill was prepared.

Tonnage carried was now down to the figures of a quarter-century earlier and less than the canal was taking in its last years. Receipts in 1884 were so low that, for the first time, the LLUC only received the minimum payment of £1,350 set out in the 1878 lease. A 5% dividend had been maintained by the LCR on its share capital since 1856 but this was only to last another year or so. The LLUC likewise was also paying a regular dividend although this dropped from 5% in the mid-seventies to between 2½% and 3½%. Nevertheless, despite not being able to repay debentures when called upon and despite the NCR's refusal to assist with the construction of the Northern Extension, optimistic plans for the future were made. A token of this optimism was the start of negotiations for the acquisition of the 'Commercial Inn' at Moorswater as a residence for Smythurst, the Traffic Superintendent. The former landlord had been killed by falling under a train at Liskeard station in December 1879. A lease at £25 a year was agreed in 1883 but repairs were needed and Smythurst had still not moved in twelve months later. Whether he eventually did is not known. Great reliance was placed on the Extension; indeed there was little else they could rely on although the suggestion of a link to Callington was made again, once more by a protégé of the L&SWR, a new Devon & Cornwall Central Railway. Much traffic was expected on the line to Launceston for beyond Trewint it would pass through a good agricultural district. Lime, apparently, was still used in quantity and fat sheep and store cattle were having to be driven on the hoof to Lydford to be put on rail. The LCR would tap this traffic at source and at Launceston its wagons could connect with and have access to the rest of the country's railway system.[5]

There was no smooth passage for this Bill however; both the GWR and the L&SWR, and also the latter's satellite Bodmin & Wadebridge Railway, opposed it. The L&SWR objected because the LCR's stated aim was to connect with the GWR but the GWR objected because it was felt, once the traffic was on the standard gauge, it would stay there and not be transshipped to the broad. The Bill originally asked for running powers over both the L&SWR and GWR to permit through running to Exeter, a high aim indeed, but in the face of the opposition this was dropped. The GWR petition was supported by ten people but their case was somewhat belittled when it was pointed out that of the ten one was a pauper on parish relief, four would not be touched by the new line and several were relations or tenants of objecting landowners. The L&SWR did not bother to be represented in Parliamentary Committee.

The Bill passed through the Lords first and in Committee in March 1884 Borlase Childs, the LCR Secretary, had quite a grilling at the hands of the GWR's opposing Counsel, Mr Pope. Childs took great pains to point out that their's was a modern railway worked by steam power and took exception to Pope's suggestion that it was a mere tramway. Much play was made by the opposition that nothing had been done under the 1882 Act but Silvanus Jenkin stated the Trewint line was staked out ready for construction and when the Bill went to the Commons in June he was able to advise that work had started on it. W. Robert Galbraith, a consulting engineer, spoke up for the LCR saying he thought the GWR were concerned that the L&SWR would work the new line but, he said, the LCR were quite capable and prosperous. [6] Galbraith had laid out many L&SWR lines in Devon and Cornwall and was, in fact, the engineer for the North Cornwall Railway.

One cannot but feel that Parliament were misled but their blessing was forthcoming and on 28 July 1884 the 9½ mile extension from Trewint to Launceston was authorised. (47-8 Victoria cap.cxcv) The capital and borrowing powers this time were £150,000 and £50,000 respectively. Also authorised by, and scheduled to, the Act was an agreement of 9 May 1884 with the LLUC whereby the LCR leased the Looe line, agreeing to work it 'continuously and vigorously' for 30 years from 1 January 1888 at a minimum rental of £1,650 per annum. A pipeline was also authorised from the Hendra stream to Polwrath for locomotive water as that at South Caradon was polluted.

Still wishing for a passenger service over the Caradon line the directors again asked Colonel

Towards the end of the life of Brunel's broad gauge, a GWR convertible saddle-tank takes a westbound train past Moorswater. In the foreground is Freeman's stone yard, out of use, and in front of it is Moorswater station. On the far right is the station building but centrally is the small square signal box erected in 1879. A double armed signal is behind it.
LISKEARD OLD CORNWALL SOCIETY

Moorswater station was in use between 1879 and 1902, being the upper terminus until the extension railway opened up to Liskeard. The sign immediately to the right of the door is that erected in 1884 giving the terms for the issue of free passes. The same sign from Tokenbury Corner survived in the Great Western Railway Museum at Swindon. See page 58.
L&GRP

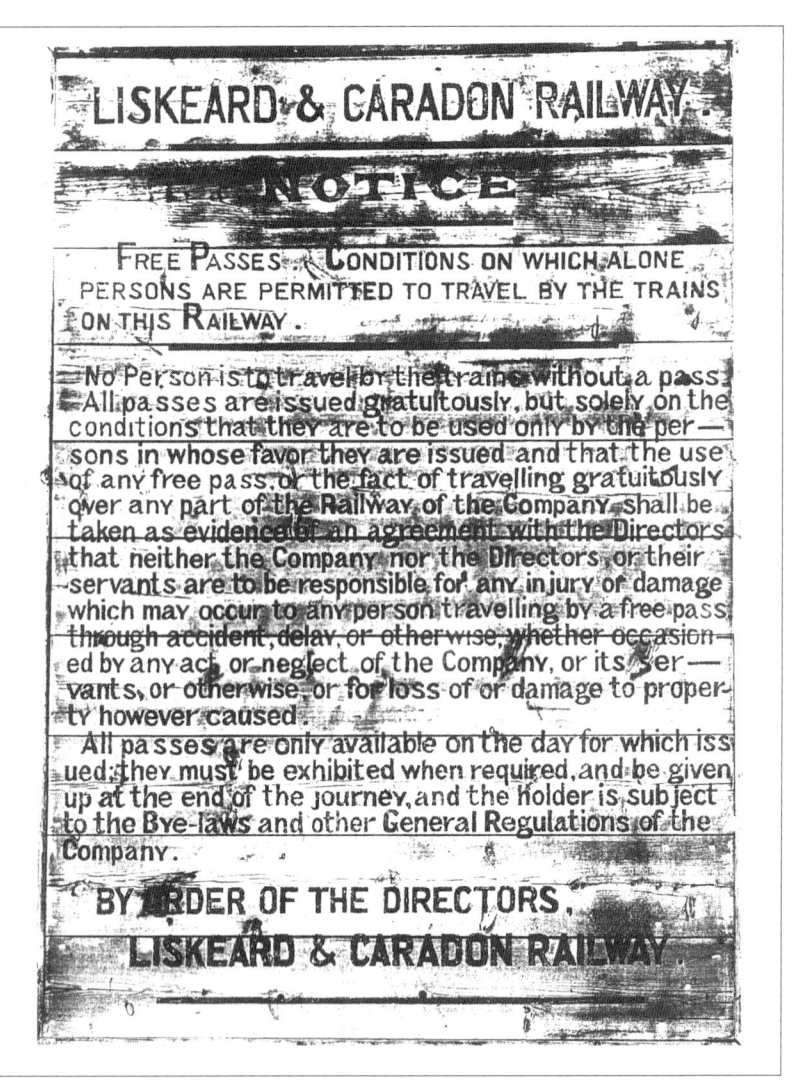

The notice board erected at Tokenbury Corner in 1884, giving the conditions for the use of free passes. Similar notices were erected along the line and can be seen in several photographs of stations. This one survived in the Great Western Museum at Swindon.
AUTHOR'S COLLECTION

Rich to inspect the line as a light railway. He did so on 9 August and a week later reported, rather critically, that the permanent way was in parts worn out, there were curves of less than five chains (110 yards) radius, and the many level crossings of public roads required gates, gatekeepers, lodges and signals. The Board of Trade's Railway Department pointed out that the railway had no authority (*vide* s.264 of the 1843 Act) to cross roads with steam locomotives and that penalties were being incurred daily. Although the 1843 Act had been repealed the Board maintained its restrictions continued. Fortunately no-one endeavoured to impose the fines. Col Rich amended his report to say the level crossings of public roads needed Parliamentary sanction and the directors responded that they had done away with three of seven level crossings since 1860. Silvanus Jenkin was instructed to remove the rest but nothing was done.

The carriage of excursion traffic has already been mentioned, as has the strict control exercised over the issue of passes. From 1862 only the LCR Secretary or the Clerk of the LLUC had been authorised to issue passes.

J. S. Hawker came up with a 'scheme for permanent and other passes' in December 1878, which appears to have involved a paper pass bearing the holder's name, but no details are recorded in the Minutes. Although it was instructed that a limited number were to be made available for pleasure on the Caradon line for the summer of 1880 these proved too cumbersome to issue in the quantities sought and instead card free passes were issued, but to obtain these the would-be passenger had first to purchase a ticket to Looe. The first class passengers paid 2s 6d and rode in the van whilst for 1s 4d the third class passengers rode in open wagons. In 1884, a month before Colonel Rich's inspection of the LCR, J. C. Isaac, an LCR director, complained regarding the 'illegal' carrying of passengers that for a few pounds profit it was not worth all ending in jail.[7] Quite what practice this complaint refers to is not known. Certainly it was Colonel Rich who suggested that excursion traffic could be carried gratuitously at the passengers' own risk and this suggestion was eagerly seized upon. Appropriate disclaimer notices were rapidly prepared and erected at Looe, Sandplace, Moorswater, Polwrath, Tokenbury and Rillaton. (That from Tokenbury survives in the Great Western Railway Museum at Swindon.) Most probably it is from this time that the practice started of charging 'passengers' for an umbrella or hat before the issue of a 'free' pass. It ceased about 1896 when the permanent way had become unsafe for freight trains, let alone passengers.[8]

School parties were always popular users of the railway and special cheap rates were given. Whilst such trains were usually of four or five wagons, as many as forty wagons hauled by two or three locomotives are said to have run on occasions, although they must have stretched the resources of the line somewhat. Even these lengthy trains returned by gravity with the locomotives following.[9]

Darite School was one user of such facilities. It was under the patronage of Lord Robartes (his wife was mineral lord of West Caradon) and his agent for the area was Silvanus Jenkin, so it is not surprising that the school's annual excursion tended to be to the Robartes' seat at Lanhydrock by wagonette or to Looe by train. The school log of 24 September 1888 records:

> Tomorrow the childred [*sic*] will assemble at 8 a.m., march to the train and be taken to Looe for their usual Summer outing.[10]

Summer excursions to Looe were also a cause of absenteeism.

HOPES AND DESPAIR

A Sunday School special returning from Looe approaches Sandplace in charge of CHEESEWRING. All the available passenger stock is on the train and eight open wagons have been pressed into service to give additional accommodation. Brake van No 4 is followed by the three Metropolitan carriages and brake van No 6. The final closed vehicle would appear to be brake van No 8 and this is the only known illustration of it. As vacuum brakes are fitted the date would be at the latter end of the 1890s. AUTHOR'S COLLECTION

CARADON & LOOE – THE CANAL, RAILWAYS AND MINES

Beneath Moorswater Viaduct and immediately opposite the passenger station was the stone yard of John Freeman & Sons. Here about 1899 CHEESEWRING propels wagons of rough stone into the yard's siding. KEN NUNN COLLECTION, LCGB

Cheesewring Quarry restarted in 1884. Freeman & Sons had stated when work stopped two years before that, if they could have a better rate for carriage on the LCR, they could ship large quantities of granite from Looe.[11] The new South Caradon Mine Ltd had frequently asked for a reduction in rates and 6d per ton was finally agreed in February 1885, reducing the toll charge to Looe to 5s per ton. This was an eleventh hour decision, though, for in January the mine had given six months notice to abandon the company and nine months later resolved to wind up.

Less than 8,000 tons of copper had been raised since taking over the sett as the old company had removed all easily accessible copper before vacating the mine and vast new sources of copper overseas had forced the price down to a level which made Cornish mining unviable. Whilst this was the primary cause, the railway came in for its share of blame as well, the mine complaining of unfair rates that were higher than for neighbouring mines.[12] Whilst a toll of about 6d per ton mile seems to have been high in comparison with similar west country lines the LCR was not making excessive profits. Such complaints had been growing in number since the copper boom passed its peak in the mid-sixties and all the mines seemed to think they were paying more than their neighbours.

As the pumping engines at South Caradon Mine came to a stand the water rose not only in its workings but in the adjoining mines also. Neither East Caradon nor Glasgow Caradon Consols, let alone the struggling New West Caradon, could cope with the influx of water and at a stroke copper mining ceased on Caradon Hill. This had enormous repercussions for the district, not least for more than four hundred employees of the mines. Some found employment at Phoenix for a few more years but most had to seek work elsewhere.

On the LCR, construction of the Trewint line was under way; tenders had been let and sixty to seventy men were employed from July 1884. Despite repeated requests both the L&SWR and the NCR had flatly refused to build the extension and the LCR Secretary, Borlase Childs, was actively trying to raise money for its finance. In London he could find neither cash to pay for the line nor a contractor to build it and he returned empty handed to try the L&SWR again. The Commercial Bank of Cornwall wanted repayment of the £4,500 that they had lent for the Parliamentary deposits and a similar request came from John F. Childs, the brother of Borlase Childs, for £1,500 lent, apparently temporarily, the previous November. The money was held by the two brothers as

Timetable October 1886

Classes	1 & 2	1, 2 & 3
Moorswater	9.50	3.55
Sandplace	10.09	4.13
Looe	10.18	4.22
Looe	10.56	5.05
Sandplace	11.05	5.14
Moorswater	11.25	5.32

Moorswater, probably in the first decade of the twentieth century. Beneath the viaduct is the chimney and buildings of Freeman's stone yard. Over the wall in the right foreground is the approach to the engine shed and the small platform that was originally intended to be Moorswater station. In fact it was built in the distance beneath the viaduct. The prominent structure with a curved corrugated iron roof was for transshipment and storage of goods.
MAURICE DART COLLECTION

On the moor above Minions, with Wheal Jenkin in the distance, CHEESEWRING waits with a short train. The wagon with its side door down, behind van 6, is fitted with seats for a party of Lewis Foster's friends. 1898. See page 144.
AUTHOR'S COLLECTION

Trustees for others and the latter shortly found himself in the position of suing himself, as LCR Secretary, for the money. No cash was available to repay the loan and the directors decided to let the legal action take its course. One director resigned at this decision, commenting on the further damage to the company's credit when they were asking the public for the money to build the Trewint line.

The directors proceeded to print prospectuses for the additional share capital needed and authorised by their Acts and managed to defer Childs' £1,500 for some months. However in July 1886 a writ was issued against the company and this was followed by several others from debenture holders who had not received their interest. In September Lewis Charles Foster, the company's treasurer since 1879 and a partner in the East Cornwall Bank, was appointed a director and a week later a writ was received from the bank for the outstanding balance of £10,201 5s. On 13 October 1886 Lewis Foster, without opposition, was appointed by the Court of Chancery as Receiver of the LCR and the railway entered into its final chapter.

Although it could not meet its long term commitments the railway until now had been making an operating surplus of between two and three thousand pounds, enough to pay the LLUC at least the agreed £1,350. From 1886 the operating surplus was insufficient even to meet this and the LLUC were unable to pay their debenture interest and share dividends or do anything about their £300 overdraft at the bank.

They hopefully offered to accept the rent, which was to be increased to £1,650 from 1 January 1888, in instalments but apart from £14,000 owing to debenture holders the LCR owed £20,000.

Action was immediately taken to effect economies by the LCR; all salaries were cut by 20% and the wages cut by 2d per day. Two of the three men at Rillaton were given notice and all gatemen were discharged, as were the gang working on the extension. A 10 m.p.h. speed limit was imposed on the Caradon line and it was instructed that the engine was not to be sent to the 'Hill' with less than six wagons at a time. On the Looe line a third class carriage was attached to all trains and 3rd class tickets issued for all trains. Wilton, the sole remaining employee at Rillaton, was left in charge of all wagons, loading and unloading, on the north part of the line and was later taken off a daily rate and paid 6d per wagon handled.

Attempts to gain new traffic were urgently made. A drastic cut in tolls and other concessions secured the contract for all of Phoenix Mine's traffic, of which previously 40% had gone by road, and new traffics were obtained from Looe to Liskeard in the forms of salt-fish and coal.

On the motive power side *Kilmar* had broken down in November 1885 leaving only *Cheesewring* serviceable. The 0-6-0 saddle tank hired from Peckett's of Bristol at that time had been promptly returned when the first writs were received, although Peckett's bill had not been met, and despite the depleted traffic a second locomotive was badly needed. A new boiler was bought for *Kilmar* and the money found to pay for it. Money was also found for yet another Act of Parliament to extend the time permitted by the 1882 Act to build the Trewint line.[13]

The Directors' Minutes cease in September 1887, significantly at the same time as the death of Richard Hawke, Chairman since 1878 and a major shareholder. Lewis Foster took the Chair and from then until the company's demise it appears to have been run by Foster as Receiver and Borlase Childs as Secretary. As a result little knowledge remains of the railway's operations during the next dozen years. Two trains a day were run to Looe and back – with extras on market days – and two up to the Cheesewring if traffic warranted it. Gravity working was certainly used as late as the 1870s, locomotives merely replacing horses to take the empty wagons back up the line, but whether this continued with no gatekeepers at the level crossings – train crews opened and closed the gates themselves – is not known but it must be doubtful.

At first a little traffic was offering still from the mines. In 1888 a Scottish company tried to take advantage of a rise in the price of copper by re-opening the four Caradon mines – West, South, East and Glasgow – but the rise was the result of massive manipulations in world markets and was short lived, the attempt foundering the following year. To the north Marke Valley had given up copper and was struggling to raise a little tin from the Wheal Jenkin part of its sett but abandonment came in 1890. Phoenix ceased to be profitable soon after the death of William West in 1879 and the shareholders were continually injecting further capital to keep up the flagging tin production. A report of 1891 said the mine was still rich but the low price of tin did not warrant further capital expenditure and failure finally came in 1898.[14] Thus by the turn of the century mining

A later view of Looe quays than that on page 37, probably in the 1890s. Granite can still be seen awaiting shipping but there is no copper or even any coal. Locomotives were not permitted on the quay so KILMAR *should not have been there.*
ROYAL INSTITUTION OF CORNWALL;
REF: LOOE H56

A card timetable was issued in 1897 and, interestingly, shows the times of train to Caradon Hill, although the note 'For the use of the Company's Servants only' is presumably to discourage casual passengers. Except on Wednesday the services could be worked by one locomotive.
GERRY BEALE COLLECTION

JUNE, 1897, and until further Notice.
LOOE RAILWAY.

DOWN TRAINS.	1 2 3	1 *2 3	1 2 3	1 *2 3
	A.M.	P.M.	P.M.	P.M.
MOORSWATER...dep.	9.50	2.0	3.30	7.35
CAUSELAND ......arr.	10.3	2.13	3.43	7.48
SANDPLACE.......arr.	10.10	2.20	3.50	7.55
LOOE .... arr.	10.20	2.30	4.0	8.5

UP TRAINS.	1 2 3	1 *2 3	1 2 3	1 *2 3
	A.M.	P.M.	P.M.	P.M.
LOOE ....dep.	11.0	2.40	5.0	8.30
SANDPLACE.......arr.	11.10	2.50	5.10	8.40
CAUSELAND ......arr.	11.17	2.57	5.17	8.47
MOORSWATER ...arr.	11.30	3.10	5.30	9.0

* Wednesdays only.

FOR THE USE OF THE COMPANY'S SERVANTS ONLY
JUNE, 1897, and until further Notice.
LISKEARD AND CARADON RAILWAY.

UP.	A.M.	P.M.
MOORSWATER............dep.	7.0	12.15
CHEESEWRING............arr.	8.0	1.15

DOWN.	A.M.	P.M.
CHEESEWRING............dep.	8.15	1.45
MOORSWATER............arr.	9.15	3.0

May 24th, 1897.

HERBERT G. T. HAWKEN,
Traffic Manager.

To S. Bone Esq/r

At Looe between 1896 and 1901. One the reverse of the print is written 'Arrival of train, 50 minutes late, in the good old days, Looe'. The locomotive is CARADON.
GRAHAM ROOSE COLLECTION

on and around Caradon Hill had ceased completely, its fall almost as fast as its rise, and in little more than half a century we have been given a rags to riches and back to rags story that has no parallel anywhere else in Cornwall.

The LCR's final Act[15] was obtained in 1892 to extend the time for constructing the line from Trewint to Launceston and to constitute that line as a separate undertaking, the Launceston Railway. This was presumably to assist raising finance for the Northern Extension by divorcing it from the destitute LCR but as before nothing was done.

The GWR had finally taken over the Cornwall Railway in 1889, having had a major hand in its running for some years, and the improvement in efficiency coupled with the conversion to standard gauge in 1892 must have presented the LCR with some competition, at least in the domestic coal market. Fed with a little traffic from Cheesewring Quarry and what coal that still came via Looe, plus 20/25,000 passengers a year, the LCR lived a hand to mouth existence. Maintenance was done as a necessity to the bare minimum and the track of both railways deteriorated considerably; so much so that the 'free' passenger service to Caradon had to stop about 1896, as did the excursion specials. In 1899 the pupils of Darite School went to Looe in four wagonettes. Excursion traffic started again when the LLR had improved standards after 1901 and Sunday School specials became popular again for a brief period.

The Board of Trade's Order that the lines adopt the block system and fit continuous brakes in 1890 caused something of a crisis for no money was available for such luxuries and the correspondence dragged on for five full years. The Board were adamant and eventually Lewis Foster fitted vacuum brakes at his own expense. Block working was dispensed with on the company giving an undertaking to work the lines on the one engine in steam principle.[16] Another bone of contention was the railway's mixed trains on the Looe line. For economy all trains were mixed with the passenger carriages at the rear to facilitate shunting at Moorswater, Sandplace and Looe. The Board could not approve of this and whilst they might license one mixed train per day the carriages had to be marshalled next to the engine. Amongst other arguments Childs stated that the carriages were not strong enough to be placed between the locomotive and coal wagons. The Board seems to have given up on this point and the railway continued running its mixed trains, even, as one writer in the *Railway Magazine* observed, propelling wagons in front of the engine, a common practice between Sandplace and Looe.[17]

Thus the Liskeard & Caradon Railway staggered towards the twentieth century while the Liskeard & Looe Union Canal's railway was preparing to awake from its slumbers to enter the new century fighting.

HOPES AND DESPAIR

CARADON and passenger train at Looe in the closing years of the nineteenth century. The longitudinal track is quite clear. To the right of the station door is the notice regarding free passes and to the left is a large Caledonian Railway poster board.
GRAHAM ROOSE COLLECTION

CHEESEWRING beside the water tower and coaling stage at Moorswater shed. The shearlegs on the right, spanning one of the shed roads, were used for heavy lifting jobs. About 1899.
KEN NUNN COLLECTION, LCGB

CHAPTER SIX
CHANGE OF DIRECTION

We'll ne'er stop the express to pick mushrooms again
While the driver and guard wait near!
We shall never step off to race the train!
Such joys have vanished, I fear.[1] ANON 1901

The Cornwall Railway could not afford their planned link to the LCR and only six years after the broad gauge opened through Liskeard the LCR directors had considered making a connection between their line and the main line. Silvanus Jenkin surveyed a line climbing continuously from Moorswater at 1 in 38 or 40 to enter Liskeard station approximately midway along the down platform but his £7,000 estimate of the cost put it out of the question. In 1877 a Bill was prepared for a connection but finance again was not available and in 1880 the Cornwall Railway were asked if they would subsidise a bus from Liskeard station to Moorswater but nothing appears to have come of this either, a fate shared by the line authorised in the 1882 Act. A stop at Coombe, the nearest point to Liskeard station, was made from about 1884. James Temple, a carrier, was appointed in 1882 to convey goods between Liskeard station, the town and Moorswater. In 1884 he was paid 2s 6d for each journey

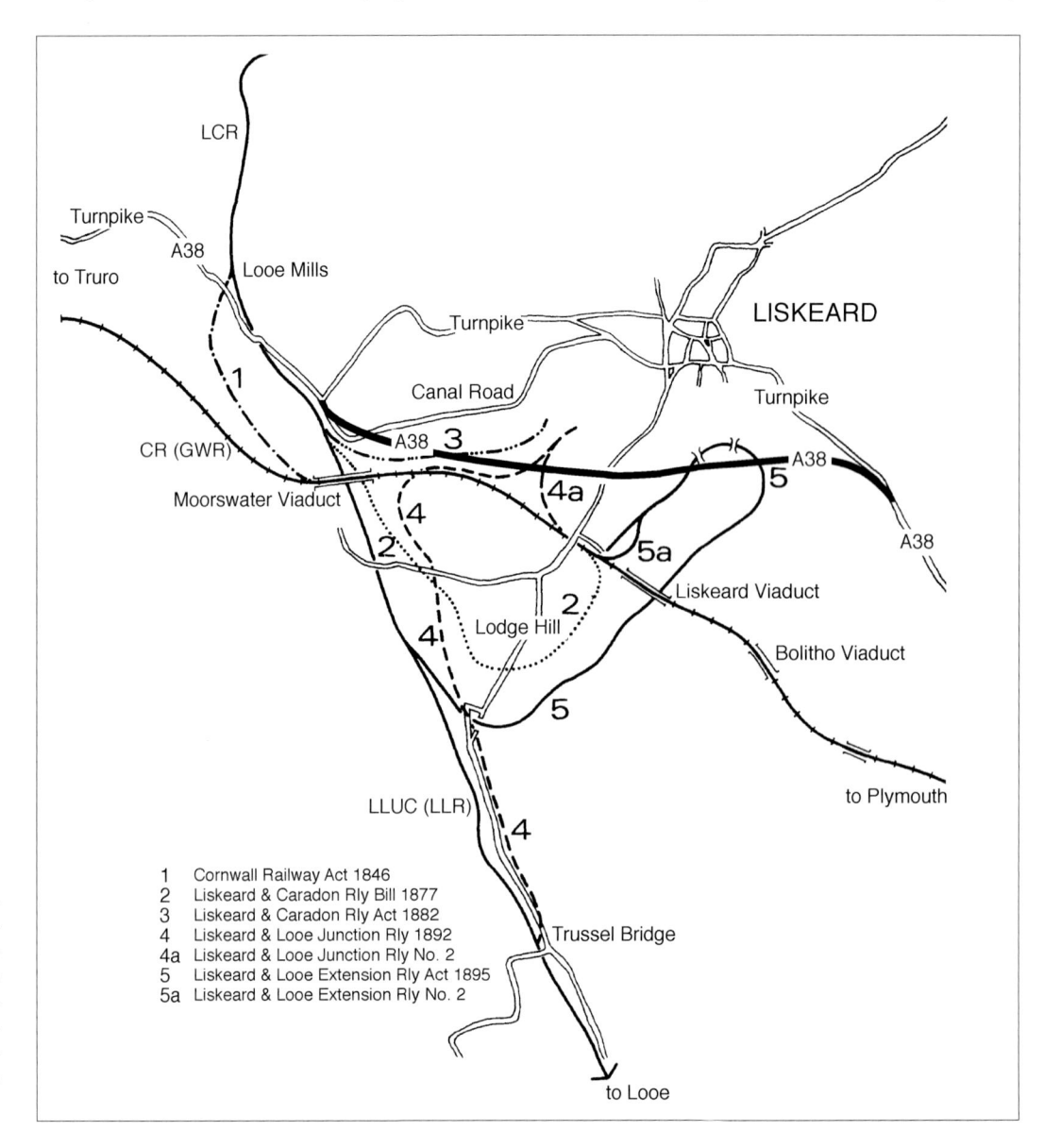

1   Cornwall Railway Act 1846
2   Liskeard & Caradon Rly Bill 1877
3   Liskeard & Caradon Rly Act 1882
4   Liskeard & Looe Junction Rly 1892
4a Liskeard & Looe Junction Rly No. 2
5   Liskeard & Looe Extension Rly Act 1895
5a Liskeard & Looe Extension Rly No. 2

Numerous suggestions were made for connecting the railways at Moorswater with the main-line above. This map shows those proposals, where details of the routes have survived.

66

between Moorswater and the main line and he specifically met the afternoon train to Looe. The Secretary showed a distinct change of thought when giving evidence to the House of Lords Committee for the 1884 Act, for he stated then that the LCR's outlet lay to the north and the two railways had interchanged with the GWR main line only about 80 tons a year for the past ten years.[2] The GWR, at a later date, thought the LCR beneath notice and showed the connection to Looe in their timetables as by horse-bus from Menheniot.[3]

With the LCR in Receivership and the LLUC reliant on the Receiver for income neither company was in a position to make the much needed connection to the outside world but a new character was to enter the scene: Joseph Thomas. Thomas was a successful civil engineer who, after a full life working around the world, now hankered after the district of his boyhood years.

His first suggestion of a connection was in 1888 with a route from the Looe line below Lodge up the Liskeard valley and across it by a substantial viaduct entering the GWR station from the south-east. The cost of the viaduct would have been prohibitive but the next idea, about 1890, would have been no less expensive. It involved a rack railway at 1 in 7 from Moorswater and the inability to provide a through connection with the main line ruled this scheme out.[4] (Although the main line was still broad gauge its conversion to standard was obviously not far off.) The third plan was prepared by Thomas with the LCR Engineer's firm of S. W. Jenkin & Son in 1892 and was prepared for Parliament under the name of the Liskeard & Looe Junction Railway. Climbing mostly at 1 in 40 it would have left the Looe line at Trussel Bridge, run through Lamellion hamlet and under the GWR at the east end of Moorswater viaduct to a reversing point behind the workhouse, later Lamellion Hospital, 1¾ miles from Trussel. Another quarter mile in the other direction, climbing at 1 in 45, would have taken the line into the GWR goods yard at the west end of Liskeard station.[5] This plan met with the approval of the Committee of Management of the Canal company and they resolved to recommend Thomas's proposal to the shareholders but time and finance did not permit promotion of the Bill in that session of Parliament. The Receiver's attitude is not recorded but there is a suggestion that agreement could not be reached with the LCR.

In 1893, having been appointed engineer to the St Ives and Mevagissey harbour schemes, Joseph Thomas moved to Looe and began a more active part in the development of Looe as a holiday resort. He built the Hannafore Estate road and aided the construction of the resort with the Hannafore Point brickworks. About this time, taking a fresh view of connecting Looe with the outside world, he proposed a line from Menheniot to the Looe line at Plashford. His enthusiasm must have fired some life back into the somnolent LLUC who, in April 1893, decided to look at its relationship with the LCR with a view to regaining control of its own railway. Joseph Thomas's next and final scheme was taken up and preparations made for the enabling Act. At first the LCR sat on the fence regarding the proposed connection, both approving the Bill and resolving to petition against it, but on 2 March 1895 agreement was reached between the LLUC, the LCR and Lewis Foster, the Receiver. The main points of the agreement were that, on the opening for passengers of the new junction railway, the Looe company would regain possession of its railway, would take over all locomotives, rolling stock and equipment of the LCR and would have the right of working the Caradon railway. Lewis Foster was to be paid a fair value for the locomotives, etc., and the Looe company had the right if the Caradon line did not pay its way for six consecutive months to cease working it. Much of the accrued debt owed to the LLUC since the Receiver was appointed was to be cancelled.[6]

The Liskeard & Looe Railway Extension Act 1895 (28-9 Victoria cap.cviii) scheduled the agreement and authorised the railway from near Coombe Gate to adjacent to the GWR Liskeard station. The capital authorised was £30,000 in new 5% preference stock and borrowing powers of up to £10,000. Additionally £14,000 preference stock could be raised to repay existing mortgages and a dividend of 3% could be paid out of capital until

The Company Seal of the Liskeard & Looe Railway.
AUTHOR'S COLLECTION

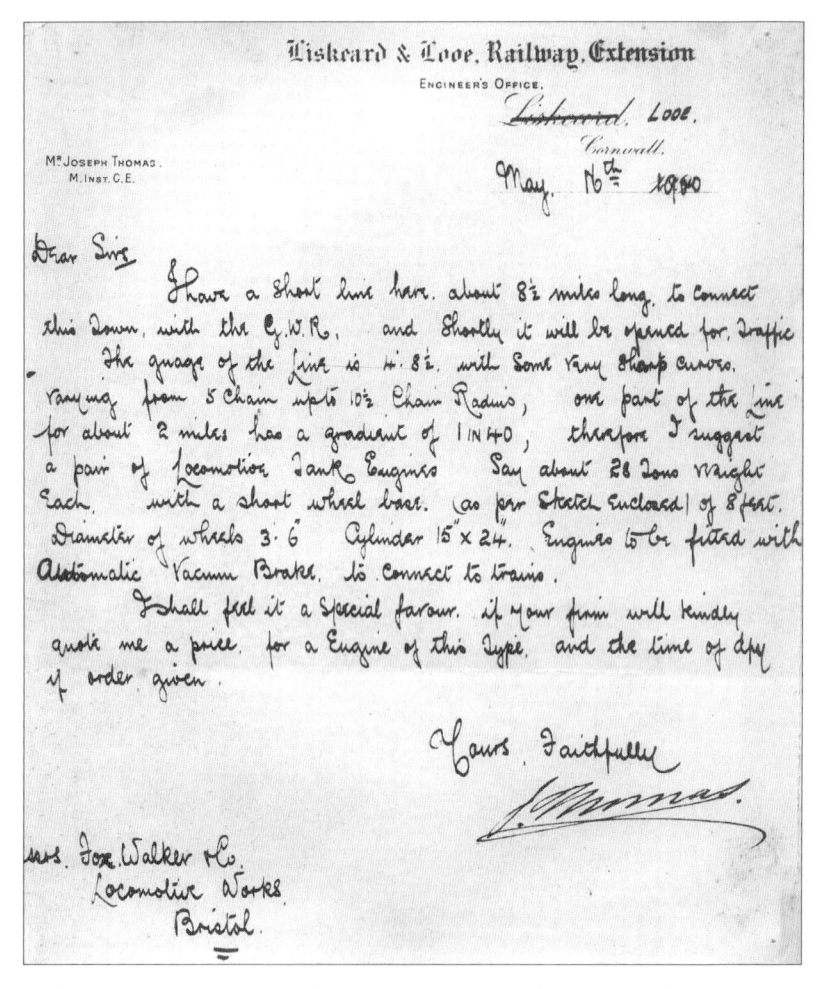

Joseph Thomas wrote to several locomotive manufacturers with his specification of what he thought would be suitable to work the steep incline up to Liskeard.
INDUSTRIAL RAILWAY SOCIETY

the railway was opened. Section 39 changed the name of the company from the Liskeard & Looe Union Canal Company to the Liskeard & Looe Railway Company so after 36 years the iron way became a railway, officially.

As usual money to build the new railway was difficult to find. For some unknown reason, perhaps lethargy, little was done until June 1897, two years after the Act was passed, when a Special General Meeting of shareholders approved the issue of the new share capital. Possibly action was only taken then as the compulsory purchase powers would expire twelve months later. A circular to shareholders detailed the additional traffic the railway would expect as a result of the new link and appended a report of Joseph Thomas showing the company's income could be more than trebled and a gross profit of £3,751 made.[7] Such an income would be more than sufficient to pay the interest on both the debentures and the preference stock, but people were still not encouraged to subscribe to the new railway; only a few thousand pounds being promised locally. The Committee appear to have offered their shares around with little success until, with Joseph Thomas's help, Captain John Edmund Percival Spicer, a former 1st Life Guards Captain who lived in Wiltshire, showed an interest. Spicer had been introduced to Thomas, through J. E. Chambers, in 1891 to help finance Thomas's developments at Looe and went on to support the railway project.[8]

Thomas's figures showing the additional traffic to be gained from coastal shipping, 'excursionists', fish and coals must have convinced the Captain that the line had potential, for he offered to take up sufficient preference stock to enable the junction line to be built. A condition of this offer was that he should be able to buy a proportionate share of the existing capital, at £6 5s per original or New £25 share. The Committee approved the offer and

LADY MARGARET climbs the 1 in 40 gradient towards Liskeard with a train of the Hurst Nelson carriages, while on the main line a GWR 4-4-0 heads westwards. 1905. L&GRP

CHANGE OF DIRECTION

recommended the shareholders to do the same.[9]

So Captain Spicer gained control of the Liskeard & Looe Railway, replacing the local ownership, and the Committee, who remained in command but with the addition of J. A. Chambers of London, gained the means to build their extension. Contracts were signed and sealed with J. C. Lang of the local contractors firm, T. Lang & Son, to build the railway and lay the permanent way. On 28 June 1898 the first sod was cut by Silvanus Jenkin and fifty of Lang's men immediately set to work. Excavation work began in earnest on 1 August at the sites of the three major cuttings, at Lodge Hill, Heathlands Lane and Gut Lane. The first was particularly hard work, through solid rock, and was the last to be completed in November 1900. The only fatality in the work occurred here when a young worker was killed by a rock fall. In the meantime two other cuttings, Trevillis and Bolitho, were completed. A landslip at the latter caused by cutting into a bed of clay resulted in an extra wide embankment under Liskeard Viaduct to dispose of the surplus fill. Five overbridges and an underbridge were constructed and all were complete by the end of 1900 when laying of the permanent way was put in hand.[10] It soon became clear that funds would not be sufficient to complete the line and purchase rolling stock but once again Captain Spicer stepped into the breach, although he had little option if his initial investment was not to be jeopardised.

The flurry of activity with which the Liskeard & Looe Railway greeted the twentieth century was intensified as the completion of the new line approached. In January 1901 Horace Holbrook was recruited from the Great Eastern Railway to be Traffic Manager (and E. T. Tucker was paid two guineas for recruiting him) at £200 per annum salary. Holbrook brought with him a number of colleagues from the GER and a certain amount of equipment was bought from that company also. By March the railway was almost ready, staff was recruited from the LCR, GWR and GER and a new locomotive and carriages were bought. Notice was given to the LCR Receiver, in accordance with the Agreement, of the LLR's intention to take over control of the two railways. A train was hired from the LCR (at £1 a trip) to inspect the new line. On Wednesday 8 May 1901 the LLR commenced operations of their own and the new railway, without any fuss or ceremony, although a considerable number of people turned up at Looe to see the first train off. As the old LCR passenger stock was used for the first week there must have been little different to see, apart from the novelty of the day's trains starting from Looe instead of Moorswater. The new stock was reserved for the formal opening on the following week.

Thus the two railway companies came under completely new management. At the same time, the focus for the combined system moved from the isolated Bodmin Moor to the connection with the outside world at Liskeard and to the burgeoning tourist industry of Looe. A change of direction in more ways than one.

The years of neglect while the line was in the Receiver's care very soon became apparent and on 11 May Thomas delivered an urgent report to the Committee on the state of the permanent way. Granite blocks still acted as sleepers for some three miles of track and 100 of the rails on these needed renewing. Of the wooden sleepers many were rotten and he considered the line was generally not safe for use. In some instances the track was 1½ inches over gauge and Thomas concluded his report by stating that the

Sent as a postcard to a friend, Horace Holbrook had written on the reverse 'My Dog & me, H.H.H. 5.6.05'. Taken on the platform at Liskeard outside his office. GRAHAM ROOSE COLLECTION

Soon after the Extension Railway was opened in May 1901, LOOE *drops down the grade from Liskeard with the three Hurst Nelson carriages. The newness of the fence and ballasting, and the lack of growth on the embankment all suggests that this photo was taken as early as May 1901.* LISKEARD OLD CORNWALL SOCIETY

69

Suffering from an unfortunate mark in its centre, this photograph shows the approach to the new Liskeard station of the LLR, soon after opening in 1902. On the left is the footpath approach from Tremeddan Terrace.
AUTHOR'S COLLECTION

KILMAR, with its rather ugly cab, at Looe between 1903 and 1907. The first vehicle in the train is the ex-GWR brake van and the next four appear to be main line wagons and a van. Beyond those is an LCR van and LCR wagons. In the distance is the carriage shed.
R. C. RILEY COLLECTION

following day, Sunday, he was taking all platelayers to patch up the line fit for use on Monday.[11] The Board of Trade inspection would only have covered the new line from Coombe to Liskeard but it is strange that no-one noticed the appalling state of the old line to Looe.

No accident involving the permanent way marred the formal opening on Wednesday 15 May 1901, although the day was not without incident. The official train left Liskeard at one o'clock arriving at Looe half-an-hour later, pausing only for *Looe*, the new locomotive, to run round the train of new 'American style' carriages at Coombe Junction. At Looe the train was met by an official reception committee and after a brief exchange of greetings all the gathered dignitaries and officials set off behind Liskeard Borough Band around the town of East Looe to the Guildhall. The procession included 400 schoolchildren and many of the inhabitants of Liskeard and of the twin towns of Looe either took part or watched with the many holiday makers. The streets and shops were decorated with bunting and mottoes, flags and a triumphal arch and the early afternoon scene that day must have left a lasting impression on those who took part. A marquee was erected on the quay for a public luncheon that was to last two and a half hours and be attended by eighty to ninety local people and friends of Joseph Thomas and the railway. The speeches, of which there were many, were all on a high note of optimism; Looe at last was on the railway map and there would now be no holding the development of the district as a holiday resort. A similar development to that at Hannafore was anticipated to the east of the towns but it was not feared the towns would be spoilt, as any development would be kept out of the old central parts by the natural barriers of hills and rivers. Great tribute was paid to Joseph Thomas and a silver bowl was presented to him in recognition of his services to Looe.[12]

More than 400 passengers travelled from Liskeard to Looe, and quite a large number of Looe people also visited Liskeard, but the day nearly ended with what the *Cornish Times* politely called a 'contretemps'. Many of the day's visitors, including a large party from Plymouth, left Looe on the 8.35 p.m. train but shortly after leaving Coombe Junction the engine ran out of steam and could not get up the bank to Liskeard. Assistance was very promptly obtained, but the delay meant the last GWR train had left for Plymouth. The timely arrival of Horace Holbrook to pay for a special train saved the day and also saved the LLR from losing a large number of friends no doubt.[13] The GWR later agreed their train should have been held and only charged 15s for the overtime of the special train's crew.

Running out of steam became a common occurrence on the new bank and *Looe* was eventually replaced but not before a number of budding poets had commemorated several occasions in verse in the *Cornish Times*. Another mishap only a week after the opening was caused by an over zealous driver running through the catch-points at Coombe before the road was set for him to back back on to his train.

Not for the first time the Committee were concerned at the financial state of the company and a row was brewing with Lewis Foster. The Looe company had taken action in the High Court to compel Foster to hand over the Caradon equipment and an order had been made on 3 May 1901. Eventually the equipment was valued at £3,850 but the LLR endeavoured to set off against this the costs of putting the Caradon and Looe lines back into good repair,

CARADON at Looe with Hurst Nelson coaches, probably about 1902.
LISKEARD OLD CORNWALL SOCIETY

71

Moorswater from the air, about 1958. Lines of wagons are on the clay company's siding and on the truncated main line to Caradon. Hodge's lime kiln stands out clearly at the top (west) of the photograph. The undergrowth in front of the clay dry and its siding marks the former canal reservoir, while the line of the Crylla feeder crosses the field on the right before turning sharp right (west) towards the reservoir after passing under the lane that formerly led to the iron foundry. Foundry Bridge is where this lane meets the main road. R. G. SPALDING COLLECTION

claiming that the Receiver was in breach of the earlier agreements. They lost the case on a point of law – they had no statutory right of set off – and the subject was to be a bone of contention for some years.[14] Foster later returned to the Court for directions as to the disposal of the £3,850 and was authorised to pay it to the debenture holders.[15]

Regarding the condition of the LCR Arthur Stride, Managing Director of the London, Tilbury & Southend Railway, inspected the line in August 1901 and reported that half the line was up to standard and half far below. The Phoenix branch was then disused.[16]

As with all previous railways built between Looe and Caradon, this new line had proved too expensive and again the Committee had overspent, exceeding their borrowing powers as the LCR had done in 1846. In addition the debenture interest was £3,000 in arrears. A memorial in November 1901 to the Privy Council for Trade secured the issue of 'The Liskeard & Looe Railway Certificate 1902' authorising a further £18,000 in preference shares and £6,000 by mortgage. This was to be spent on the Receiver (£3,850), new locomotives and rolling stock (£7,570) and repairing and completing the railway (£6,000). £1,000 went on legal expenses and the remainder to reserve.

Traffic carried in the first year showed the line had the promise hoped of it. Although mineral traffic was almost as low a figure as that carried in the horse-drawn days of half a century before, much more merchandise was conveyed and, of course, the number of passengers showed great increase on LCR days. In 1902, the first full year, over 55,000 passengers were carried and this figure increased to more than 70,000 in the next five years, compared with an average of 24,000 per year before the junction line was built. Over the same period merchandise increased from 3,800 tons to 5,500 tons. Some 11,500 tons of coal and Cheesewring granite were carried and a useful addition to the mineral traffic came in 1902 when the St Neot Clay Company commenced building their clay dry at Moorswater, just below the iron foundry. Several hundred tons of granite from Cheesewring Quarry, now being worked by Harry Hawkey, and sand from East Caradon were carried as infilling and a siding was laid into the site.

The clay pit was at Parsons Park, high on Bodmin Moor, between St Neot and Bolventor, and a pipe for the liquid clay slurry was laid on a sinuous course via Draynes, Redgate,

Trewartha, Pellagenna and Landazzard to Moorswater, dropping more than 550 feet in altitude on the way and permitting the slurry to run entirely by gravity. Construction continued through 1903 and 1904 and on 16 November 1904 the first shipment of china clay went down to Looe. It is an interesting thought that, if Silvanus Jenkin's plans of 1873 for the Temple Mineral Railway had been successful, Parsons Park would have been connected to the Bodmin & Wadebridge Railway's Wenford branch and neither the pipeline nor the Moorswater dry would have been built.

The locomotive *Looe* was sold in 1902, having proved inadequate for the work, and a 2-4-0 tank, *Lady Margaret*, was bought from Andrew Barclay, Captain Spicer paying the cost. The original LCR locomotives had seen very little maintenance for some years and in common with the rest of the railway were in a very run down state. To maintain services GWR 4-4-0 saddletank No 13 was hired for the first time and the engine was to become a regular visitor to Looe. A slight boost to traffic was given by the opening of St Keyne station on 1 September 1902 and, as at the opening of Sandplace, the suggestion that Causeland be closed was not proceeded with in deference to local requests. The new carriages, like *Looe*, were not proving satisfactory and the opportunity was taken, on the electrification of the Mersey

GWR No 13 at Looe with the three Hurst Nelson carriages, about 1902/03. Horace Holbrook stands on the front of the engine with stationmaster Herbert Hawes below him..
R. C. RILEY
COLLECTION

Holbrook's efforts to promote traffic resulted in posters such as this, of June 1905. Alas, the Liskeard & Caradon Railway was no longer in a fit state for excursions and passengers were met at Liskeard by horse-brakes.

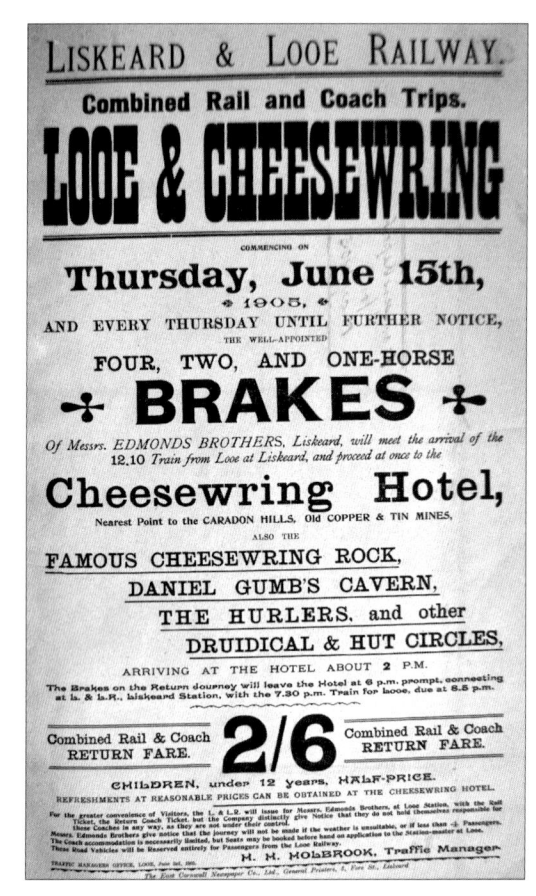

Railway, to purchase some of their old passenger stock, Holbrook being sent to Liverpool to inspect. On the freight side a shortage of wagons was complained of (like the LCR before) and the clay company's wagons were borrowed from time to time.

Captain Spicer seems to have become a little disenchanted with his investment, for in 1904, and again in 1906, he obtained High Court Judgements against the LLR for unpaid interest. Although making an operating surplus of several hundred pounds, the railway had insufficient to pay dividends on the shares or interest on the debentures. This was not for want of trying on the part of Horace Holbrook who took every opportunity of gaining traffic. Excursions were encouraged, carrying, amongst others, football teams and their followers and school outings. An innovation in 1905 was combined waggonette and rail trips to the Cheesewring at a special fare of 2s 6d of which the railway took 1s. The reconstruction of St Germans Viaduct on the GWR with Cheesewring granite added to the mineral traffic and the company was even selling withies from the canal bed at 8d a bundle to add to income. A pictorial poster was issued in 1905 for the first time to advertise the line and special services were run every bank holiday. Four or five trains were run each way daily with extras on Saturdays and market days, but eight or more ran on bank holidays.

The passenger service was maintained by one engine manned by two sets of train crew stationed at Looe. Another locomotive and one crew working from Moorswater looked after shunting there and any mineral traffic. The enginemen worked an 11 hour day but the mechanics at Moorswater worked a 51 hour week of 5½ days.[17]

Early in 1905 the carrier who delivered goods and parcels at Looe resigned and the company took on the task themselves. Perhaps as a result of this, thought was given to using 'motors' for the collection of passengers and goods and Holbrook was despatched to Lowestoft to inspect the Great Eastern Railway's bus services. He delivered a lengthy report in June but no action was taken, although an Atkinson lorry may have been hired briefly. (Alternatively the payment shown in the Minute Books may have been for a horse-drawn van that was eventually purchased for £25 – it is not clear.)

One of Cornwall's most spectacular railway accidents occurred in June 1906, fortunately without loss of life. On Thursday 14 June a special train for Looe Wesleyan Sunday School

CHANGE OF DIRECTION

CARADON leaving South Caradon reversing point with a train of granite from Cheesewring Quarry. The first six wagons are GWR ones and the last four LCR. The centre two LCR wagons are low-sided stone wagons, one of which has a lever brake, and all the LCR wagon have dumb buffers at one end. The brake van was numbered 9 when it was bought from the GWR in 1903. The photograph was taken between the GWR approval of 1906 for its rolling stock to run on the Caradon line and the withdrawal of CARADON in 1907. On the hillside above the train is the stone wall supporting the Cheesewring branch before it passed beneath the dumps of West Caradon Mine and reached the Gonamena incline. L&GRP

had been run, consisting of eleven carriages, and on the following day six of these ex-Mersey Railway carriages, which were reserved for excursion traffic, were brought back to Liskeard behind *Kilmar*. The guard, J.Horrell, had been unable to find any vacuum coupling hoses for the carriages so the continuous brake was disconnected and on stopping at Liskeard the carriages ran back on the gradient pulling the couplings tight. Horrell placed the largest stones he could find under four wheels but, in easing up to slacken the couplings so the carriages could be uncoupled, *Kilmar* pushed them over the stones and off they went towards Coombe Junction. All available staff ran after them, optimistically putting stones under the wheels, and *Kilmar* also joined in the chase, but to no avail. Rapidly gathering speed the carriages left all behind but fortunately the signalman thought to telephone Coombe Junction Signal Box. With great presence of mind signalman Marsh, at the foot of the incline there, set the road for Moorswater and rushed out to stop the passenger train from Looe, which was already in

A Sunday School special at Darite, Railway Terrace, on the Caradon line, about 1903. Hauled by CARADON, the wagons are numbers 70, 56 and 66 and brake van No 4. There is a brakesman on each wagon, balanced on the buffers, and the driver and fireman are believed to be Messrs Chaston and Bray. This must have been one of the last such specials but is probably typical of many of years past. AUTHOR'S COLLECTION

75

CARADON & LOOE – THE CANAL, RAILWAYS AND MINES

The Cornish Times, *in its hastily published Special 'Railway Smash' Edition, included these sketches of wrecked carriages at Moorswater. On the left appears to be one of the Hurst Nelson coaches and the point of impact is discreetly veiled with a tarpaulin.*

sight. Had he used the track provided for runaways, the carriages would have run straight into a road where children were playing, but instead they passed him at an estimated 60 m.p.h. to Moorswater where, with a sound like thunder, they demolished the carriage shed, smashed three carriages and damaged three more. Four of those of the train were hardly damaged at all. Carpenters had been working that day raising the engine shed roof and painting a carriage but as luck would have it they had finished work early and there was no injury to anybody.

Poor Horrell, who was only a porter-signalman but often acted as second goods guard, got all the blame and was suspended. Signalman Husband at Liskeard would have been suspended for not running the train into a siding, but was let off because of his quick action in phoning Marsh at Coombe Junction. Edward Marsh received due commendation. The event caused no little excitement locally and the *Cornish Times* rushed out a Special 'Railway Smash' Edition.[18]

Although much attention was paid to trackwork it was deteriorating, particularly on the LCR, almost faster than it could be attended to. There were still many lengths of granite blocks on the Looe line and the trackbed was very wet. The average cost of maintenance on an English trunk railway was 7½d per train mile but the LLR was costing 8½d and the LCR no less than 1s 10½d.[19]

Fresh hopes for traffic on the Caradon line came in 1907 when an Australian company, Cosmopolitan Proprietory Ltd, took on a lease of Phoenix Mine while hard on their heels another company took South Phoenix, just north of Rillaton, and commenced pumping. This latter company, Cornish Consolidated Tin Mines Ltd, did not do very well; the gas engine they installed failed and was replaced at the manufacturer's expense but work soon ceased and the engine found its way to Hingston Down Mine near Callington.[20] At Phoenix in May a completely new shaft commenced sinking near the end of the disused branch line and the

A rare view of CARADON *in the goods yard at Liskeard, about 1905. The building behind is the store of N. S. Lander & Son, who operated St Keyne Roller Flour Mills, at Lametton Mill.*
MAURICE DART COLLECTION

Prince of Wales' Shaft engine house under construction at Phoenix Mine in 1907. The temporary headgear is for shaft sinking and through it can be seen Cheesewring Quarry and its dumps.
G. J. CHILDS COLLECTION

South Phoenix Mine was re-worked briefly and unsuccessfully from 1906 to 1908. This is Prosper Shaft, a few yards north of Minions village.
AUTHOR'S COLLECTION

Top Left: *Three Lancashire boilers provided the power for the 80-inch engine at Prince of Wales' Shaft. All appear to be second-hand from 'up-country' and were brought up the winding railway then down the near derelict Phoenix branch. Here they are installed temporarily and the boiler house is being built around them. Alas the maker's plate on the centre boiler cannot be read but the winch is brand new, supplied by Redruth Foundry in 1907.*

Top right: *The 80-inch diameter cylinder lies outside the engine house at Phoenix. The arch of the cylinder window, immediately behind it and through which it will be installed in the house, still has its supporting timbers.*

Bottom left: *A Lancashire boiler waits on its Midland Railway boiler truck on the Phoenix branch until its foundations are ready for it to be installed.*

Bottom right: *The engine house is complete, apart from the bob platform, and the beam engine installed. The pump rods, lying in the foreground, have yet to be installed in the shaft but the permanent headgear is in course of construction with the temporary shaft sinking frame still within it. This was the last major Cornish pumping engine to be installed in Cornwall. It was designed by Nicholas Trestrail and built by Holman Bros, of Camborne.*

G. J. CHILDS COLLECTION

Liskeard firm of Runnalls & Son secured the contract to build the engine house and stack for the Cornish engine that was to be erected.

Progress was fast. By October the shaft was 66 feet deep and the engine house near completion. Much heavy machinery and plant had arrived on site including three Lancashire boilers, probably second-hand, and a 19-ton casting. These came on London & North Western Railway 75-feet-long boiler wagons and a GWR six-wheeled wagon respectively and getting them to Phoenix safely must have been an achievement in itself. At Treworgey the curves, of 3½ chains (77 yards) radius, had a super-elevation of up to 11 inches and the Phoenix branch, disused for six years, was laid

Everybody in this posed Looe scene is looking at the camera. LADY MARGARET *has a full head of steam and the blower on, to give an impression of motion. The train consists of brake van 4, two Metropolitan coaches and a Hurst Nelson carriage. The barrels could contain fish or merchandise as they were frequently used for carrying all sorts of goods. About 1903 and probably taken by Mr Raddy, of Looe.* LISKEARD OLD CORNWALL SOCIETY

with worn 40 lb rail on blocks, probably untouched since 1869. Also brought up the line had been a Holman steam compressor, a 30-hp Robey engine to sink the shaft, several more boilers, including one on a Midland Railway boiler wagon, and a ventilation engine and fan. Materials for the mine justified running a train every day, sometimes two, with an average of ten wagons on each. Some trouble had been had with Runnalls during the construction of the engine house. They borrowed a couple of wagons to move their materials about and would insist on letting them run down the steep branch by gravity. Damage was frequent and finally in July Runnalls ruefully wrote that one 'looks to be a good bit smashed'.

This incident was insignificant, however, in comparison with the problems that were pending. The LLR had been unable to pay interest on the debentures for six years and early in 1907 Lewis Foster, as a private holder of £5,500, called for a Receiver to be appointed. This was interpreted as a move to enable the North Cornwall Railway, of which Foster was Chairman, or the L&SWR to acquire the line cheaply. A legal error in the way debentures had been issued thwarted Foster and the LLR approached the GWR for help.[21] Close relationships had developed between the LLR and their large neighbour helped by the friendship of J. A. Chambers and James Inglis, the GWR General Manager, and the two companies were on good terms. The GWR were still very sensitive of the threat of the L&SWR, who for years had been driving westwards into GWR territory, and did not wish them, through the NCR, to make their way to Looe. An agreement was hastily prepared to work the Looe line from 1 July 1907 but this was not proceeded with as it was felt the NCR could still get a foothold on east Cornwall by purchasing the LCR and building the Launceston Railway to connect. One has to say that, despite the sensitivity of the GWR, neither the L&SWR nor the NCR ever showed any interest in purchasing the LCR or in building the Northern Extension. At this time they were much more focussed on reaching Truro.

Plans had already been set for the acquisition of the LCR by the GWR, for in early March Captain Spicer and the GWR had come to an agreement whereby the former would acquire debentures in the LCR in his own name but with GWR money.[22] Pressure was put on the Receiver in June when the LLR gave notice of their intention to discontinue working the LCR. The reasons given were the likely cessation of granite traffic and the fact that the state of the permanent way put too much risk on the engines, rolling stock and the company's servants. At the same time Captain Spicer made an outright offer of £10,500 for the LCR. The companies' solicitors exchanged letters in which the poor state of the LCR was gone into in some

Looe station about 1906 with stationmaster Herbert Hawes prominent in the centre and a train of Mersey stock.
M. E. J. DART

detail. Much of the line needed relaying, wooden sleepers needed replacing while the granite blocks needed to be 're-plugged and re-dogged'. Derailments were an everyday occurrence. Although Foster was anxious to let the L&SWR gain control of his railway, he was even keener to give up the Receivership, a post he had now held for 20 years, but had to decline Spicer's offer as he had no powers to sell the line.

The Captain had already bought £14,000 of LLR debentures with GWR money and in November for £4,700 he obtained LCR debentures with a face value of £6,000 and on which £2,640 interest was owing. With a Mr White he acquired the entire £14,000 debentures issued by the LCR and finally he purchased for £5 the Judgement Debt of £10,201 5s under which Lewis Foster had been appointed Receiver. The way was then clear for Foster to withdraw and Arthur Charlesworth, who unbeknown to Foster was a GWR nominee, was appointed in his place in December 1908. Lewis Foster remained as Chairman.

All this surreptitious intrigue of dubious legality had been deliberately kept from the GWR Board until it was a *fait accompli*. T. R. Bolitho, a director of the GWR, had been a partner with Foster in the East Cornwall Bank and, since the bank had been taken over by

Liskeard branch platform with LADY MARGARET *waiting to depart for Looe. Driver Chaston and fireman Menhenick are with their engine. On the right is the original footpath access from Tremeddan Terrace.*
AUTHOR'S COLLECTION

Barclays Bank in 1905, they had been Local Directors together. Also the Bolithos and Fosters were related by marriage. so with some justification it was feared details of the dealings would get back.[23] What Lewis Foster felt and thought when he found he had in fact been bought out by the Great Western is not recorded but doubtless he was not very pleased.

Now controlling the debenture stock, the GWR was able to make a public offer for the LCR and Charlesworth, a receiver appointed by the debenture holders unlike Foster, had the power to sell the railway. Accordingly the takeover was agreed with effect from 1 July 1909. The debentures were to be repaid in full plus 1s in the pound of the outstanding interest, although as they were all held by nominees of the GWR this was an academic point. The creditors, with debts totalling £26,888, were to get 1s in the pound (5%) in full discharge and the ordinary shareholders received 1% of the face value of their holdings. The directors' last duties were on 18 February 1909 to approve the Bill to sell their undertaking to the GWR.

The GWR had taken a large hand in the running of the LLR from 1907 and, having ensured the L&SWR could not enter the scene, it was agreed they should work the LLR from 1 January 1909, on which date they also took responsibility for maintenance on the LCR. An Act with the somewhat lengthy title of the Great Western Railway, Liskeard & Looe and Liskeard & Caradon Railways Act 1909 (9 Edward 7 cap.xiii) was obtained on 25 May 1909 and confirmed the vesting of the LCR and the working of the LLR. The new LCR Receiver, Charlesworth, was to be liquidator and paid £2,350 for his costs.

The GWR was to work the LLR and pay over a percentage of the total receipts, varying between 28% and 34%, but with a minimum of £1,200 to ensure that there was sufficient to pay $3^{1}/_{2}$% interest on the debentures. Captain Spicer now held all £24,000 of these, having been advanced £14,570 by the GWR to purchase those he did not already hold, and nearly £7,000 accrued interest was owing. He agreed to forgo the outstanding interest and accept $3^{1}/_{2}$% in future; the debentures had originally been issued at 4%, $4^{1}/_{2}$% and 5%. The Act also provided that the Members of the Committee of Management were now to be styled directors and the Clerk was to be called the Secretary.

So with their railway now controlled and operated by up-country people the last vestiges of the old canal company were dispensed with and soon there would be little to distinguish the individual and local Looe railway from most other Great Western branch lines.

Liskeard station from the air, about 1965. A single unit railcar is in the branch platform and the loop has been lifted but the goods yard is mainly intact.
COLLECTION R. G. SPALDING

CHAPTER SEVEN
THE GREAT WESTERN AND AFTER

'The staff will don Great Western uniforms – many of them seem much in need of new uniforms of some kind.'
RAILWAY MAGAZINE 1909

Underneath the train crew and station staff is GWR No 13, at Looe after the GWR takeover. From left to right, in front of the smokebox, are driver W. J. Chaston, who came from the GER in 1901, fireman H. Menhenick and driver Bill Vincent. Amongst the faces to the right are guard H. Menhenick and Edward Marsh, the hero of the 1906 accident.
AUTHOR'S COLLECTION

£3,000 had already been advanced by the GWR to improve the permanent way which still included some two miles of granite blocks. The surviving locomotives – *Caradon* had already been scrapped by the LLR – were to see service for some years longer, but most of the rolling stock was condemned as unfit to run on the GWR. After nearly a year's argument Silvanus Jenkin was persuaded to part with the plans, which he regarded as his own property, of the two railways for £50 and 1½ tons of records and papers in the LCR office were destroyed (to the chagrin of this writer but also to his relief!). Despite having obtained Jenkin's plans, or perhaps as a result of, the GWR set about making their own very full survey of the railways, giving rise to local speculation that they were about to start building the Northern Extension. An inspection was made of the area served by the LCR with a view to operating a passenger service and an engine and two carriages sent up the line as a trial. The GWR thought the line not suitable for passengers but that a Motor Car Service would be worthwhile as the area was more populous than that served by the Looe line. Some re-laying was done to the permanent way of the LCR, which below South Caradon was still mainly on granite blocks, and the Phoenix Mine branch was relaid to cope with the increasing traffic to the mine. All permanent way work and matters dealing with locomotives and rolling stock were transferred to GWR depots elsewhere - Plymouth, Par and Lostwithiel - leaving just enginemen and cleaners on the line.

Five of the six the overbridges between Coombe and Looe were rebuilt in 1910 to permit GWR stock to run down to Looe. Previously they had had a headway of up to 14 feet 6 inches and a span of 11 feet 8 inches. At St Cleer a goods loop was installed, possibly not so much for traffic there but to give somewhere for a

A nicely posed group at Looe, about 1911. The names are believed to be, from left to right (back row) W. J. Chaston (driver), Dick Grant, Hocking, Bill Vincent (driver), Harry Cox, unknown, (seated) H. Menhenick (passenger guard), Ted Hunter, Alfred Burridge (stationmaster), unknown, (seated) Bowden, Jack Pengelly, unknown. Young Pengelly wears a cap with the visible name '...MAN & SONS', perhaps Freeman & Sons.
R. C. RILEY COLLECTION

locomotive to run round. This was authorised in June 1910 and first appeared in the GWR service timetable in October 1911, as 'St Cleer Loop'. St Cleer was not listed at all until then. Most of the staff were transferred to the GWR but Holbrook left the district shortly afterwards.

At Phoenix a new company, Phoenix Mines (Cornwall) Ltd, with local Cornish interests and a capital of £160,000 had taken over and the new shaft was down to 540 feet. The last major new Cornish engine built in the county, a massive 80-inch beam engine by Holman Bros.

of Camborne to the designs of Nicholas Trestrail, was officially started on 9 June 1909 by HRH the Prince of Wales (later King George V). It proved inadequate to deal with the water and a couple of air pumps had to be installed to assist. Seccombe's and Stow's Shafts were cleared and timbered for re-use and the construction of the mill commenced, a secondhand mill engine already being on site. Up to 150 men had found employment. By the time Prince of Wales Shaft, as the new shaft had been named, had reached 1,200 feet in depth a

0-6-0ST 1941 at Looe with a train of Great Western four- and six-wheeled carriages in the early days of GWR ownership. July 1924.
H. C. CASSERLEY

83

The Looe branch page of the GWR's Service Time Table for the winter of 1920/21, commencing October 1920.

substantial tin lode was evident but, alas, the ore was not of commercial value. The company had already spent well in excess of its capital and more cash was needed for further development. The outbreak of the Great War in August 1914 defeated the enterprise and mining finally ceased in the Caradon district – apart from an unproductive attempt during the Second World War – as the pitwork was withdrawn from Prince of Wales Shaft. The engine was bought by the Duchy of Cornwall, the mineral lords at Phoenix, and kept maintained until the 1930s in case a revival should occur but it was finally broken up.[1]

What the GWR now called its Caradon branch was served by a daily goods train, although it only ran on Tuesdays and Thursdays if there was a need. By 1915 it was only timetabled for three days a week, and then only ran as far as was required. A little granite kept the branch going a short time longer but late in the Great War the line was requisitioned, along with several others in Cornwall, and the GWR announced its 'temporary' closure to assist the war effort from 1 January 1917. Track lifting had commenced some weeks before; the rails were said to have gone to France, although their value must be questioned and it is more likely they were melted down as scrap. There was some hope of re-opening the line after the cessation of hostilities. Clay deposits were one possible source of traffic and Freemans returned to Cheesewring Quarry in 1919 but nothing made it worthwhile. The GWR continued paying a nominal rent of £1 a year for the Phoenix and Kilmar lines to the Duchy until 1933[2] and legal abandonment came in 1931 as part of the GWR's 1931 Act.[3]

Forty years later, in 1972, it looked as though life might return to the Caradon line when a narrow gauge tourist attraction was mooted. The track would have been laid from Tokenbury Corner on the old bed to Sharptor and thence across the moor to Siblyback Reservoir. Restaurants, bars, pony rides and the exploration of old mines were some of the delights offered but, despite the backing of the English Tourist Board, all came to nought and this corner of Bodmin Moor was left in peace.

Reverting to the Looe line, the directors of the LLR had very little to occupy them. They had a steady income of between twelve and thirteen hundred pounds from the GWR each year which gave them a gross profit of more than they had received in almost any year since the 1870s. This was enough not only to pay the debenture interest but also from 1913 a modest dividend of between ½% and 1% on the preference shares. The track was brought up to scratch by the GWR and their locomotives and rolling stock operated the services, thus stripping the line of much individuality. The LLR directors did observe one aspect of this loss and wrote to the GWR saying that they were

> sorry to see that so much of the wood and undergrowth adjoining the railway has been cut down as this adds to the picturesque character of the line and is very attractive to visitors and suggest that the cutting of the undergrowth above referred to should be limited as far as possible in the future.[4]

The precursors to the 45xx class were the 44xx class of 2-6-2 tank locomotives. Here 4401 is at Looe with a set of GWR clerestorey stock, probably in the 1930s.
M. E. J. DART COLLECTION

The Great War brought Government control of the railways but as income was guaranteed at a pre-war level it made little difference to the Looe line, bar a drop in freight coming in to Looe by coastal shipping. The final problem to face the directors was how to get the best out of the GWR under the Grouping, the reorganisation authorised by the Railways Act 1921. They joined the Association of Smaller Railways and also sought advice from the Cambrian and Furness Railways but it was Chambers' good relations with Paddington that gained an improved offer. This was for each £100 3½% debenture stock, £87 10s GWR 4% debenture stock; for each £100 5% new preference shares (issued 1897/98), £34 4s 1d in cash, while the ordinary shares issued in 1825 and 1858 were cancelled as worthless. This was approved, the directors voted themselves £400 as compensation for loss of office and on 1 January 1923, after 98 years as a separate entity, the Liskeard & Looe Railway Company ceased to exist.

It was only its distinctive physical features in the long curving descent from Liskeard to Coombe Junction, the reversal at the latter station and the twisting course to Looe that

A view across Moorswater from the foot of Canal Road (the later main road) probably after 1909. The china clay dry opened in 1904. The brake van to the right of the GWR wagon is not of LCR origin and is presumably a GWR one. The incline ramp is still in place at Hodges limekiln but not in use.
LISKEARD OLD CORNWALL SOCIETY

The home signal is 'off', its water tanks are full to overflowing and 5531 is almost ready to leave Looe for Liskeard. 9 September 1961.
M. J. MESSENGER

Between the wars Looe was promoted by GWR posters such as this, much to the benefit of the tourist trade.
SOUTH DEVON RAILWAY TRUST

prevented the line being now just another Great Western branch. As Looe prospered as a seaside resort so the line prospered. Looe station platform was extended in 1928, at a cost of £150, to accommodate greater traffic, as was Liskeard in 1924 and 1937. The service during the inter-war years was seven or eight passenger trains each way daily, with small variations. A Sunday service was re-introduced in 1933, until the Second World War.

A 1926 GWR report into the viability of the company's branch lines[5] gave the receipts for the branch in 1925 as £21,502 against expenditure of £12,788. Clearly the branch was profitable, despite the fact that only Looe's traffic was counted, the rest being attributed to Liskeard and the main line. The principal goods traffic at this time was coal, grain, manure (fertilisers) and livestock. Whilst fish traffic is not specifically mentioned there was doubtless some of that too. On average each day Looe received four wagons of coal and nine of general goods, whilst despatching three of the latter category. This justified a daily goods train each way and one of the eight passenger trains could be mixed in the down direction. About 12,000 tons was carried each year, almost equally divided between coal and general goods, along with 3,512 cans of milk and 176 wagons of livestock.

The General Strike, euphemistically referred to as 'Labour Troubles', saw an emergency timetable of four trains each way introduced in June 1926.

In the early thirties the number of tickets issued at Looe declined sharply, from more than 50,000 in 1929 to less than half that five years later, and continued declining thereafter. This represented a loss in local traffic rather than holiday visitors who bought their tickets up-country. Freight traffic declined from the end of the Great War as coastal shipping decreased. Initially 2,000 tons of china clay a year were shipped from Looe, another 1,000 tons went by rail on the main line, but gradually all was taken from Moorswater up to the main line railway. Eventually almost the only freight was clay from Moorswater to Liskeard and coal to Moorswater, for the engine shed and the clay kiln, and to Looe, for domestic use. The main line connection at Liskeard was strengthened in 1935 to give heavier stock access to the branch line. Staff at Looe numbered ten throughout the inter-war period and the wages bill averaged about £1,400 a year.[6]

An interesting development appeared in 1935 when the GWR proposed to build a new seven mile branch to Looe, spending part of thirty million pounds to be made available by the Government to meet the problem of

LISKEARD AND LOOE. (Week Days only.)

	a.m.	a.m.	a.m.	a.m.	a.m.	a.m.	p.m.	p.m.	p.m.	p.m.	p.m.
Liskeard .... dep.	4 40	6 8 0	7 15	8 8 40	8G 55	10 0	12 33	2 0	4 45	5 55	7 45
Coombe Junction .... ,,	..	..	7 23	8 48	9G 3	10 9	12 41	2 8	4 54	6 4	7 54
St. Keyne .... ,,	..	..	7 28	8 53	9G 8	10 13	12 46	2 13	4 58	6 8	7 58
Causeland .... ,,	..	..	7 32	8 57	9G 12	10 17	12 50	2 17	5 2	6 12	8 2
Sandplace .... ,,	..	..	7 37	9 3 2	9G 17	10 22	12 55	2 22	5 7	6 17	8 7
Looe .... arr.	5 5	6 25	7 42	9 3 7	9G 22	10 27	1 0	2 27	5 12	6 22	8 12

	a.m.	a.m.	a.m.	a.m.	a.m.	a.m.	p.m.	p.m.	p.m.	p.m.	p.m.
Looe .... dep.	6 40	8 0	8G 15	9D 25	..	9 45	11 45	1 10	4 0	5 23	6 40	8 30
Sandplace .... ,,	..	8 6	8G 21	..	..	9 51	11 51	1 16	4 6	..	6 46	8 36
Causeland .... ,,	..	8 10	8G 25	..	..	9 55	11 55	1 20	4 10	..	6 50	8 40
St. Keyne .... ,,	..	8 14	8G 29	..	..	9 59	11 59	1 24	4 14	..	6 54	8 44
Coombe Junction .... ,,	..	8 21	8G 36	..	..	10 6	12 6	1 31	4 21	..	7 1	8 51
Liskeard .... arr.	7 6	8 31	8G 43	9D 50	..	10 13	12 13	1 38	4 28	5 46	7 8	8 58

The last GWR summer timetable, for 1947, a few months before nationalisation.

unemployment. The new line would have run from a junction at Trerulefoot, west of St Germans, to the coast at Seaton and thence to a terminus high above Looe. Extensive earthworks and engineering would have been needed including three tunnels, one more than a mile long, and two masonry viaducts. Millendreath Viaduct was to have had 12 spans over a total length of 287 yards and a height of 123 feet. Keverall Viaduct was to be even larger with 13 spans over 343 yards and 144 feet in height. Stations would have been at Looe, Millendreath and Downderry and the service operated by the new GWR streamlined diesel railcars running from Plymouth. The journey time from Plymouth to Looe would have been 35 minutes and it is quite likely the new branch would have sounded the death knell of the old line from Liskeard. Although the contract for the Looe to Keverall section was let and much of the line marked out, only a little preparatory work was done before the scheme was dropped.[7]

During the Second World War the railways again came under Government control, in the form of the Railway Executive Committee, but once again the Looe branch was little affected. Services were reduced, to conserve the nation's supplies of coal, but at the same time public

Summer trains pass at Coombe Junction on an August morning in 1958. 4585 has just arrived in the platform from Looe whilst another 45xx leaves from the loop, having brought its train down from Liskeard, run around and moved into the loop to make way for the up train. The low building between the platform and the former tweed mill is built on the bed of the canal. PETER W. GRAY

Climbing Joseph Thomas's steep connection to Liskeard, the 8.40 a.m. from Looe passes under Liskeard Viaduct hauled by 4565. The coaches are a standard 'B' set such as provided most of the branch services from 1930 until the end of steam. All coaches used on the branch were restricted to short, seven feet, wheelbase bogies. 15 August 1959.
PETER W. GRAY

transport was an essential part of the war effort. The peace after the war brought nationalisation and the Great Western Railway became the Western Region of British Railways. It also brought changing travel habits and a more road-conscious public. As early as 1956, when the water-wheel at Moorswater shed needed repairing, there were doubts whether the branch would be open long enough to justify the cost. 1963 saw the publication of the 'Beeching Report' and the Looe branch, losing £1,037, was among those listed for total closure.[8] Goods trains had ceased calling at Sandplace from 18 June 1951 but all freight traffic stopped from 4 November 1963, with the exception of clay traffic from Moorswater. Steam power had given way to diesel on 11 September 1961, after just over a century. Various economies took place. Liskeard branch signal box was closed early in 1964, and demolished later in the year, and the signal instruments for the section to Coombe Junction were transferred to the main line box. The section from Coombe Junction to Looe was reduced to one engine in steam status, whilst Looe station was placed under the control of the Liskeard stationmaster.

On 7 October 1965 notice was published of the British Railways Board's intention to close the line to all traffic and the first formal objection was received just four days later. In 1965 passenger journeys averaged 199 daily in winter and 532 in summer. Earnings were £7,100 plus £6,600 generated elsewhere, presumably from through bookings, but direct costs totalled £26,900. A Liskeard/Looe Rail Preservation Committee was formed, based at the Looe Urban District Council's offices at the Guildhall, and 195 objections to the closure were eventually received.

Evidence presented to the Transport Users Consultative Committee hearing included details of Looe's reliance on the holiday trade, the poor bus services and the impact of the additional traffic on the rural Cornish roads. In many ways, the local Western National bus services were not competition for the branch line; an unusual situation for an English railway. Unable to use the direct route between Liskeard and Looe, because of the narrowness of the lanes, buses were forced to take a more roundabout route, so they took longer and were more expensive than the train. The bus timetable made no provision for commuters between the two towns.

As a result of the evidence on 20 September 1966 the Minister of Transport, Barbara Castle, refused closure and just six weeks later BR produced a report of the branch's potential and

By the early 1960s the pressure of the motor car was being felt in Looe and in August 1963 a splendid selection of what are now 'classic' cars were parked in the goods yard. Riley, Ford, Austin and Standard cars can be picked out. The left hand line, with the buffer stop, formerly ran on to Looe quay.
P. J. GARLAND

The signalman leans out of Liskeard Branch Signal Box to take the single line token from the driver of 4522 as the train arrives from Coombe Junction. The town of Liskeard, with the tower of St Martin's prominent, is beyond.
R. C. RILEY

The tide is well out as 5531 takes an afternoon train out of Looe. Terras Crossing 9 September 1961.
M. J. MESSENGER

Paper tickets were issued on the trains by the guard, particularly to cater for traffic from the intermediate halts. AUTHOR'S COLLECTION.

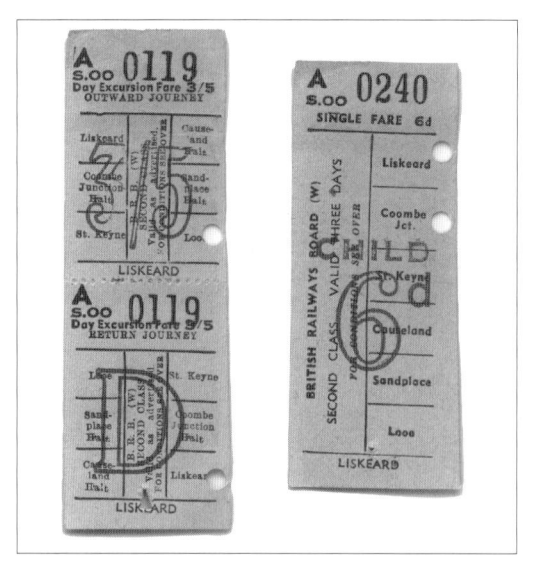

suggested savings of in excess of £10,000. The report covered the needs of local industries and schools and noted that a population of 7,660 lived within one mile of the line's stations. Of these 3,900 were at Liskeard, 3,100 at Looe and just 20 at Causeland. By retiming trains to make better connections and lowering fares, which were already less than bus, it was thought earnings could be increased by £800. At the same time savings in expenses totalling £9,800 were aimed for by such means as de-staffing Looe, then manned by two porters, eliminating Coombe Junction signal box, unmanning Coombe and Terras level crossings and stabling the diesel unit at Liskeard rather than St Blazey.[9]

Most of the economies were implemented, although not as rapidly as the report. It is sad that such economies were not considered before closure was proposed, and refused. Looe station became unstaffed on 30 September 1968, since when tickets have been issued on the train by the guard. The buildings had been demolished in May that year and replaced by what was described as a halt-type structure on the up end of the platform. Only space was left for a two-car multiple unit and the rest of the track to the south was lifted, thus reducing the length of the branch by a quarter of a mile.

After 1963 the only freight traffic had been china clay from English China Clay's dry at Moorswater. In 1974 the rail layout within the dry was altered giving a loop and two sidings and a road tractor, with buffing beams, undertook shunting until 1990 when an 0-4-0 diesel hydraulic locomotive, named *Sharon*, was transferred from Marsh Mills, outside Plymouth. Some 35,000 tons of freight travelled to and from Moorswater clay dry[10] but in 1996 ECC decided to concentrate production at fewer plants and Parsons Park clay pit and Moorswater dry were closed and mothballed. Stockpiled clay at Moorswater continued to be shipped until later in 1997. *Sharon* was transferred to Wiltshire in March that year. Since then the dry sidings have been used intermittently for stone and cement traffic. although this has now ceased.

The new end of the line at Looe. Track has been lifted and buildings demolished, and the bulldozer is busy shortening the platform. 1968. GRAHAM ROOSE

Coombe Junction signal box immediately prior to demolition in May 1981. The level crossing gates have been removed and British Rail's S & T Department crew are about to start work.
JOHN L. RAPSON

Bottom left: The engine shed has now lost its roof and in the inspection pit lies the remains of the small water wheel that pumped water up into the tank outside the shed door. October 1967.
M. J. MESSENGER

Bottom right: The end is near for the former carriage shed and wagon works at Moorswater in May 1967. The tracks have been lifted and the roof stripped of slates. Close to the marks of the lifted wooden sleepers can be seen stone sleeper blocks still in situ.
M. J. MESSENGER

From 1969 the branch received a government subsidy in the form of a passenger grant equal to the operating deficit. This varied from £35,000 to £60,000 per annum (considerably more than the original cost of the line) and ensured the line's survival to date. Present politics are not in favour of such subsidies and are moving towards eliminating grants entirely.

In the late 1980s initiatives were commenced to publicise and encourage the survival of several west country branch lines. These culminated in the Devon & Cornwall Rail Partnership, a non-profit community rail project with the object of promoting several west country branch lines. It is funded by Cornwall, Devon County and Plymouth City Councils, the University of Plymouth and, at the moment, First Great Western. The Looe line is additionally supported by Looe and Liskeard

North British type 2 diesel hydraulic locomotive D6320 approaches Coombe Junction with a clay train from Moorswater. A little later, without moving from the spot, the photographer would have seen the same train heading westwards towards Fowey across Moorswater viaduct, in the background. July 1963. R. C. RILEY

In July 1967 the Looe branch service was worked by two single unit railcars coupled together. ARTHUR R. WILSON/MAURICE DART COLLECTION

Taken from a similar viewpoint as the photograph opposite but showing the changes that had taken place in 26 years. Motive power is now in the hands of a class 37, 37673 in Railfreight livery, and the clay is carried in fairly new 50 tonne CDA wagons, replacing the ageing wooden bodied 'clay hoods' opposite. The ditch to right is the route of the old canal. 6 May 1989.
JOHN VAUGHAN

Town Councils and the South East Cornwall Tourism Association. The main issues handled are promotion and marketing but station improvements and service matters also come within their remit.[11]

The franchise holder operating the passenger service today (2015) is First Great Western and consists of up to twelve trains in each direction, probably the best the line has ever seen. It is designed to be provided by one unit and two crews, the unit working out each day from St Blazey and returning each night for servicing. The crews are also based at St Blazey and change at midday, travelling from their home depot by passenger train to Liskeard. A Sunday service is now provided in summer and, since 2004, a ticket office is open at Looe for the summer.

Since the end of the twentieth century passenger journeys have just about doubled to almost 120,000 a year (2014) and passengers are actively encouraged, with attractive publicity, good signposting and free parking at Liskeard. The park and ride facility offers visitors an excellent alternative to driving their cars into crowded Looe. Surprisingly, Causeland's passenger journeys now are well over 3,000 a year but Coombe is one of the country's least used stations. The chances of the line's survival are now probably better than at any time in the past 40 years.[12]

An unusual, and totally untypical, visitor to the Looe branch in November 2012 was the reconstructed GWR steam rail-motor. Such vehicles never normally worked to Looe but made an interesting excursion.
MICHAEL MESSENGER

93

CHAPTER EIGHT
FROM SEA TO THE MOOR

'Hallo! here is a rough tramroad ... let us follow it.'
J. R. LEIFCHILD 1857[1]

Most of the railways and the canal were built from the north southwards but for convenience we shall start at the sea, as the mileposts do, and follow the lines, and the mineral traffic, to their source.

The quays at West Looe have changed greatly from a century ago. Where once copper ores, coal and granite were piled high, cars now park and the rails have given way to tarmac. The harbour, once thronged with schooners laying side by side because there was insufficient quay room for them all, now is full of power boats, motor yachts and fishing boats, and the streets in season echo to the urban accents of London and Birmingham whose owners are attracted by the charm and character of the town and district.

Across the end of Looe Bridge what was the LLR goods yard is now occupied by a recent development that includes a health centre, police station, petrol filling station and car park. Much of this site was reclaimed from the river, apparently without anybody's leave, in the 1890s and the early twentieth century using stone from the former canal locks and buildings. As well as a weighbridge, crane and cattle pens

An unusual view of Looe station in the mid-twentieth century, showing the passing loop south of the station and the entry to the goods yard. Note the towels laid out to dry on the wall in front of the guest houses.
HMRS COLLECTION M1059

The line of the siding onto Looe quays can be clearly seen on this commercial postcard but the ore quays are empty. In the bottom right is Freeman's granite yard. The goods yard has not yet been built, or the river bank filled in, between the harbour and station, thus dating this view as before 1900.
AUTHOR'S COLLECTION

94

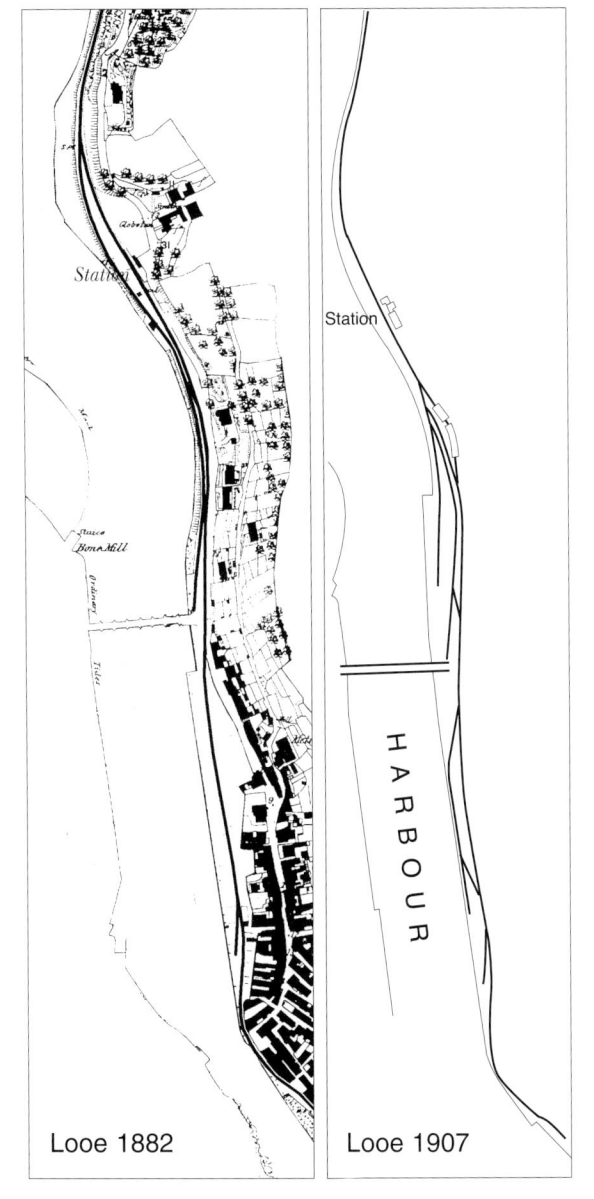

there were also a corrugated iron carriage shed and an engine shed. Both were erected in 1901, the latter costing £305, as the new timetable called for a locomotive to be stabled overnight at Looe. The engine shed was sold in 1920 for £25.

Looe station is also much changed. The platform here was lengthened from 75 feet to 200 in 1901 and by a further 96 feet in 1928. Until 1901 the station building comprised simply a booking office and waiting room with a lavatory and small goods shed tacked on at each end, but with the opening of the Liskeard extension a ladies' waiting room was added and an awning carried over the platform. All this has now gone, having been replaced with much simpler accommodation. Initially, in 1968 when the platform was shortened, a sectional building provided a ticket office and mess room but staffing ceased at the end of the 1969 summer season. The 'bus-shelter' style then provided has now been replaced by a slightly larger shelter that includes a room for the use of the train crew. The platform was shortened at the Looe end and the track now simply ends in a dead-end at a buffer stop as diesel railcars, the present service, need no run-round. A plaque records Joseph Thomas's part in connecting the old railways with the GWR at Liskeard.

Looe station in its final form, before 'down-sizing'. The centre section, between the chimney pots, is the original building of 1879 and to its right is the extension added by the LLR in 1901, when the canopy was also added. The GWR extended in the opposite direction, to the left, probably in the late-1930s. 9 September 1961.
M. J. MESSENGER

The water tower at Looe dated from before 1900 and replaced that installed in 1860. Pictured in September 1961.
M. J. MESSENGER

Alongside the East Looe River, 4552 heads for Liskeard. July 1960. R. C. RILEY

Recently decanted from London suburban workings, 2-car Class 117 DMU No. L708 in Network South East livery is reflected in the estuary of the East Looe River at Terras Pill, south of Sandplace, as it runs down from Liskeard to Looe on 22 April 1993. The road sign seems to be slightly misleading! JOHN VAUGHAN

Sandplace halt, with what may be GWR officials, and No 13 pulling in with a train of GWR stock. The baulks of timber and planking suggest some rebuilding going on nearby. Post 1910. L&GRP

The West and East Looe Rivers meet just opposite Looe station and it is alongside the latter river that the line runs, curving around past Shutta Point. The site of Looe Gas Works, one of the line's customers, is passed on the right and shortly afterwards the road comes to run parallel to the railway. At Steps the end of the Morval Valley is passed and it is near the head of this valley that the Buller family lived at Morval House. On the river here John Francis Buller had a quay which was destroyed by the railway works in 1859. The approach to the canal is soon reached where a small arch bridge carries the railway over what now appears to be a mere side stream. It was at this bridge on a November morning in 1884 that Buller's solicitors met the representatives of the two railways to witness a barge entering the canal. The railway is now on a stone embankment with the East Looe River on the left, and the channel of the canal on the right. In a few more yards Terras level crossing is reached, now unmanned and gateless although the iron cottage bought for the gatekeeper by the LLR in 1902 for £66 10s remains, now somewhat modified. The gates were installed from 24 November 1902 but were removed in July 1970 as part of the economy measures taken on the branch. Across the river on the south side of Terras Bridge a limekiln was once served by the river barges. Alongside the level crossing a small bridge carries the road over the canal, and between the railway and the iron cottage, is Terras lock, the entry to the canal, now derelict but still recognizable with the remains of the lock gates and with the addition of a sluice. In canal days there was a small lodge here where the check in respect of the cargo was handed in.

Between Terras and Sandplace the canal and river twist together from one side of the valley floor to the other as the valley itself takes a double bend. The railway cuts off both corners, crossing the canal on two bridges, New Bridge and Salt Park Bridge respectively, both of twelve feet span like that south of Terras, while the river was diverted to save two more bridges. New Bridge was rebuilt by Railtrack in the mid-1990s. Nowadays the tide does not normally go beyond this point although formerly it flowed beyond Sandplace. At Sandplace the basin where the canal terminated after the railway was built is overgrown and difficult to find, as is the site of the nearby loop siding put in for J. F. Buller in 1879 and removed 23 August 1956. The hamlet of Sandplace is alongside the railway and several of the limekilns put out of business by the opening of the canal or of the railway can be seen. The Bullers Arms is now a private house.

Sandplace station is a couple of hundred yards further on beside Highercliff Bridge. The over-bridges were numbered in 1907 for the GWR's benefit and this became No 1. More modestly described today as a halt the short platform was graced by little beyond a clapboard hut installed when the station was opened. Early in 1998 a new shelter in a pastiche traditional railway style was erected. Across the river can be seen another limekiln and a small quay cut into the river bank. Doubtless it was the passage of barges up to this point that caused Priestley in 1831 to state the canal had a branch of one mile to Sandplace; the branch being in fact the river.[2]

Sandplace halt in 1909. The wooden hut has given way to corrugated iron and has a GWR cast-iron notice attached. The bridge is in original condition, prior to rebuilding by the GWR in 1910. L&GRP

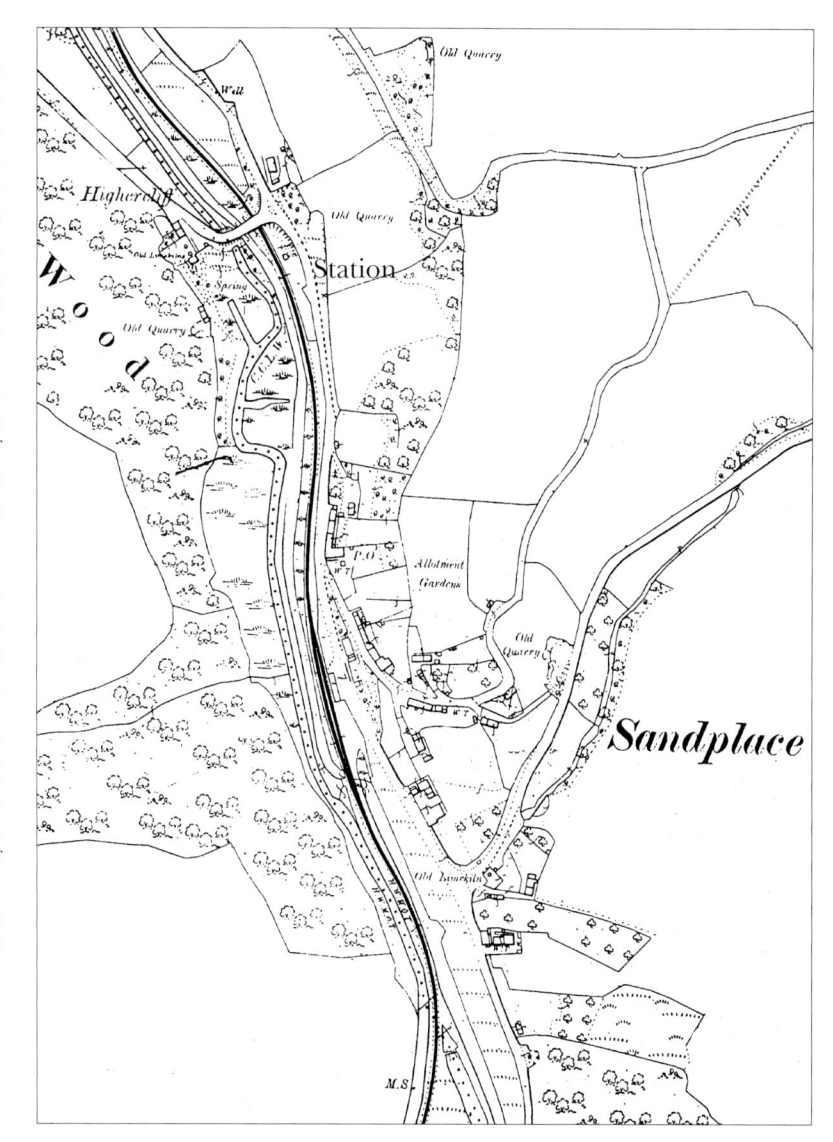

Sandplace station is below Highercliff bridge where the canal is between railway and river. Just south of the double ended siding put in for the Buller estate the canal is culverted under the railway to emerge on the east side. A small goods shed can be seen alongside the siding. [BASED ON THE ORDNANCE SURVEY, CROWN COPYRIGHT RESERVED]

Causeland station, as shown on the 1907 map. It was not marked on the 1882 survey. The canal is to the left (west) of the railway. [BASED ON THE ORDNANCE SURVEY, CROWN COPYRIGHT RESERVED]

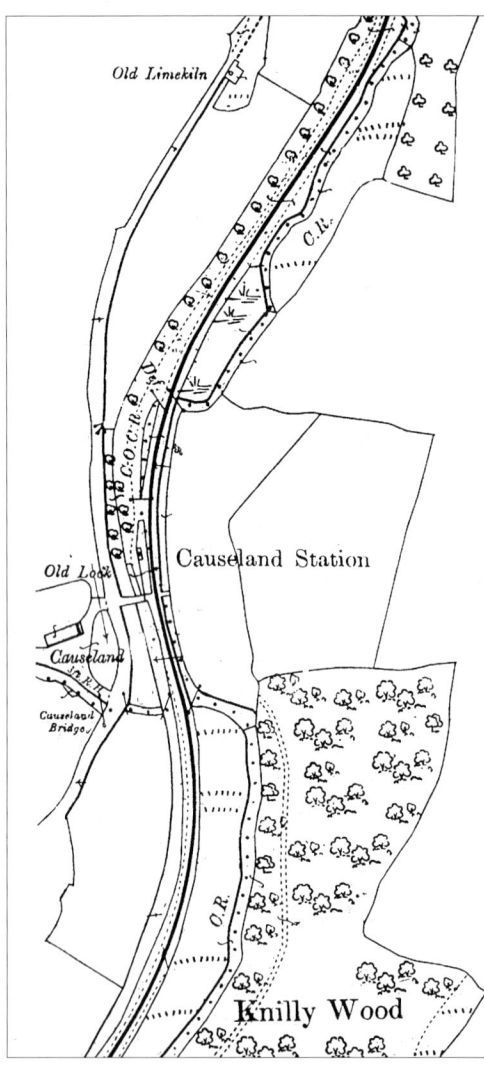

Causeland station, about the end of the nineteenth century, when it had a wide reputation of being the smallest station in the kingdom, even being featured in the national magazine Tit-bits. Note the light flat bottom rail fixed to stone sleeper blocks and the coarse ballasting. COLLECTION GRAHAM ROOSE

The next two bridges are Tregarland and Plashford (Bridge Nos 2 and 3). Tregarland is unlike all other over-bridges on the LLR in that it is a plate girder bridge rather than a three arch stone bridge. It was constructed in 1862 by Silvanus Jenkin to replace a level crossing but whether its present form is original is not known. The bridges span railway and canal and in most examples there is a canal lock within the arch. The centre arch is blind and where the GWR rebuilt the rail arch after 1909 they encroached on the centre arch.

At Tregarland the river has been diverted into the canal, now on the left, west, side of the railway, for a couple of hundred yards and at the bridge is the site of the first lock above Terras. Elsewhere the canal is often deep in undergrowth but carries a trickle of water still. The locks, now very ruinous, can often be detected by the tinkling of the little stream of water as it tumbles through the locks and over the granite sills of the lockgates. One lock is at Plashford Bridge and a couple more can be seen in the undergrowth between there and Causeland. A short distance below Causeland some of the old milestones from the Caradon line can be found embedded in the trackbed. The original granite milestones were still in place beside the Looe line in 1935.

Causeland station, the original intermediate stop on the line, stands quiet and lonely beside a lock and small bridge over the canal, and one cannot help wondering why the station should have been built here. Apart from the nearby farm from which it takes its name, there is little traffic in the immediate vicinity. On the first edition large scale Ordnance Survey of the 1880s the station was so insignificant it was not marked. On the opening to passengers it was described as a 'flag station', where trains stopped on request, and in 1898 it was said to have 'only a few feet of platform and a shed (built of old railway sleepers) which will hold six people comfortably'[3]. When a new building was promised in 1901 the *Cornish Times* thought it might 'lose its unique distinction of being the smallest railway station in the Kingdom'. On both the openings of Sandplace and St Keyne the closure of Causeland was mooted but local residents successfully petitioned against it. The building was a hut of similar style to Sandplace but has been replaced by a simple block built building with corrugated iron roof.

All the way to Moorswater the canal, railway and river run close together up the narrow valley following every curve and bend. The lock at Landlooe Bridge (4) is within the arch of the bridge and is in good condition. Above Landlooe the valley opens up a little and the

St Keyne Halt in LLR days, between 1902 and 1909, with stone blocked track. The overbridge was later rebuilt by the GWR. Opposite the platform, in the undergrowth, is the remains of St Keyne lock of the canal. On the far left can be glimpsed a wall of the limekiln. EDWIN COURSE COLLECTION

St Keyne station, close to Lametton Mill, opened in 1901. [BASED ON THE ORDNANCE SURVEY, CROWN COPYRIGHT RESERVED]

sides are not so steep but it loses none of its intimateness. Between here and St Keyne the canal moves to the east side of the railway but the bridge taking the latter over the former is no longer clear. The need to keep traffic moving on the canal whilst the railway was being built would necessitate a bridge big enough to clear a barge. At a later date a section of railway appears to have been re-aligned onto the canal bed. Some of the track on this section was still laid on stone blocks in 1901.

St Keyne station is named after the famous holy well a half-mile to the south but is now better known for the organ museum in what was Lametton Mill. In 1886 a siding was considered here to serve the mill and again in 1901 but in the event the halt was built, opening 1 September 1902. A limekiln stood on the site from 1833 until it was destroyed by the new station. A shelter of the same style as Sandplace was erected here also in 1998. The canal and a lock can be seen clearly on the opposite side of the track with the earlier bridge that crossed the

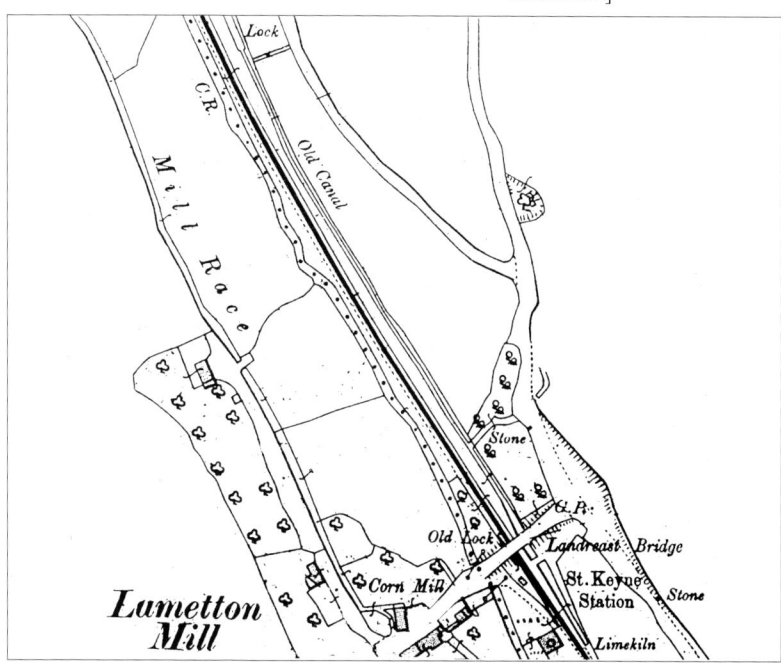

The substantial remains of the former limekiln are prominent beyond the platform at St Keyne in August 1936.
R. K. COPE, ROGER CARPENTER COLLECTION

On the right an arch survives across the remains of the canal at St Keyne. This was superceded in 1860 by the Silvanus Jenkin designed bridge beyond. 4565 is pulling in with a Looe train, August 1959. PETER HAY

canal before that carrying the road across the railway and canal was built (5). This is Landreast Bridge and from here it is a fairly straight run to Trussel Bridge (6), where Joseph Thomas's 1892 junction line would have climbed away to the right (east). Where the Liskeard valley runs in at right-angles from the north-east an occupation road to Lodge Barton crosses the railway and a solitary sidewall of a lock stands just beyond, beside the track. The extension line from Liskeard drops down on the right to join the Looe line at Coombe Junction and all trace of the canal is obliterated for a quarter-mile.

The level crossing at Coombe carries a private road to Coombe House, once the home of Lewis Foster, and caused some trouble in

100

Coombe Junction, August 1959. On the signal box balcony is a 15 m.p.h. speed limit warning and just beyond the box is the token exchange apparatus. 4565 is making a vigorous departure to build up speed to climb the bank to Liskeard.
PETER W. GRAY

1902 when the tenant of Coombe was complaining bitterly that the LLR were locking the gates against the road and cutting off his access. Wicket gates were installed and the matter resolved. To the north of the level crossing, on the west side of the railway, was Coombe Junction signal box, now demolished, and on the opposite side of the railway another lock can be seen.

The extension line joins the Looe line just before the level crossing and the combined line runs into Coombe. A stop was suggested here in 1884 for the convenience of passengers going to the Great Western station in Liskeard and the suggestion was probably taken up straight away; certainly the halt was in use by 1896 when trains would stop on notice to the guard. The platform here was originally crudely built of sleepers. In

4508 climbs away from Coombe Junction towards Liskeard. The Looe line can be seen left dropping down the valley. Coombe House, where Lewis Foster lived, is in the trees behind the signal box. July 1955.
R. C. RILEY

5531 arriving at Coombe Junction from Liskeard. The steep climb of the descending line can be seen in comparison with the line to Looe dropping down the valley. August 1961.
M. J. MESSENGER

Coombe Junction halt, in 1922. The bracket signal on the right is one of those installed by Saxby & Farmer in 1901 for the L&LR. That in the distance, controlling entry to Moorswater, is a standard GWR signal. A disc signal is in the left foreground. Dominating the background is the former Duchy Tweed Mill, opened as a woollen mill by J. H. Blamey in the 1880s.
L&GRP

1901 Coombe was provided with a lengthy passing loop, about 650 feet in all, and a centre crossover enabled two trains to gain access to the platform and pass each other. This was removed at the end of 1928 and trains had to shunt from side to side of the loop when passing. Following dieselisation, the platform line was reduced to a dead end as reversal simply involved the driver walking from one end to the other of his train taking his control handle with him. In May 1981 the layout was further simplified by slewing the platform line to join that to Moorswater and eliminating the dead end. The junction points are now changed by the train crew and as often as not the train merely clears the points and does not run into the platform. Coombe is now shown as a station stop for only a few trains in the public timetable.

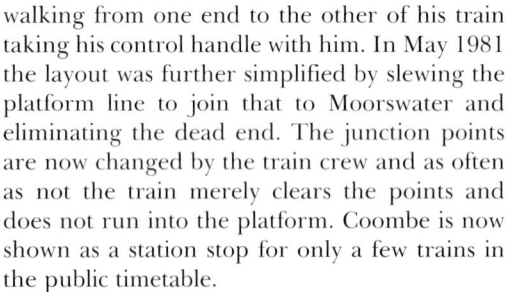

Having reversed direction, the Liskeard-bound train starts climbing at 1 in 40 almost as soon as it leaves Coombe, shortly passing over Coombe and under Lodge bridges (8 and 9). The roads that used these two bridges both had to be re-aligned. Curving sharply left now, on a 10½ chain radius curve, the line turns through 90 degrees through a cutting until it is pointing north-east and continues the steep climb up the side of the Liskeard valley. Ahead to the right can be seen Bolitho Viaduct, named after a local landowner, on the Cornish main line. A small farm over-bridge, Trevillis or Bolitho (10), is passed and then a large embankment takes the railway across the valley to pass under Liskeard Viaduct with the main line metals 80 feet above. The LLR paid an annual wayleave of £3 for the privilege of passing under the main line although under an earlier agreement with the Cornwall Railway they were only paid £1 for the main line to cross their earlier line at Moorswater.

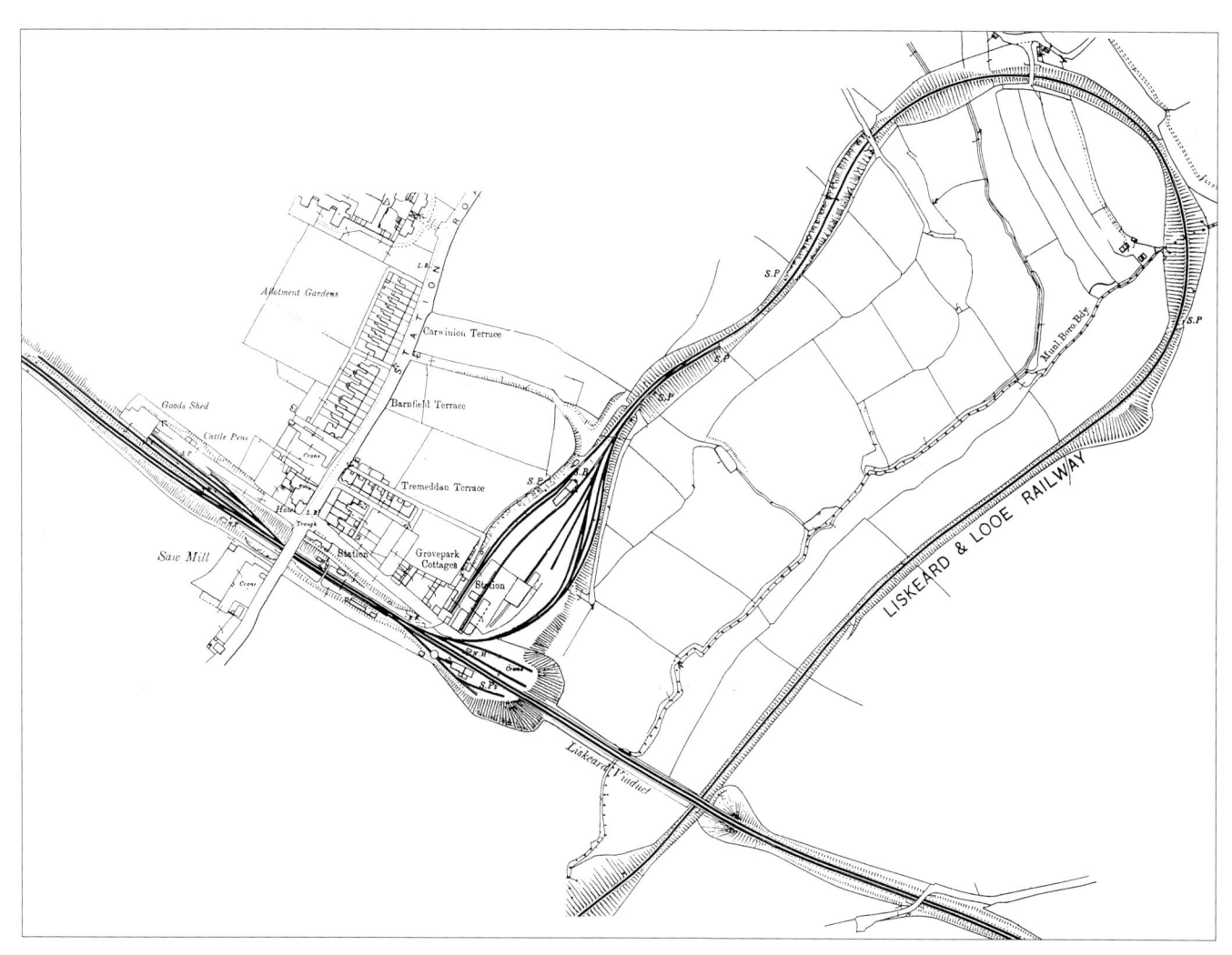

As the extension line approaches the head of the valley and Liskeard town, it passes through Bolitho cutting and under the Liskeard By-Pass (now the A38) and begins curving left under Gut Lane Bridge (11) until, by the time it passes under East Lane Bridge (12), the line has turned through more than 180 degrees and is facing south-west. This incredible curve is but eight chains (176 yards) radius. A couple of temporary level crossings were installed on this section in 1974 for contractors building the Liskeard By-Pass. A few yards further, still at 1 in 40, under the By-Pass again, then another small underbridge (13) and the line is in Liskeard station at a level with, but at right-angles to, the main line. Such was Joseph Thomas's answer to the problem of connecting the Looe line with the outside world – an expensively engineered railway with steep gradients, sharp curves and extensive earthworks – but the 1¾ mile link served its purpose well.

Liskeard station was the pride and joy of the Liskeard & Looe Railway in 1901. Outside of Truro it had the largest goods yard in Cornwall with generous siding accommodation and, of course, a brand new passenger station, all lit by gas. The latter was designed by local architect, John Sansom, and the *Cornish Times* described the facilities:

> At the northern end is the booking-hall with its ticket window opening into the booking office, which is also the Stationmaster's office. This little sanctum, surrounded by a dado of pitchpine, has a counter of the same wood, completely fitted with drawers, shelves, and cupboards, and a fireplace and writing table, with seats, complete the room, which also opens into the parcel office, which has a separate entrance from the platform. The next door leads into the general waiting-room, the furniture of which is worthy of note, a table and three benches being constructed of solid

Liskeard in 1907, showing the remarkable horseshoe curve by which Joseph Thomas engineered the approach to Liskeard.
[BASED ON THE ORDNANCE SURVEY, CROWN COPYRIGHT RESERVED]

This photograph is captioned, in Holbrook's writing, 'Liskeard station L&LRy' and may have been taken by him very soon after opening. Stationmaster Burridge stands in the doorway.
GRAHAM ROOSE COLLECTION

English oak, very massive and substantial. The ladies' waiting room adjoining is also a comfortable little apartment, furnished with a lounge upholstered in red pegamoid, a table and fireplace, with lavatory adjoining. The platform widens out into a big recess, with a seat running all round, which forms a large covered arcade, large enough to accommodate plenty of passengers in wet weather.[4]

The connecting line to the GWR, Railway No 2 in the 1895 Act, passed through the goods yard and via a curve of five chains (110 yards) radius joined the main line at the east end of the main line station. This link was connected to the GWR on 25 February 1901 and, whilst construction materials for the new railway may have used it, it would not have been used for goods traffic until after the line had been opened for passengers as until then the LLR had no locomotives or rolling stock. A footpath linked the passenger station with Station Road by way of Tremeddan Terrace, while goods traffic was catered for by a road from the end of Carwinion Terrace to the goods yard, but these were soon abandoned in favour of the Great Western road which served the LLR just as well. It was found necessary to extend the passenger platform twice, first in 1924 from 225 feet to 405 feet and again in 1937 to 640 feet. Although some sidings and the loop line have been lifted and the signal box demolished, at the time of writing Liskeard branch station is not too much changed.

To revert to Coombe Junction, the line to Moorswater continues north under Lamellion Bridge (7). This bridge, on the site of a lock, was not rebuilt and is in original 1859 condition. To the east of the bridge is Lamellion Mill, once owned by the canal company, and on the left of the railway, in the field immediately beyond the bridge, the remains of a side cut of the canal can be seen, where it served a limekiln. The main canal channel, parallel to the railway, is now occupied by a concrete invert, installed in 1983 for flood relief.

The notice guarding the link between the main line and the branch. June 1961.
M. J. MESSENGER

Liskeard Branch Signal Box, 1961. Mopeds were then essential transport for signalmen and other railway workers. The box was demolished after the token instrument was transferred to the main line box in 1964.
M. J. MESSENGER

Liskeard branch platform in 1961. This building, designed by local architect John Sansom, was erected in 1901 and survives very well.
M. J. MESSENGER

Moorswater Viaduct, arguably Cornwall's most elegant, now dominates the scene. Immediately below the viaduct was a stone yard served by a siding. It was originally used by the Cheesewring Granite Company for storing stone prior to transshipment to the canal but, after the railway to Looe was opened, it was equipped as a workyard with steam powered machinery to finally shape, finish and polish the granite. Freemans closed it about 1930 and the site has since been used by the County Council.[5]

Opposite the stone yard was Moorswater passenger station. The platform on the east side of the track was only 75 feet long, like Looe, and the buildings were identical to those at Looe, being of wood and roofed with corrugated iron.[6] It existed in 1935 as a bungalow and the remains of the platform can still be seen in the undergrowth. A neat square signal box sat just off the south end of the platform.

Moorswater was the upper terminus of the canal and of the Looe railway and the lower

Moorswater station in August 1928 when it was in use as a bungalow. After it ceased to be a station in 1901 one of the railway employees, Jonathan Symons, lived here.
R. C. RILEY COLLECTION

CARADON & LOOE – THE CANAL, RAILWAYS AND MINES

Although suffering from movement this photograph is worth including as it shows limekilns on both sides of the valley at Moorswater. The south end of Hodge's kiln, in the background, has since collapsed. The pillar that supported the plateway incline can also be seen. The top of the nearer kiln appears to have become an extension of the considerable vegetable plot in the foreground. A 45xx class locomotive is bustling about with some wagons. 27 August 1936.
R. K. COPE,
ROGER CARPENTER
COLLECTION

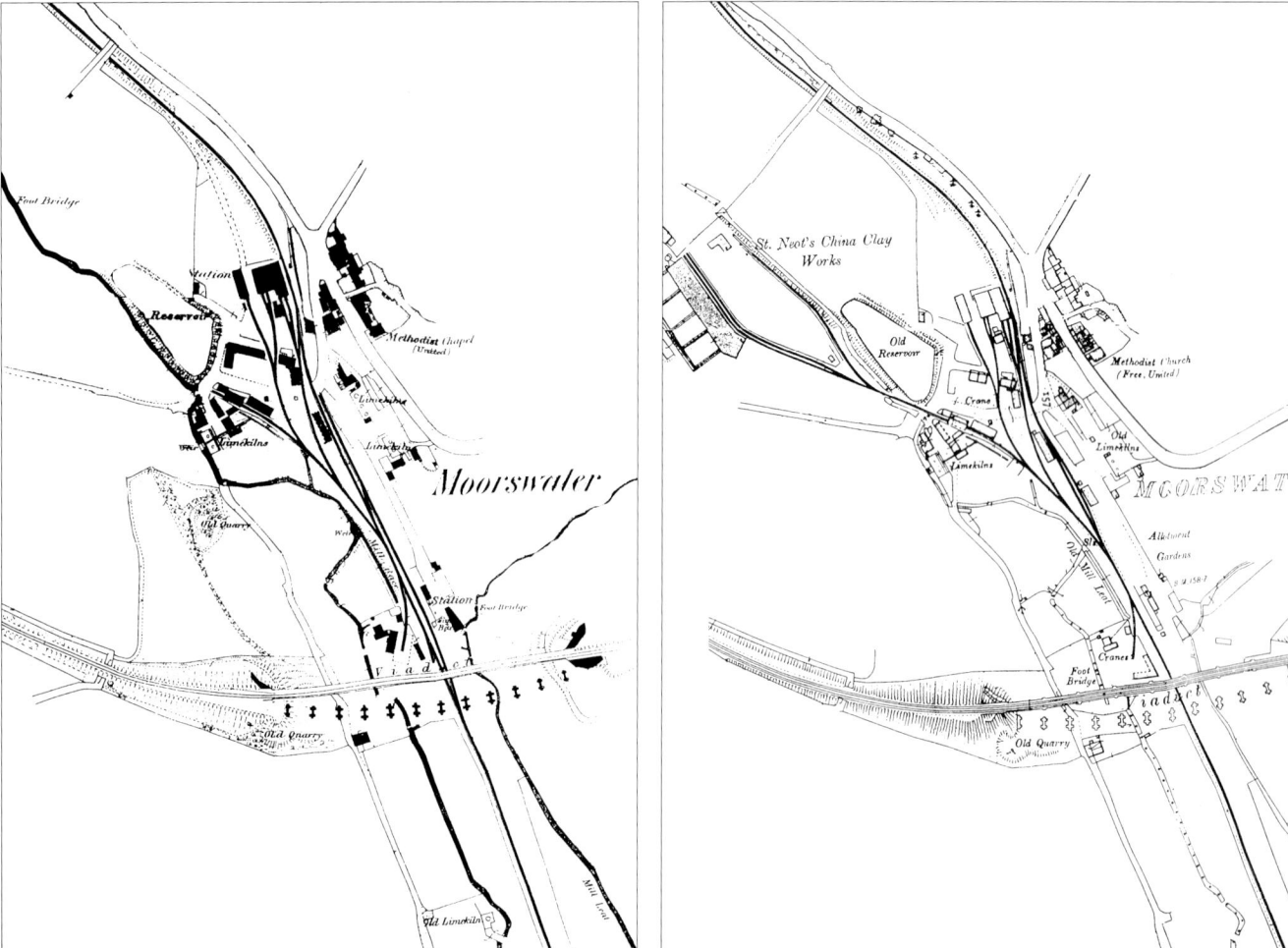

Development at Moorswater between 1882 and 1907 was slight and subtle, the most noticeable change being the extension into the china clay dry. Compare with the plans of Moorswater in canal days in Chapter 2. [BASED ON THE ORDNANCE SURVEY, CROWN COPYRIGHT RESERVED]

A view of Moorswater from a passing main line train in June 1965. The tracks into the shed and across the weighbridge have been lifted. The line to the clay dry can be seen crossing to the left. Without the by-pass and the industrial estate the scene, in the late afternoon sun, is one of sylvan tranquillity. Even the main road, passing through Moorswater village looks quiet and devoid of traffic.
M. J. MESSENGER

terminus of the Caradon railway but has suffered a great deal in recent years. The biggest devastation was caused by the Liskeard By-Pass work in the summer of 1974 and the industrial estate has overlain a good deal, but there is still much of interest at this historic site.

The canal split into two terminal basins flanked by coal and lime stores, and later ore and granite yards. On either side of the valley limekilns were built and some of each of these survive. That on the west side, William Hodge's, is particularly interesting for behind it, in the river, are the remains of the undershot waterwheel that, by means of a winch in the back of the kiln, hauled limestone and culm up the tramroad incline from the canal side to the top. The plateway turntable that turned the wagons to discharge into either of the two wells survives atop the kiln at what was the head of the incline. Across the road behind the building that is now a car workshop can be found one of the canal basins, flanked on the far side by the present siding to the clay works. On the other side of the valley two banks of limekilns, one of which survives, were similarly served by an incline between them, also powered by a waterwheel. The incline and waterwheel were owned by or leased to the occupant of one bank of limekilns but the occupant of the other bank had a right to use them on payment of a wayleave or toll.[7] Little else can be seen of the canal period, the subsequent railways having overlaid much. The reservoir has now been built on and many of the canal buildings went to fill the river bank at Looe at the beginning of the twentieth century.

The Caradon line curved down from the east side of the valley and ore yards were established on this side of the canal. One line ran over the basin to permit the loads of ore to be dropped straight into barges. As the horses were hired, both by canal and railway, stables were not provided by the companies but the

Moorswater shed showing the wagon works and smiths shop.
AUTHOR'S COLLECTION

107

Moorswater shed in April 1961, the last year of steam, was a peaceful place during the daytime when its resident was out, working the branch passenger service. Although the coaling stage has gone the scene has changed little in seventy years.
M. J. MESSENGER

advent of steam haulage needed accommodation. The first proper engine shed seems to have been built by the LCR in 1863 and it was enlarged in 1878. In 1909 the block of stone buildings included a two road locomotive shed 40 feet long with a machine shop at the rear, a carriage repair shop also of two roads but 100 feet long and a blacksmiths shop in between. Outside the shed was a pair of sheerlegs (rotten in 1909) and a water tower and coal stage. Coal was dealt with by dint of throwing it on the ground from wagons and wheeling it onto the coal stage to be shovelled onto the engines.[8]

The line to Caradon ran between the shed, on its east side, and two of the features that added much to the character of Moorswater. In a sunken pit in a small stream that ran from the former fishponds across the main road was a small waterwheel, six feet diameter and four feet breast, that drove a twenty feet long shaft under the LCR and into the shed where a tiny pump kept the water tank topped up. The wheel was repaired at Swindon works in 1956 at a cost of £100. Straddling the stream a little further down was an old firebox, widely held to be off *Caradon*, and, fitted with a wooden seat and a door, it served a most useful function for many years. Appropriately the stream it spanned ran into the Looe river. The firebox was rescued when the buildings were demolished. Another waterwheel may have existed at one time to drive the workshop machinery but was gone by 1909.

The only track that now remains, that to the china clay dry, is an extension of an earlier siding and was laid by the LLR at the clay company's expense. A loop just short of the road crossing enables locomotives to run round their trains and replaces that formerly just south of the engine shed. Beyond the road crossing the line is the property of the clay company. The dry functioned until 1996, as part of English China Clays Ltd, and is now mothballed. All railway buildings at Moorswater have now been demolished. The approaches to the Liskeard By-Pass likewise have caused the demolition of most of Moorswater village, leaving just a couple of cottages on the eastern side of the valley.

A few yards beyond the engine sheds was Foundry Bridge (14) which carried a road to the old iron foundry and this bridge, long hidden under dense undergrowth, was revealed by the By-Pass work. Looe Mills Bridge (15), under the former turnpike, disappeared in early 1960 when the main road (A38) was widened. A board from this bridge lettered 'T.R. 7m 38ch' is now in the Royal Cornwall Museum, in Truro. TR stands for turnpike road and the distance is from Looe Quay. Both these bridges were altered in 1861 to accommodate locomotives. Beyond this the railway track bed can be seen above the lay-by that was once the main road.

One contrast between the Looe and Caradon railways soon becomes apparent. Although the Looe line has been twisting and turning during its course up the East Looe valley it has at least generally maintained a south-north direction. The Caradon line, barely a mile north of Moorswater turns out of the main valley until it is almost facing east. This change of direction takes place in High Wood, the Duchy plantation that caused the line so

Track at Higher Tremarcombe, about 1908. The stone sleepers have been replaced with wood but still lie beside the track.
AUTHOR'S COLLECTION

The guide post and stone at Canal Cross, June 1970.
M. J. MESSENGER

Remains of the level crossing at St Cleer with the goods shed in the background. L&GRP

much trouble in its early days. The troubles continued later also for after the introduction of steam power in 1862 there were numerous fires in the wood and the company sought the Duchy's permission to keep the undergrowth trimmed to lessen the fire risk. As the line leaves High Wood a level crossing takes it over a minor road and a few hundred yards further on Woodhill Bridge is reached. Most of the LCR's original road crossings were made on the level at first and converted to bridges as the funds became available or when the Board of Trade complained, as the original Act forbad steam locomotives to cross roads on the level. Woodhill Bridge (16) was built over the Liskeard to St Cleer road in about 1867 with a brick skew arch and many sleeper blocks incorporated in the granite facings and wing walls. It is still (2015) marked with the distance from Looe quays; 9 miles 6 chains. The earlier level crossing and its rail approaches were to the south.

Leaving Woodhill the railway is heading approximately north-east but in half-a-mile it has turned due north, only to turn again to the west as it follows the contours around the head of the valley approaching Old Treworgey. Here is one of the line's many startling features; a reverse curve to gain height that is a mere three chains (66 yards) radius. It is small wonder the centre pair of driving wheels of the locomotives were flangeless. As planned, the curve would have been even tighter as it was not intended to cross the road but to have run on the south side of the road to Tremabe. As it is, the line runs parallel to the road on its north side. The site of the level crossing is clearly discernable, the remains of a gateman's hut, a gate and also a distinct hump in the road survive, but the track bed in the fields beyond has been obliterated.

To deviate here slightly, approximately ¾ mile to the west is Canal Cross, the junction of the lanes from St Cleer, Treworgey and Looe Mills. As well as a modern fingerpost there was a stone with its three faces inscribed, respectively, ST. CLEER, LISK[D]. and CANAL, a relic of the days when the narrow Cornish lanes would be full of carts and packhorses carrying lime and ores. Both fingerpost and stone have been removed in recent years.

Tremabe was the nominal terminus of the LCR for some months after the formal opening of the line but this brief glory has left no trace.

The caption on this commercial postcard reads: 'Darite, formerly Railway Terrace, the latter name arising from the fact that the houses are situated on natural terraces, above the railway shown in the foreground, which is a portion of the mineral line connecting the celebrated Caradon and Phoenix Mines, the Cheesewring Granite Quarries, etc., with Liskeard and Looe.' The tracks are the loop siding at Polwrath immediately prior to the line splitting for the Cheesewring and South Caradon.
AUTHOR'S COLLECTION

A finger post near St Cleer points to Cheesewring Railway, one of the former names of Minions.
ROGER CARPENTER COLLECTION

The overbridge at Tremar carried the turnpike road over the railway and was the location of the temporary terminus for the first few months of the railway. 1922.
H. C. CASSERLEY

In a deep cutting the railway passed under the former turnpike at Tremabe Bridge (17), which was demolished and filled in to widen the road in 1985. A plaque and a length of bridge rail commemorates its passing. At the end of the cutting there was originally a level crossing but by 1884 the road from Tremar was diverted to the west to cross by the bridge. There was also a siding here at one time. The railway follows the contours and climbs continuously to Newhouse (also called Challacott) where the bridge (18) was built in 1884 in substitution for another level crossing. To the north are Tremar and Tremarcoombe and the LCR passes between these two former mining villages and the much older St Cleer, whose church gives its name to the parish that included the Caradon copper mines. The site of the level crossing over Tremar Lane is quite clear and beside the next crossing, below St Cleer Well, stands the former coal store. Across the road, where the Memorial Hall now stands, was the location of the short lived St Cleer Loop.

On this part of the route the railway is becoming more difficult to find as many parts of the course have been incorporated into fields by the removal of one or both hedges. From St Cleer it swings to the west, then northwards and then northeast, crossing a minor lane in the process as it climbs steadily, having gained 400 feet above Moorswater as it passes close to Trecarne Farm. The next level crossing was Tremar, which sported a circular gatekeeper's hut, and a couple of hundred yards beyond this is the site of the level crossing that until 1861 preceded Polwrath Bridge (19). The latter has now disappeared completely.

At Polwrath goods depot was a double ended loop siding and here also the line divided for South Caradon and the Cheesewring. The two lines ran parallel below Railway Terrace, that for the Cheesewring climbing steeply, and both turned north into the Seaton gully between the once great West and South Caradon mines. The Cheesewring branch as planned would have been higher up the hillside and on a level with West Caradon Mine. Strangely, roughly on the

FROM SEA TO THE MOOR

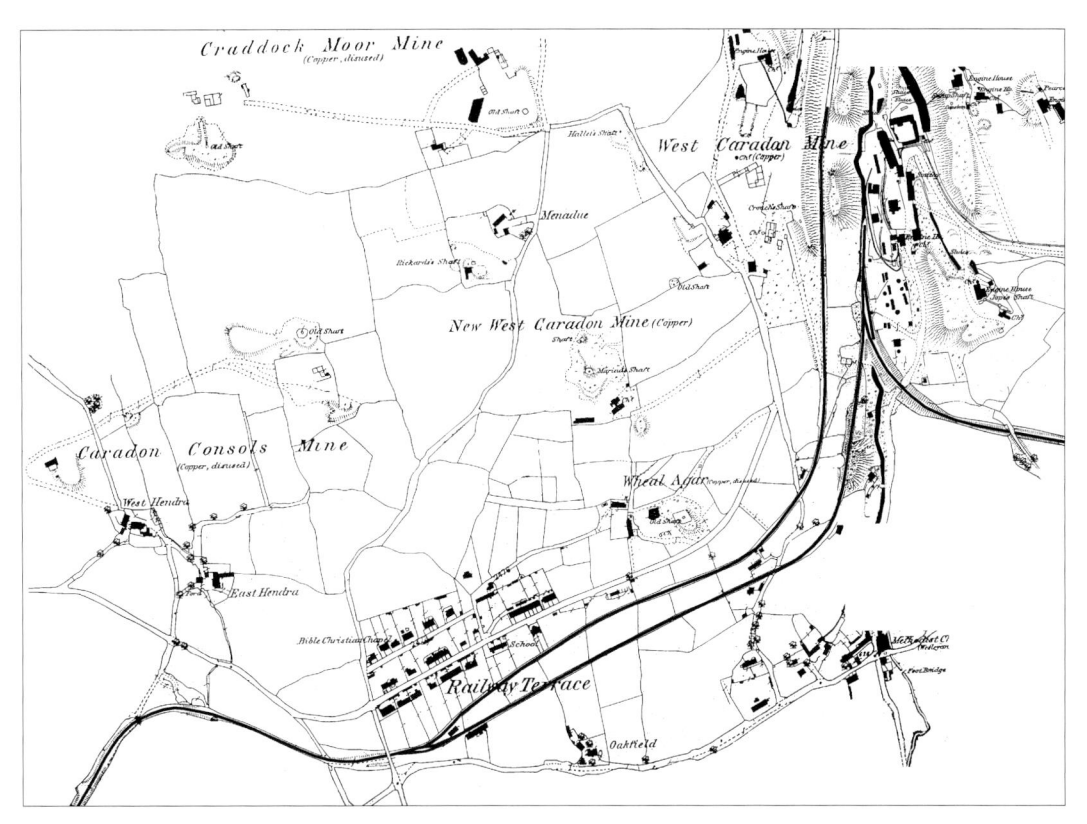

At Railway Terrace, or Polwrath as the LCR referred to it, the line split. The upper route ran around the base of West Caradon Mine to Gonamena and the Cheesewring, whilst the lower line ran into the dressing floors of South Caradon Mine before reversing back to Tokenbury. This map was surveyed about 1882 and shows the railways at that time. The incline up to West Caradon Mine can also be seen.
[BASED ON THE ORDNANCE SURVEY, CROWN COPYRIGHT RESERVED]

An aerial view of the Seaton Valley, with West Caradon Mine on the far side of it and South Caradon Mine nearer. The lower level of the LCR running into South Caradon's dressing floors and reversing out toward Tokenbury can be clearly seen. At a higher level on the valley side is the Cheesewring branch, running through the dumps of West Caradon, and turning to climb the Gonamena incline. The head of the incline is just where the cloud shadow starts. Also to be seen is the incline from the Cheesewring branch up to West Caradon Mine and, just in the cloud shadow, the abortive branch towards Craddock Moor Mine. Running eastwards in the foreground are the tramway and cart tracks leading to the eastern parts of the South Caradon sett. April 1987. COPYRIGHT: CORNWALL ARCHAEOLOGICAL UNIT

LCR boundary stone alongside the Gonamena incline. R. DEREK SACH

Caradon Hill and the moors to the north showing railways, built and proposed, and mine and quarry tramways.

line of this planned route, the St Cleer Parish Tithe Map shows a field named 'Railway Park' and one cannot but help conjecture at a possible connection with the railway. The map, however, was surveyed in the early 1840s and was too early to show either the LCR route or West Caradon Mine. In the total lack of any evidence for this field name any thoughts about it are pure speculation.

The South Caradon line terminated in a dead end virtually on the dressing floors of the mine while, at a higher level, the Cheesewring branch continued up the narrowing valley. To the left ran a private branch line up a 1 in 6 incline to West Caradon Mine, now partly obliterated by the dumps of that mine which themselves have been removed in part. Apart from the count house little remains of the second great copper mine of Caradon. It was from this point that Wilkie Collins' account of South Caradon (and/or J. R. Leifchild's) was observed and indeed there is still an excellent view over the remains of the dressing floors, stores, smithy and miners' dries now picturesquely ruined and overgrown on the valley floor below. Above them stands the sentinel of the engine house of Engine Shaft and to the south Jope's Shaft engine house keeps vigil over the entrance to the valley. Beyond, the track bed of the former tramway (gauge about 3 or 3½ feet) runs eastwards towards Rule's Shaft and North Engine Shaft and on to Kittow's Shaft, following the line of the lode. The LCR line to Tokenbury Corner trails off the South Caradon line to run eastwards around the Hill but we will return to that later.

Back on the Cheesewring branch, a double row of sleeper blocks leads to the foot of the Gonamena incline, soon reached after leaving South Caradon Mine behind, and the track bed climbs steadily at 1 in 11 up to the head of the valley. On the right is the ancient farm house that gives its name to the incline and to the very old mine to the north and east. The footpath here picking its way along the overgrown track bed between the tumbled sleeper blocks is very pleasant for a sunny summer stroll but could not have been so in the depths of winter for the children from Minions to whom, at the end of the nineteenth century, it was the only way to school at Darite.

Partway up the incline a cutting through rock was crossed by an overbridge. This was removed and the cutting filled at that point in 1919 by the GWR at the request of a local farmer. The arch was 16 feet high and 20 feet wide and presumably it was becoming unsafe. A little beyond the bridge on the right (east) a stone marked 'LCR' records the boundary of the company's property.

Little documentary evidence seems to have survived regarding the Gonamena incline and this has to be added to the archaeological evidence and one's knowledge of this type of railway feature in an endeavour to suggest how it was constructed and worked. The Minute Books only refer to the renewal of ropes in 1853, at a cost of £93 11s 6d, and in 1861, suggesting they lasted eight years. The only plan to be located showing any track in situ on the incline is an underground map of Old Sump Shaft at South Caradon Mine dated 1875 that by coincidence shows the foot of the incline on the surface with a double track descending and merging into one.[9] A simple double track would have been the most likely layout at the time the line was built. The plans dated 1859 deposited in connection with the 1860 Act show the head of the incline but neither track nor the winding house, despite showing other buildings such as the nearby stables. Whilst the lack of track is not unusual in plans of this nature the lack of a building is more significant. By the time the Ordnance Survey reached the area in 1882 to prepare the 25 inch Survey the track had been

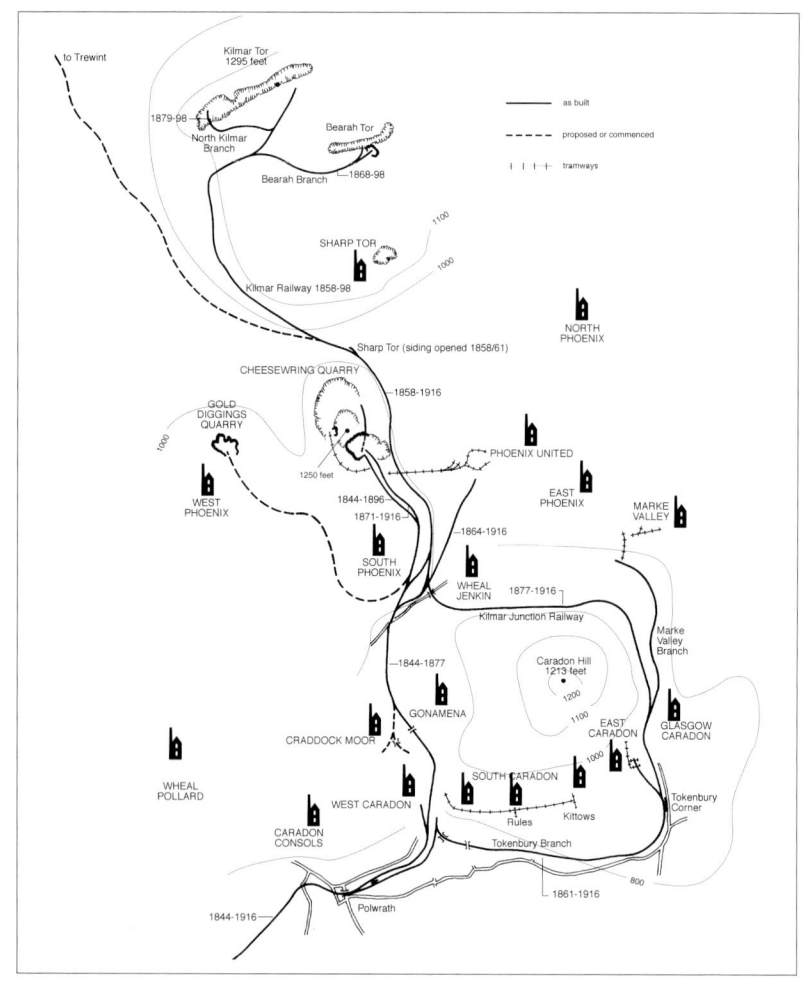

112

lifted and again no building such as a winding house was charted.

On the incline today many of the granite blocks have been disturbed but it is apparent that only one line, on the west side, survives. The line ceased to be used at the end of 1877 and the North Kilmar branch was laid in 1879. The blocks on the latter line have identical markings to those remaining on the incline and, assuming from the 1875 plan there was a double track throughout, they would seem to have been lifted from the eastern track; the disused incline proving no doubt a useful source of materials. Many of the blocks have had rails spiked in two places and also bear the impression of a chair from when the line was relaid with heavier rail. There would have been rollers for the ropes to run on between the tracks but no indications of supports for these have been found by the writer, but they may have been of timber.

There is no obvious indication of a winding house on the ground at the head of the incline, either above or below ground and, as it seems unlikely that the 1859 plans would miss it or that it would have been demolished between the line closing and the arrival of the Ordnance Survey, it is probable that there was not one. It has been suggested that a horse whim was used[10] and with the limited means of the railway in 1844, and the fact that the engineers were doubtless more familiar with mining than railway practice, some structure of this style is a distinct possibility. Downhill traffic was in excess of uphill, so unpowered counterbalanced working was quite possible on a double track incline. A wooden overhead frame similar to a horse whim could adequately support a braked winding drum and would leave no trace. Such a frame was in use at the time on the Weare Giffard incline of the Rolle Canal in North Devon and, from an earlier date, at the head of the Dalkey Quarry incline outside Dublin.

The nearest railway inclines to Liskeard were then on J. T. Treffry's tramways at Fowey Consols Mine (two) and Carmears, both north east of St Blazey, and Caffamill Pill, at Fowey; all were waterwheel powered. Further west the Hayle Railway operated four inclines in various manners.

The line now climbs towards Minions but on the left (west) near Pontius Piece earthworks can be seen running alongside the railway. This was the abortive attempt following the 1860 Act to build a deviation to avoid the Gonamena incline. Curving away southwards the abutments of a bridge over the lane to Gonamena can be seen but the embankment peters out in the next field. No reason for this is known but the projected line, like the original 1843 route,

would have taken it directly through West Caradon Mine and even at this late date the mine was still sufficiently active to object, no doubt, to such an intrusion. A few years later, in 1864, the first part of the route was used for a projected branch to Craddock Moor Mine but this too was not completed, although the line of an earthworks reaching across a field towards the mine remains.

The main line continues on a comparatively level and straight course to Minions and to the north of the village on the moor is a network of earthworks and track beds that take some unravelling. But before crossing the road onto the moor we will return to South Caradon to follow the later line around the Hill.

The Tokenbury branch was built when traffic from the mines on the east side of the Hill justified it and powers for the line were renewed by the 1860 Act. The original Act envisaged a facing junction shortly before South Caradon, and a route a little to the north of that built, but in the event a trailing junction was constructed with trains having to reverse out of the dead end at South Caradon. Almost immediately the line crosses the valley on a large stone embankment through which the road passes under the arch of Crows Nest Bridge (20), nearly 25 feet high. Shortly after is Stanton over-bridge (21) and the line heads eastwards between the fields. A strangely shaped enclosure constructed of

The head of the incline at Dalky Quarry, near Dublin, may be similar to what was at Gonamena.
DR DAN MCCARTHY

The branch to Tokenbury opened in 1861 and was soon extended on to East Caradon Mine. In 1877 it was extended northwards to Marke Valley Mine (right) and around Caradon Hill to Minions (left). [BASED ON THE ORDNANCE SURVEY, CROWN COPYRIGHT RESERVED]

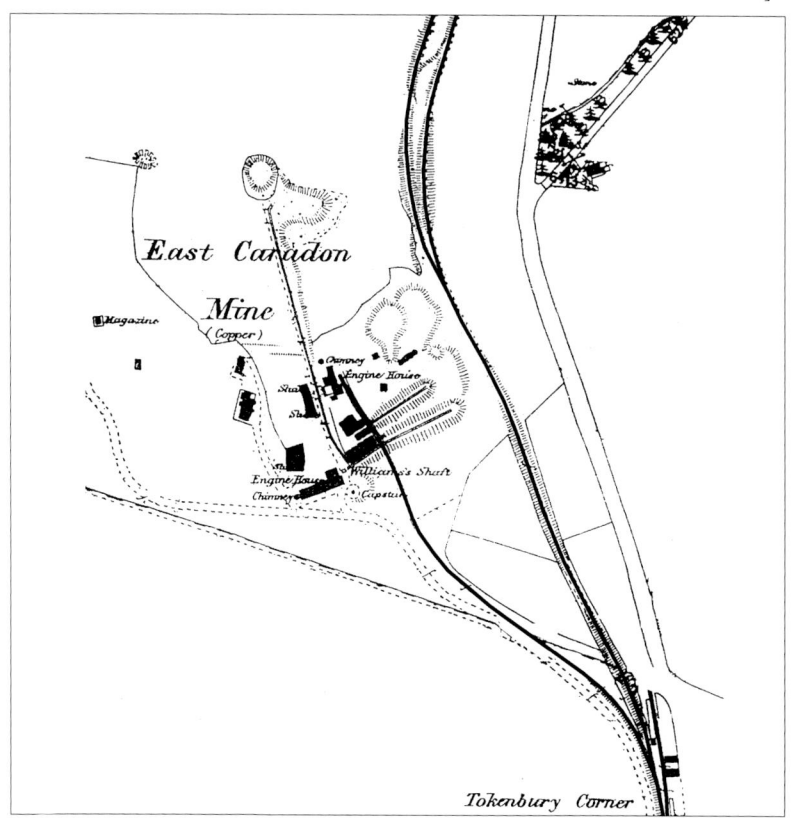

The extensive depot at Tokenbury included a goods shed and a depot for the local Co-operative Society. 1934. L&GRP

Milepost 15 at Tokenbury Corner, April 1970.
M. J. MESSENGER

The bridge at Rillaton carrying the Kilmar Junction Railway over the Minions to Upton road was demolished in 1947. The building on the left has been described as a coal store and is now a private dwelling. 1934. L&GRP

massive granite blocks stands beside the line where the lane to Higher Tretharrup crosses. This was the coal store for Rule's Shaft and was built in 1876 when South Caradon Mine started having coal delivered to the shaft instead of to Tokenbury Corner. After passing south of Wheal Hooper (due south of Kittow's Shaft) the line emerges on to the open moor and curves north to Tokenbury Corner. Here were erected a goods shed and a coal store (often erroneously referred to as stables) served by a siding, and the line was very soon extended into East Caradon Mine by a 400 yards long siding to the dressing floors. Several extensions were made to the facilities at Tokenbury which remained the terminus of the branch for 16 years until it was decided to extend the line around the Hill.

The buildings at Tokenbury have now been demolished and a new house built in their place. Some granite blocks have been incorporated and the granite 15 milepost now stands beside the road, the cutting it formerly stood in having been filled in to make a garden.

A double line of stone sleeper blocks below East Caradon's fast diminishing dumps suggests the line ran this far before work started on the extension in 1872. The impecunious state of the Company meant little progress was made for some years and the emphasis was placed on reaching Marke Valley Mine anyway. The Kilmar Junction Railway, as the new line was known, was ready for use by the end of November 1877 but the Marke Valley branch appears to have been ready a few months before.

The new line heads roughly north from here and the Marke Valley branch soon leaves on the right (east), falling away below following the contours for three-quarters of a mile to terminate above the mine. Tramways connected it with the shafts but the whole area is now green and overgrown with the engine houses in ruins. On a clear day there are superb views to the east and north, past Kit Hill and on to Dartmoor. 200 feet above the terminus of the branch the KJR turns to the west and runs straight towards Minions now giving good views to the north across Phoenix Mine and beyond to the Moors. At Wheal Jenkin, marked by the fine engine house of 1886, a tiny underbridge took a tramway to the dressing floors on the north side of the track. The line curves north again and crossed the Minions to Upton road on what was Rillaton Bridge (22) until its demolition by the army in March 1945. A few more yards and the KJR meets up with the earlier tracks and the circuit of Caradon Hill is complete.

Cheesewring Village near Liskeard.

The track from the head of the Gonamena incline used to emerge from the right of the Cheesewring Hotel and cross the road to the right, much to the annoyance of local residents. Amongst others, John Gerry, owner of the Cheesewring Hotel, had complained. The hotel was also known as the Railway Hotel at the end of the nineteenth century.
AUTHOR'S COLLECTION

When, in 1844, the LCR first crossed the Dobwalls to Upton Cross road near the ancient tumulus called Minions Mound there was not a single habitation at this spot. With the growth of quarrying and mining a small village grew up which is still thriving today. Variously known as Rillaton, Gerry's Corner (after a local resident) and Cheesewring Railway, it is now established as Minions. The Cheesewring Hotel was built in 1874 as a private residence and became the highest hotel in Cornwall at a little below 1,000 feet above sea level. The railway crosses the road and is soon on the open moor, known as Smith's Moor when the line was built, heading north towards Cheesewring Quarry and passing Houseman's Shaft of South Phoenix Mine. This is the original line of the railway of 1844. The later depot at Rillaton is dealt with below.

The trackbed is very clear at this point, passing many remains of South Phoenix Mine, including extensive dressing floors, and fine views can be had of Phoenix Mine, below to the

Cheese Wring Village, near Liskeard

The LCR track had long ceased to cross the road at Minions when this photograph was taken. On the skyline in the centre is the LCR's Rillaton depot.
AUTHOR'S COLLECTION

CARADON & LOOE – THE CANAL, RAILWAYS AND MINES

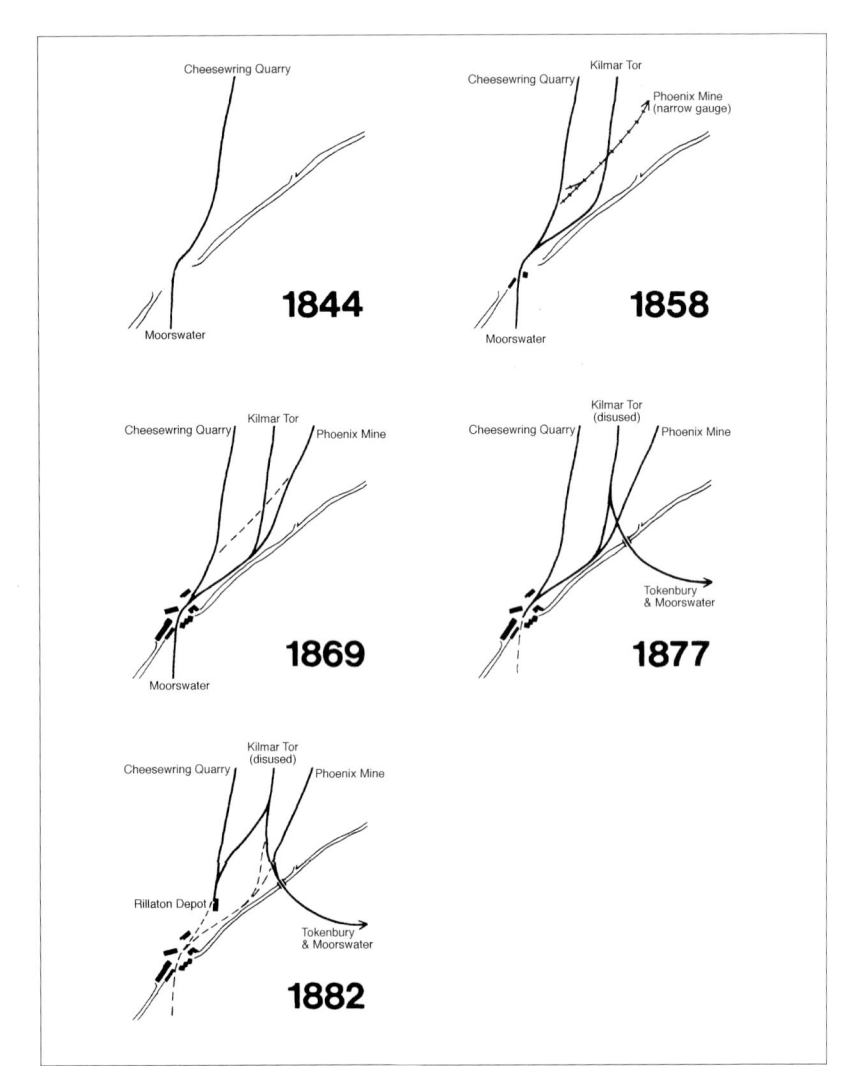

An early commercial postcard of the Cheesewring.
AUTHOR'S COLLECTION

The present village of Minions, known as Cheesewring Railway through much of the nineteenth century, saw many changes in the railway arrangements there. These drawings show developments from 1844, when there was no village at all, to 1882 when the railway reached its peak.

Cheesewring Quarry about 1900, a not very active time.
AUTHOR'S COLLECTION

116

Looking along the Kilmar Railway in 1948 with the Cheesewring, the quarry and the dumps dominating the view. Cheesewring Cottages were built for quarrymen in 1864 and demolished soon after this photograph was taken. The Kilmar Railway ran below the dumps and around the flank of Stow's Hill.
ROGER CARPENTER COLLECTION.

east. Shortly after curving to the north west an embankment can be seen climbing and diverging away to the left. This is the original route into the quarry and the lower track was that laid in 1871 to enable Freemans to extract granite at a lower level. Rails remained on the old line until about 1898 and it can be seen continuing beyond the quarry for a short distance. Evidently, since it does not serve an excavation, it ran past the original small quarry mouth, to reach surface deposits of loose moorstone. That there was a quarry and not mere surface workings when the line was built is implied by a reference to John Trethewey having tramways of his own at the Cheesewring.[11] A deep cutting runs close to the railway south of the quarry and the standard gauge tramway that once used it runs to a small quarry on the west side of the hill. This could have been part of Trethewey's workings. The evidence on the ground suggests strongly that it connected with the Cheesewring branch just south of the quarry. It was unrecognisable as a tramway to the Ordnance Survey mappers when they reached Stow's Hill in 1882.

What was once an impressive monument to the Cornish granite industry was badly mauled in 1984 when the impressive dumps at Cheesewring Quarry were raided for stone to reinforce Mount Batten Breakwater at Plymouth. At the same time much of the archaeological evidence of tramways, crane and machinery bases on the quarry floor was destroyed or buried, although some rails remain visible in the quarry entrance. Some 100 men and boys worked here at the quarry's peak in the 1860s but now, in summer at least, it is visitors to the novel Cheesewring itself above the quarry and budding mountaineers who spread fly-like across the granite face who prevent the quarry becoming too silent and desolate.

In 1858 the Kilmar Railway was constructed by the Cheesewring Granite Company to serve their quarries deep in the moor. It made a junction with the Cheesewring branch just north of the Minions road crossing and ran behind what is now a row of cottages and the Primitive Methodist Chapel of 1863 to briefly touch the road before turning north and heading for the moor, running parallel to but

The lower, 1871, entrance to Cheesewring Quarry, looking out. The rails are still in place at the time of writing.
AUTHOR'S COLLECTION

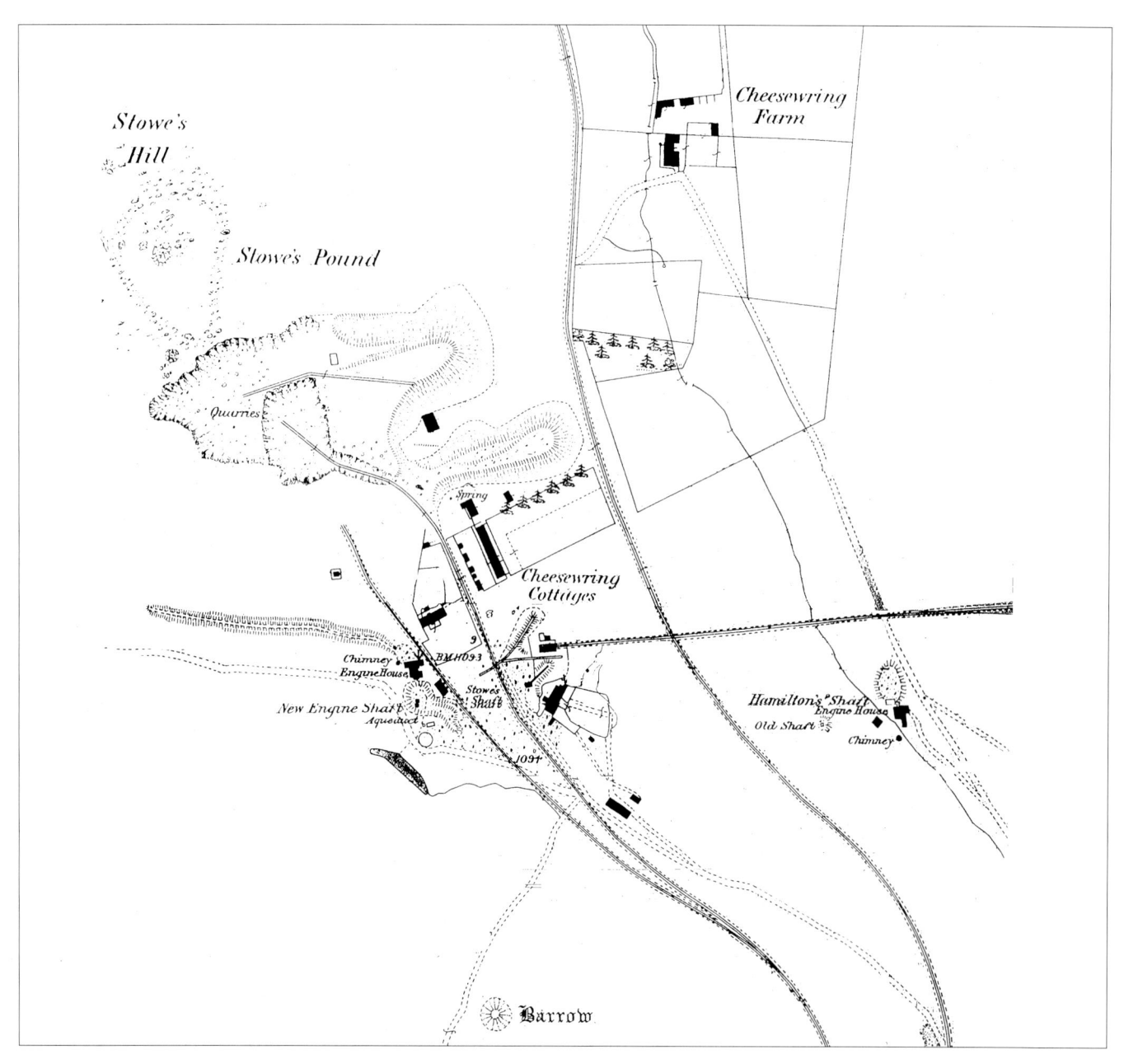

Cheesewring Quarry, 1882. The left hand line is the Cheesewring Quarry branch, with the original 1844 line and the later 1871 route into the Quarry shown, and the right hand line is the Kilmar Railway of 1858. Running across the map is the incline connecting Stowe's Shaft with Phoenix Mine.
[BASED ON THE ORDNANCE SURVEY, CROWN COPYRIGHT RESERVED]

fifty to seventy-five feet below the Cheesewring branch. Mileposts were erected at quarter mile intervals and these are still extant for the first mile.

The narrow gauge tramway built about 1850 to link Phoenix Mine with the LCR ran from the site of the later Rillaton depot north-east to the mine. In 1869 it was replaced by a standard gauge branch that left the Kilmar Railway close to the road and took over part of the narrow gauge trackbed. Little trace remains of the former line and the standard gauge line has in its turn been partly overlaid by the minor road to Henwood; nevertheless the route of the latter line can be easily followed down to the massive Prince of Wales Shaft engine house.

When the KJR entered the scene in 1877 it crossed the Phoenix branch on the level and connected with the Kilmar Railway. This meant trains for both the Cheesewring and Phoenix (and this was all traffic, for the Kilmar Railway was by then otherwise out of use) had to reverse twice and in the case of the former this involved blocking the road in the centre of Minions village. After numerous complaints a new link from the Kilmar Railway to the Cheesewring branch was built about 1884 (authorised by the 1882 Act) and probably about the same time a link was built permitting trains to run directly on to the Phoenix branch. A new depot was built north of Minions and named Rillaton (the narrow gauge connected depot on the same site

118

had been called Phoenix Road). The only other unexplained earthwork in this area is one indicating a short siding to a shaft of South Phoenix Mine close to Rillaton depot.

The Kilmar Railway had a short working life although it was hoped it would play a large part in the LCR expansion schemes. The leasehold was purchased from Freemans in 1879 but neither the LCR nor the GWR got around to buying the freehold from the Duchy, although it was offered several times.

The route ran round the side of Stow's Hill at a lower level than the Cheesewring branch. A few yards before the ¾ mile-stone is reached the line was crossed by an incline tramway connecting West Phoenix with Phoenix United. This was constructed during the 1870s but was not noted in the LCR Minutes until 1883 when the Kilmar line was about to be brought back into use for the construction of the Northern Extension. The incline crossed the track on the level and was simply laid on top of the standard gauge line.

Below the despoiled dumps of Cheesewring Quarry the sleeper blocks have been disturbed by the workmen removing stone in 1984. In another half mile the line reaches Sharptor and the site of another siding and coal depot. The granite sleeper blocks are very prominent on this section and the layout of a loop can be clearly seen. There were very few loops on the LCR; Moorswater, Polwrath, a double-ended siding at Kilmar Tor and a passing loop on the Bearah Quarry branch were the others. Even the Marke Valley branch terminated in a dead end without even a siding. Rope shunting must have been used to get the locomotive from one end of its train to the other. To the east of the loop are the ruined remains of a coal-yard and a siding once ran into this with the track presumably on trestles. Both the store and siding were built in 1859 or 1860 at his own expense by Thomas Lowry.[12] When the rails north of this point were removed in the last years of the nineteenth century, Sharptor (sometimes referred to as Sargents or Windyeats Corner) became the northern terminus, although it saw very little use. The loop survived until 1905 but had gone by 1910.

200 yards beyond Sharptor the Northern Extension was intended to diverge but progressed little beyond initial construction. On leaving North Wardbrook the first section, to the crossing of the Withey Brook, is not too clear

The depot at Rillaton (Minions) was erected in 1884 when the track layout there was re-aligned to prevent the road being obstructed by trains. The store was demolished after this photograph was taken in the mid-1930s but its site is clear to see.
ROGER CARPENTER
COLLECTION

This commercial postcard of Phoenix Mine, taken about 1907, is full of interesting detail. In the foreground the stone-blocked track of the LCR leads to a stub point for the siding to the engine house. The Holman-built Cornish engine has not yet been installed but the temporary ramp has been built up to the door through which the beam will be hauled and later the cylinder will be taken. The temporary shaft sinking headgear is still in place with power coming from the small building on the right.
AUTHOR'S COLLECTION

The Kilmar Railway's milestones recorded the distance from Minions. The quarter miles were simply numbered 1, 2 and 3 whilst the one-mile stone was lettered 1M. They only survive for the first mile. April, 1973.
M. J. MESSENGER

as it was the last to be tendered out and only the minimum of excavation was completed when the financial situation stopped work. After bridging the brook, however, the earthworks are virtually complete and easily followed, particularly the section that has been converted to a forestry road. Most of this section was bought for ten shillings from a friendly landowner. Afforestation has detracted considerably from the character and atmosphere of the moor along much of the route here but to the east one can look across to Kilmar and Trewortha Tors. Four cattle creeps can be found passing under the railway and, of prehistoric interest, hut circles abound close to the line. A tumulus was destroyed by the railway in its progress. It is interesting to note that between the railway and the Withey Brook lies the projected route of the Cornwall Railway's 1845 branch to Launceston (from near Doublebois) although this is the only point where the routes coincide. A few yards short of

Rusheyford Gate, and the boundary of Altarnun parish, the line's initial destination, it runs into a rock cutting. The cutting is now flooded as a reservoir but the excavation never emerged and here ended the northern aspirations of the Liskeard & Caradon Railway. Only a line of surveyor's pegs continued the directors' hopes across the moor towards Trewint.

To return to North Wardbrook and the Kilmar Railway, from Minions the latter has been roughly level, following the 1,000 feet contour, but here the line starts climbing around the side of Langstone Down. Below, the abandoned route to Trewint can be clearly discerned making its way north-west, while the Kilmar line climbs first north-west and then turns to the east. Beside the line is the ruin of the former blacksmith's shop where the quarrymen's tools were sharpened. It is hard to credit that, in 1868, nearly eighty men worked on the slopes of Kilmar Tor while another sixty were at nearby Bearah Tor.

Shortly after passing a boundary stone of the Duchy of Cornwall Manor of Rillaton a junction is reached and the branch to Bearah Tor diverges to the right. Whether this branch was ever owned by the LCR is uncertain; they were considering buying it (or the leasehold) with the Kilmar Railway from Freemans in 1876 but the GWR was subsequently of the opinion that they did not, and they were probably correct. It was laid about 1868 after the quarry at Bearah was opened[13] and the GWR records it was Freemans who removed the rails. There was a passing loop partway and the line ended in two short sidings, now obliterated by the dumps of the quarry.

The Kilmar Railway proper heads north-east towards Kilmar Tor and terminates in open moorland with no sign of a quarry and no immediate reason for the railway finishing there, The answer can be found in the many tons of loose rock, moorstone, that still lie tumbled about the surface of the moor. The rock was split where it lay and the blocks loaded on to the railway by the many ramps, or platforms, that line the track on this final section. Another short branch trailed off to run to a small quarry at the west end of the Tor and this line, laid by the LCR in 1879 at Freeman's request, must surely be one of the last railways to be laid on stone sleeper blocks, lifted from the Gonamena incline.

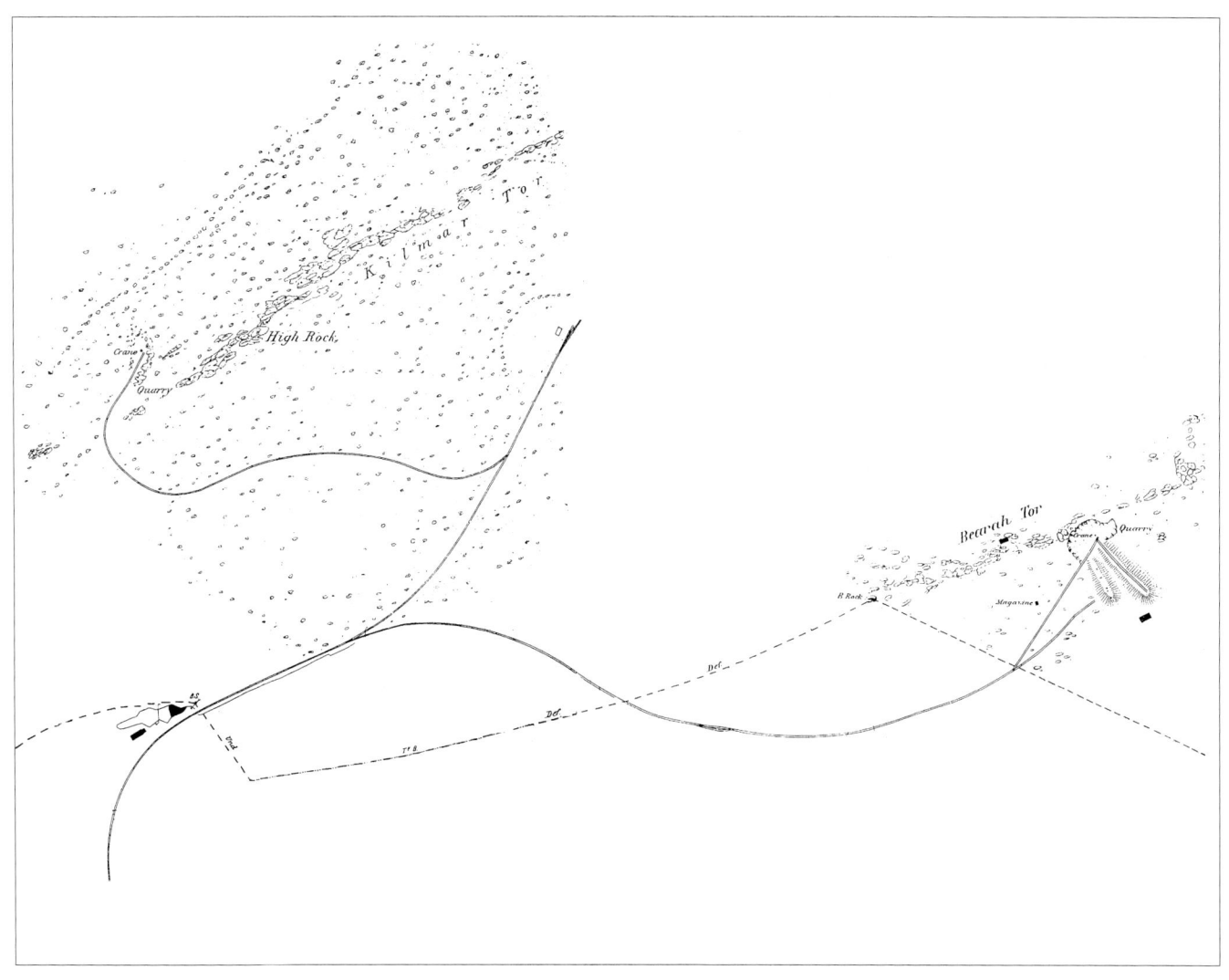

The terminus of the Kilmar Railway was apparently extended slightly as the quarrymen moved on to fresh deposits of stone and another loop, or double-ended siding, can be seen just short of the finish. Nearby lies a massive boulder, partly split and with rows of holes ready drilled for the quarryman's feathers and wedges. They were never inserted and the rock remains cracked but *in situ*. Perhaps it had a flaw that rendered it useless or possibly it marks the finish of quarrying work at Kilmar Tor. Either way it remains as a mute witness to man's activity.

At Kilmar Tor the railway reaches approximately 1,150 feet above Looe and sea level, its highest point, and the contrast with the lush wooded East Looe Valley thirteen miles due south could not be more complete. It is a beautiful place at which to reflect on the urge and the industry that drove man to lay his iron rails deep into the heart of nature to plunder her produce, for this land has never been tilled and is much as it has been for thousands of years. But all is now quiet, the wound has healed with but a minimum of scar, and the railway's abandoned earth and stone works now blend into the moor with the abandoned relics of earlier invaders, the hut circles and tumuli of the first industrious men.

The Kilmar Railway, with its branches to North Kilmar (left) and Bearah Tor (right) terminated on the open moors. [BASED ON THE ORDNANCE SURVEY, CROWN COPYRIGHT RESERVED]

CHAPTER NINE
LOCOMOTIVES AND ROLLING STOCK

'We have the best class of trucks, worked by locomotives ...'
SILVANUS JENKIN 1884

Motive power on both the canal and, initially, the LCR was horse (plus gravity on the latter) but when the LLUC built their railway it was their intention to use locomotive power. Silvanus Jenkin reported on 8 February 1859 that the LCR should also consider steam power and thus, when it was agreed that the two railways should be worked together, the LCR provided the wagons and the LLUC the engine. This was not found altogether satisfactory and the LCR soon took over the motive power, providing more locomotives themselves, and this situation remained until 8 May 1901 when the LLR took control of both railways and all locomotives and rolling stock. On 1 January 1909 the GWR took responsibility and substituted its own vehicles.

LOCOMOTIVES

Unable to afford the purchase of a locomotive the LLUC hired one from James Murphy, civil engineer and railway wagon maker, of Newport, south Wales, who provided *Liskeard*. Little is definitely known of the locomotive. It was a four-wheeled tank, probably saddle-tank, engine said to weigh 15 tons and was 'of the type till lately used on the London & Birmingham Railway for goods trains' having been converted by Murphy from a tender to a tank engine.[1] It may be assumed with some safety that *Liskeard* was originally a Bury locomotive of which the L&BR had a large number and which were disposed of in many directions before 1860. There were several types of Bury 0-4-0 with 13, 14 and 15 inch diameter cylinders and driving wheels of four and five feet, built between 1838 and 1846.[2]

Liskeard arrived at its namesake town *via* the Cornwall Railway on 18 December 1860 and the following day was taken by 28 horses down the road to Moorswater. There had been a heavy fall of snow and teams of men were employed to hold it back on the descent of the Canal Road. Several times all went flying on the slides created in the snow by the skids.[3] It was put on the rails and satisfactorily hauled the inaugural train to Looe on 27 December. Murphy quoted to supply and work the locomotive for 2s per mile per day (although this was later reported as £3 per day), the LLUC providing a shed and water. They had an option to purchase within 12 months at £700 and in September 1861 it was agreed to purchase *Liskeard* for £600. After the Joint Committee meeting in March 1862 when it was decided the LCR should work all traffic, the LLUC sold it to them for the same price but in

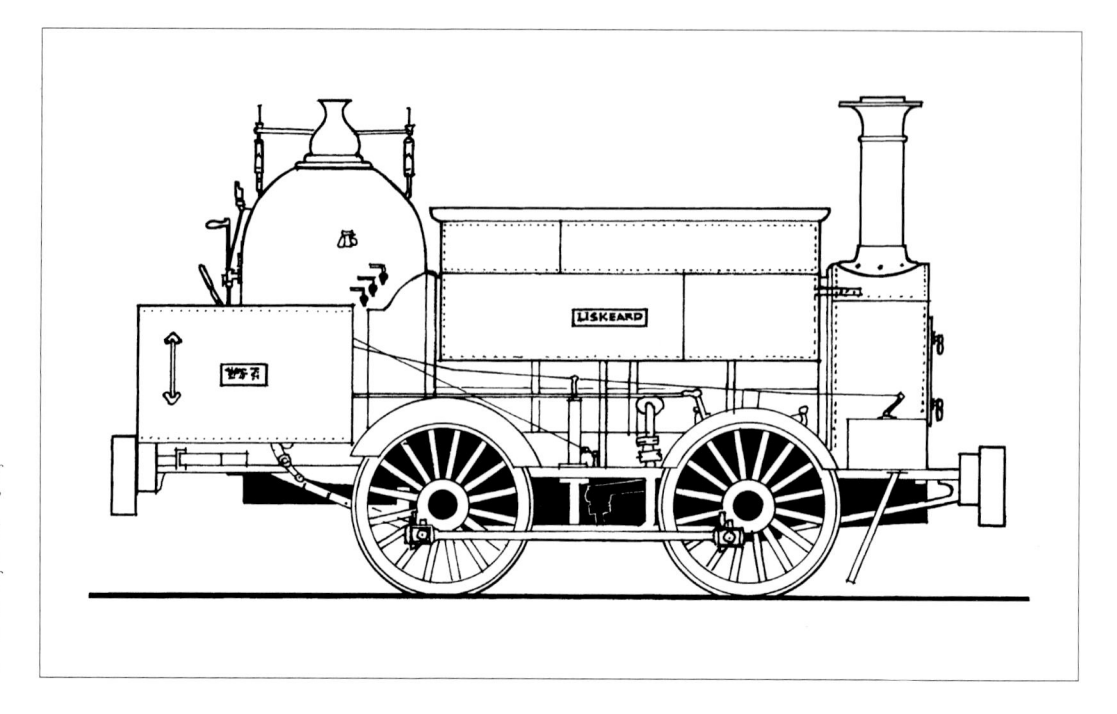

A conjectural drawing of LISKEARD, the railways' first steam locomotive. It was thought to be a Bury 0-4-0 locomotive of about 1840 to which a saddle tank had been added.

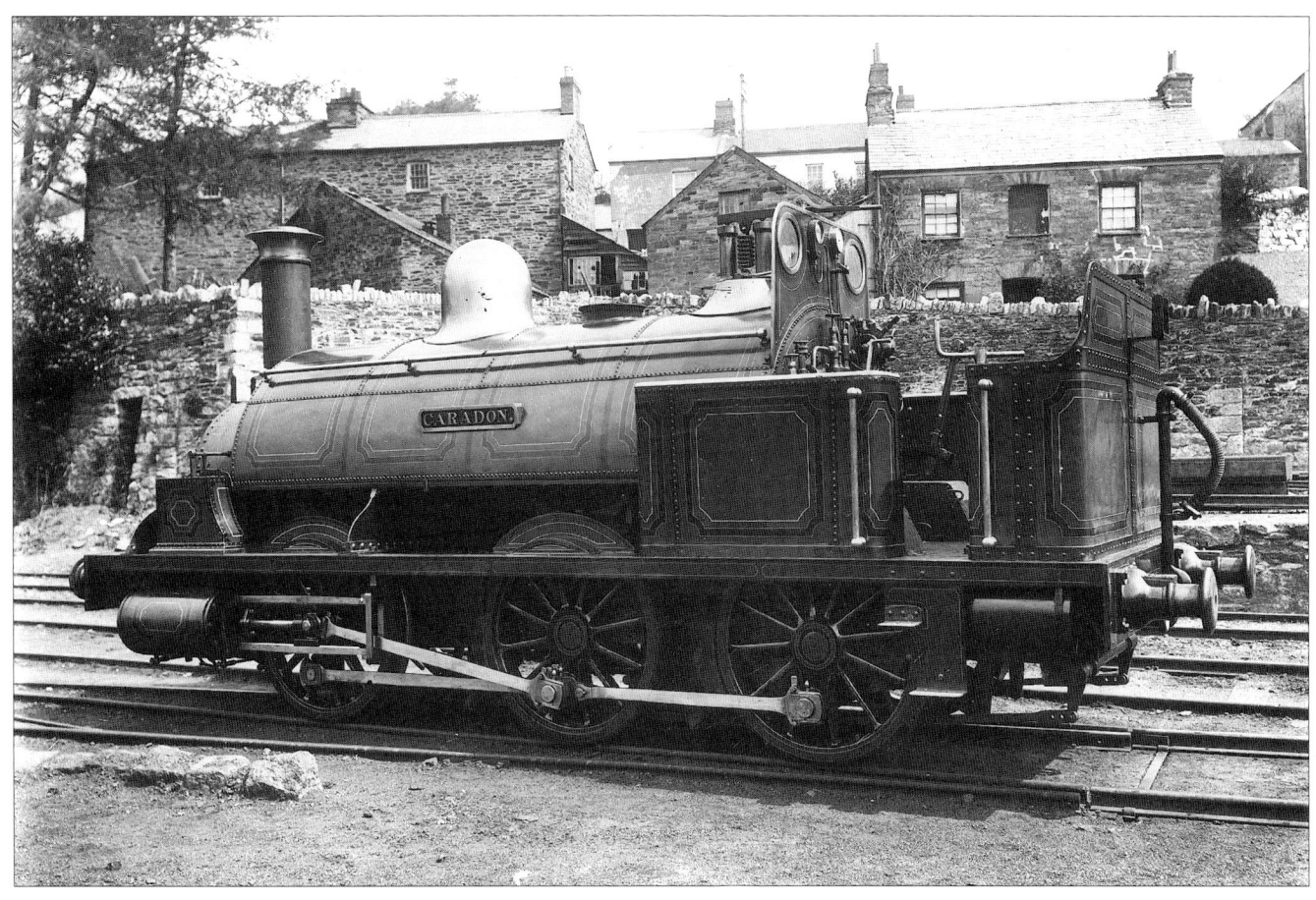

August, after receiving a report from Mr Wright, Locomotive Superintendent of the South Devon and Cornwall Railways, on its 'state' it was decided to sell or exchange the engine. *Caradon* had just been delivered and, with the benefit of twenty years' progress in steam technology, was doubtless proving a far superior machine. The final reference in the Minute Books to *Liskeard* is in August 1866 when Murphy offered to purchase 'the old locomotive engine' and Silvanus Jenkin was instructed to negotiate for the best terms. However, the statutory returns until that for 31 December 1871 show an extra unaccountable locomotive and possibly *Liskeard* lingered at Moorswater until then. It has been suggested that the extra locomotive was hired but the only evidence appears to be substantial payments to the Avonside Engine Company which could equally be for repairs to the other engines.

When it came to purchasing their own locomotives the LCR turned to the Tees Engine Works of Middlesbrough. This firm was established in 1845 as Gilkes Wilson & Co and had very good connections with the Stockton & Darlington Railway. Between 1847 and 1875 they built more than 200 locomotives, almost half of which were for the S&DR or its successor, the North Eastern Railway. Quite why Silvanus Jenkin went so far away for a locomotive builder is not clear but there may have been a Quaker connection. The partnership changed in 1865 to Hopkins Gilkes & Co and the firm moved into bridge building. This, coupled with the end of locomotive manufacturing, was to be their downfall for they built the ill-fated Tay Bridge, which collapsed disastrously in 1879. The firm's assets were sold in 1881.[4]

Locomotives built by the Tees Engine Works almost all had a number of distinctive features. The smokebox wingplates were extended to the edge of the footplate and cylinders were placed horizontally. Another distinctive detail was the placing of a full stop after a locomotive's name, whether on a cast plate or painted. The three LCR locomotives all shared these features.

The first, *Caradon*, was despatched from Middlesbrough in July 1862 to the order of Jenkin & Trathan. It was an 0-6-0 saddle-tank with outside cylinders driving the flangeless centre pair of wheels. Six months later six wheels on axles were ordered from Middlesbrough indicating something unsatisfactory but nothing is recorded. Indeed little is recorded of any of the locomotives and only clues can be gleaned from the minutes and

CARADON at Moorswater outside the engine shed in April 1901, having been photographed by the GWR, possibly in connection with the transfer from LCR to LLR. The spartan footplate facilities for the crew are readily apparent. Note the stub point the locomotive is standing on. The low platform behind the engine was originally intended as the passenger terminus until vetoed by Colonel Rich in 1879. Possibly it was used informally before that.
BRITISH RAILWAYS

A broad-side view of CARADON *at Moorswater taken in the early 1880s. The conical safety valve cover was later replaced and exposed spring safety valves fitted.*
JOHN ALSOP COLLECTION

CHEESEWRING posed at Moorswater for the GWR photographer in 1901, when nearly forty years old. CHEESEWRING *is quite different to* CARADON.
BRITISH RAILWAYS

odd reports. *Caradon* appears to have received a new firebox in 1885 from Vulcan Foundry and is reported to have been rebuilt in 1899. However in 1906 it was stated to need constant attention, the frame was split, and it was withdrawn in 1907. A reminder of *Caradon* survived at Moorswater until the 1970s in the form of a firebox, with wooden door, suspended over, appropriately, a feeder of the East Looe River where it catered for one of man's basic functions. This is now with the Bodmin & Wenford Railway at Bodmin General Station but, alas, no longer provides a service.

Cheesewring was the second new locomotive, despatched in March 1865 at a cost of £1,900, although the cost of putting it in working order was deducted from the builder's bill. It was very different from *Caradon*, with a longer boiler and a very short wheelbase of 8 feet 8 inches, resulting in the firebox being behind the rearmost axle. The centre driving wheels were again flangeless but it was the rear axle that was

124

LOCOMOTIVES AND ROLLING STOCK

Seen here in the unlikely surroundings of Old Oak Common locomotive depot, outside Paddington, is CHEESEWRING *in the guise of GWR no 1311. It was allocated to work a nearby munitions depot until scrapped in 1919.*
MAURICE DART COLLECTION

driven. In 1885 it was the only fit engine on the railway and in 1890 was rebuilt with a new boiler.[5] New tubes were fitted in 1902 and in 1904 the LLR granted the loco fitter and his assistant a £1 gratuity each for their 'exceptional work' on the engine. In 1906 it was past repair in the company's own workshops and after failing to get a low enough quote from Pecketts was despatched to Swindon in 1907 for a general overhaul. In 1909 *Cheesewring* became GWR No 1311 and spent the Great War working a munitions depot in London, being based at Old Oak Common. It was withdrawn in 1919.[6]

In 1868, in response to an enquiry by Silvanus Jenkin, Hopkins, Gilkes & Co offered 'to construct a locomotive engine equal in character to the *Cheesewring* for £200 less price.' This was accepted and *Kilmar* was duly despatched in March 1869, to broadly the same dimensions as *Cheesewring*. The most noticeable difference was the location of the steam dome, with safety valves on top, on the rear ring of the boiler. *Cheesewring* had followed *Caradon* in

The novelty of the GWR photographer at Moorswater had drawn an audience when he took this view of KILMAR *outside the engine shed. Although the tank and boiler fittings differ* KILMAR *is basically similar to* CHEESEWRING.
BRITISH RAILWAYS

125

CARADON & LOOE – THE CANAL, RAILWAYS AND MINES

A magnificent official GWR photograph of KILMAR, probably taken after it had had heavy repairs at Swindon in 1908.
BRITISH RAILWAYS

having the steam dome conventionally on the centre ring and the valves over the firebox. As a result *Kilmar*'s 750 gallon saddle-tank sat ahead of the dome. There was some initial trouble and again two years later when £312-worth of repairs were made. *Kilmar* broke down in 1885 and appears to have remained out of use until early in 1887 when a new boiler was bought from Vulcan Foundry of Newton-le-Willows, Lancashire. In 1902 it went to the Avonside Engine Co, Bristol, for major repairs but was still needing constant attention, like *Caradon*, in 1906. Two years later the GWR made heavy repairs at Swindon which enabled it to survive as GWR No 1312 until 1914. *Kilmar* was the only LCR locomotive to provide cover for its crew, possessing a large cab from about 1902 to 1908; it was probably fitted at Bristol.

H. H. Holbrook was evidently very fond of his dog and with it on the footplate, he poses in front of KILMAR at Looe. The ungainly cab was probably added by the Avonside Engine Company in 1902.
L&GRP

126

LOCOMOTIVES AND ROLLING STOCK

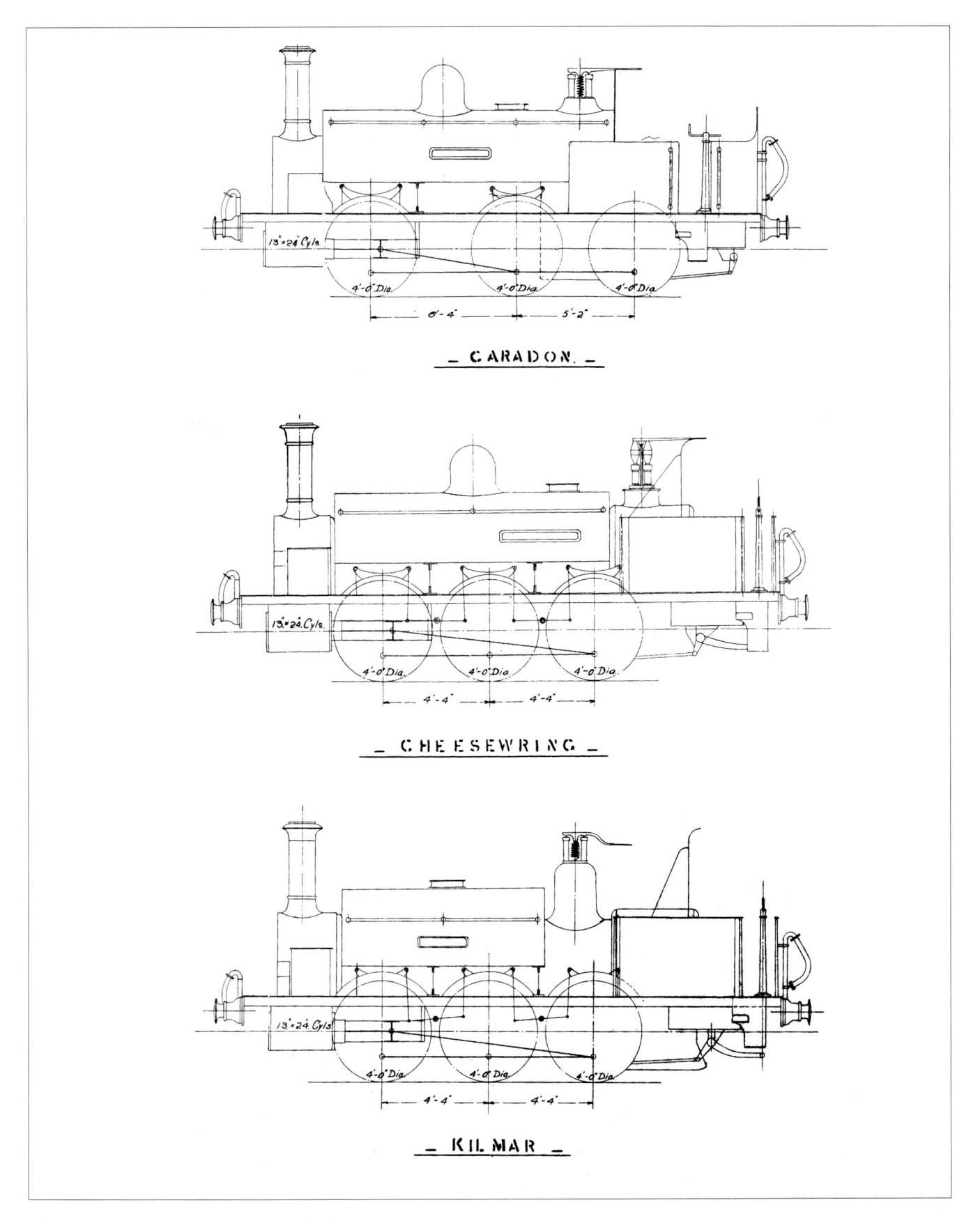

The GWR's official diagrams of the Caradon locomotives.

In 1885 the LCR hired a locomotive from Peckett & Sons. The original intention was to hire No 428, of Peckett's class B1, seen here, but in the event No 444 was hired.
FRANK JONES

The short wheelbase and sturdy appearance of Robert Stephenson & Co's LOOE is apparent in this photograph (unfortunately from a damaged glass plate). The date must be between May 1901 and April 1902 and is probably at Looe. L&GRP

From 1869 several payments to the Avonside Engine Co can be found in the Minute Books and they would appear to have been doing much of the heavy repair work that was beyond the local fitters and equipment. In 1877 a boiler was brought down from Bristol but like most of the other references it is not known which locomotive it was supplied for.

In 1885 *Caradon* was having a new firebox fitted when *Kilmar* broke down leaving *Cheesewring* to carry all the traffic and a locomotive was hired from Peckett & Sons of Bristol. Although the first choice was for Peckett No 428 it appears No 444 was supplied. This was of Peckett's class B1 and was built in 1885, an 0-6-0 saddle-tank with 14-inch cylinders and 3 feet 6½ inch diameter driving wheels.[7] It was returned to Pecketts as soon as the writ was received from Lewis Foster in September 1886. This locomotive was subsequently sold to the Nailstone Colliery Co Ltd in Leicester where it carried the name *Phoenix*. It would be very pleasing to think that this name, which goes so well with *Caradon*, *Cheesewring* and *Kilmar*, was acquired during the engine's few months on the LCR but it is not likely.

The LLR turned to Pecketts in 1900 when seeking a new locomotive to work the Liskeard Extension. They wrote to other builders also, but it is the correspondence with Pecketts that survives. Joseph Thomas envisaged a locomotive much on the lines of the LCR's 0-6-0s but heavier and with larger cylinders to cope with the gradients. Pecketts eventually suggested a six-coupled tank engine with 16 inch by 22 inch cylinders, 3 feet 10 inch wheels and an 11 feet wheelbase. The cost quoted was £1,850 but the wheelbase was considered too long and the order went to Robert Stephenson & Co in Darlington.

Looe arrived in time for the opening of the new line in May 1901 but did not prove a great success, like the coaches bought at the same time. *Looe* was an 0-6-0 saddle-tank with 16 inch diameter cylinders driving the centre pair of the 3 feet 6 inch driving wheels. The wheelbase was only eight feet and with the comparatively high-set boiler it must have been a little unsteady on the rough granite-blocked Looe trackwork. Whilst the small wheels and large cylinders made *Looe* powerful enough, the boiler could not continuously generate enough steam when the demand was high, as on the climb to Liskeard, and it soon developed a habit of running out of steam. In October 1901 Pecketts were written to with a specification of a locomotive such as the LLR required and this is of interest in that it shows the lessons learnt with

Andrew Barclay's erecting shop at the Caledonia Works, Kilmarnock, south west of Glasgow, about October 1902. Just about complete and ready to leave, side to the camera, is LADY MARGARET. HUNSLET-BARCLAY LTD.

Looe. It called for a side-tank engine with rear coal bunker, inside cylinders, a 2-4-0 wheel arrangement with 4 feet diameter driving wheels, and 'to be able to draw 90 tons up an incline of 1 in 40 and 1½ mile long'. Pecketts had nothing suitable and, when *Looe* was sold to the London & India Docks Co for £1,400, at a loss of nearly £600, in April 1902, GWR No 13 was hired. Quotes had been obtained from several manufacturers for a replacement and the order went to Andrew Barclay & Co, of Kilmarnock, Scotland. Their quote was £1,570 compared with £1,800 by Robert Stephenson & Co for a 2-4-0 side-tank.

Lady Margaret, named after Captain Spicer's wife, a daughter of the 12th Earl of Westmoreland, was built according to the specification with 14½ inch cylinders and seems to have been quite a success. The delay between the sale of *Looe* and the purchase of *Lady Margaret* was no doubt due to a lack of cash. Captain Spicer had paid for *Looe* and the £1,400 raised by its sale was needed to pay for its replacement. Holbrook was instructed to affix a

LADY MARGARET *poses at Looe with the station staff; stationmaster Herbert Hawes on the far right. Although fairly new the paintwork on the side tanks shows damage, suggesting an accident of some sort. About 1903/04.* L&GRP

CARADON & LOOE – THE CANAL, RAILWAYS AND MINES

After the GWR take-over LADY MARGARET *became 1308 on that railway and was used on a number of their branch lines that needed smaller locomotives, in particular the Tanat Valley in north Wales. Here in 1928 it is on the Culm Valley Light Railway, the Hemyock branch, after rebuilding with a large cab, boiler and GWR boiler fittings.* AUTHOR'S COLLECTION

plate reading 'The property of Capt. J. E. Spicer' to *Lady Margaret*. Obviously better suited for the job than the industrial type *Looe*, *Lady Margaret* needed little attention, apart from the installation of a brick arch in 1905, with scant success. It became GWR No 1308 in 1909 and soon after was removed from the Looe line. It was rebuilt in May 1929 with a new top-feed boiler. The GWR had inherited a number of lines that called for light engines and *Lady Margaret* was of use on these. It was on the Culm Valley line, in east Devon, after its rebuild and withdrawal came in 1948 whilst at Oswestry for the Tanat Valley branch. Strangely *Looe* lasted longer, being withdrawn by the Port of London Authority in 1950.

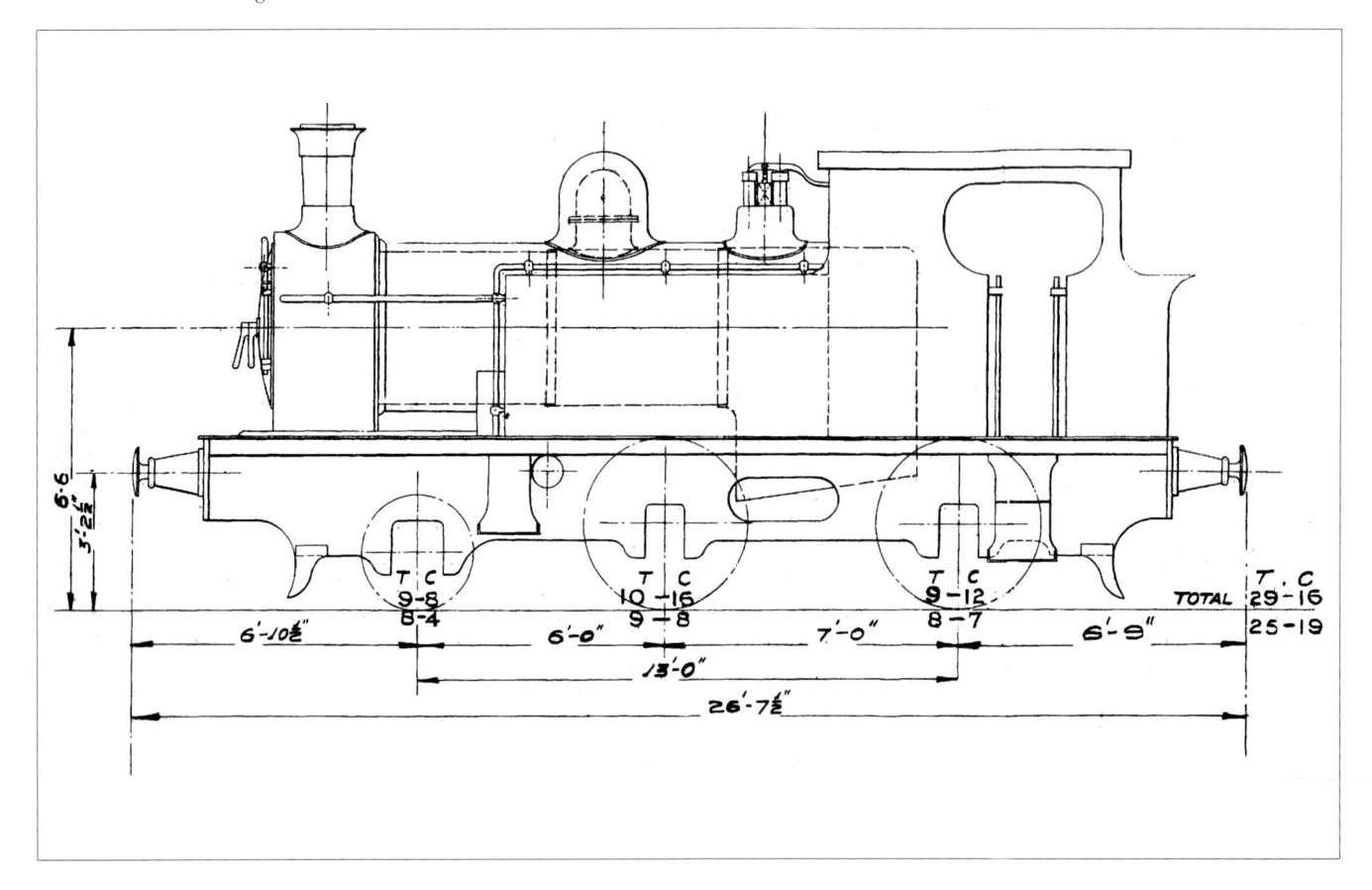

GWR diagrams of LADY MARGARET, *before rebuilding.*

130

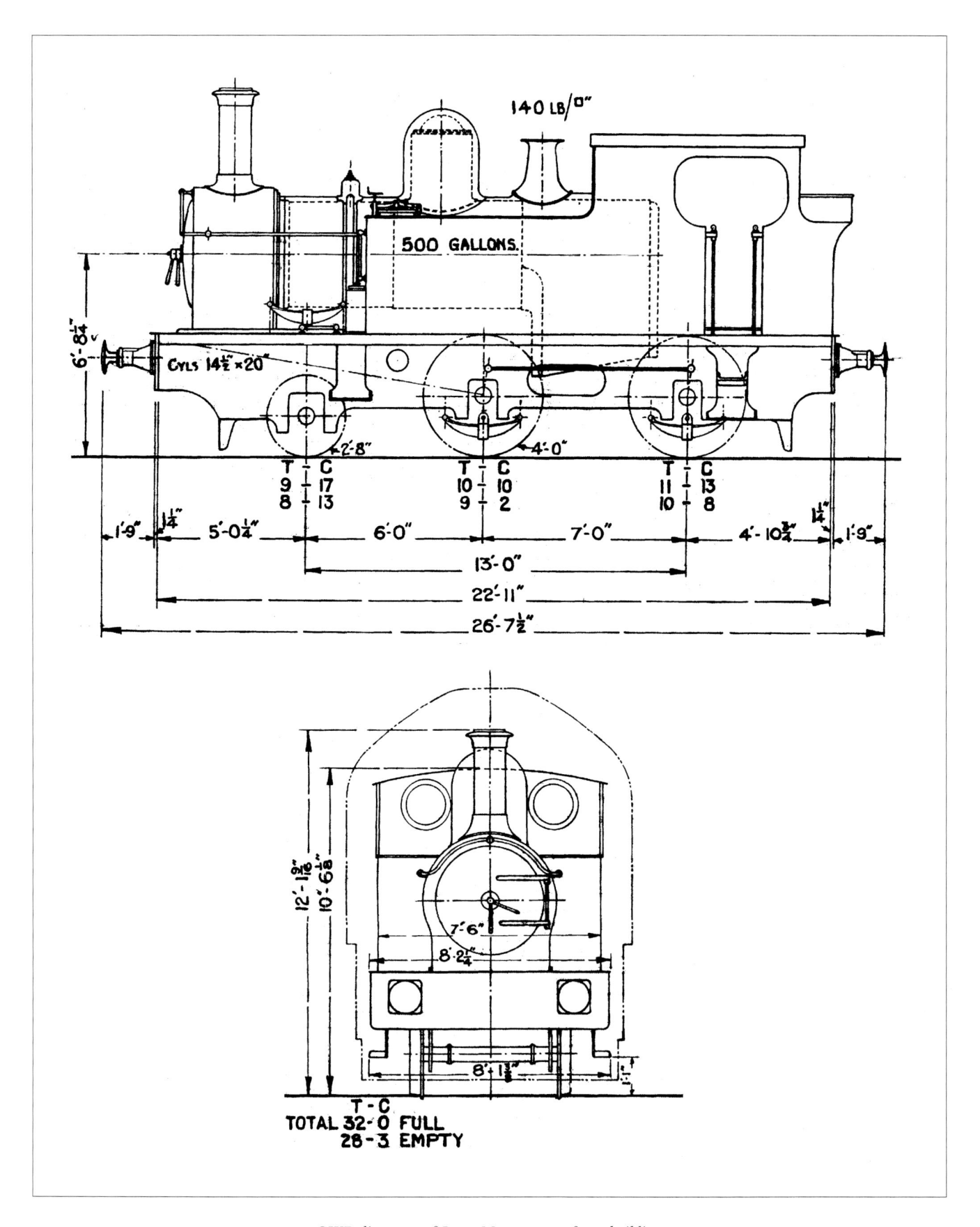

GWR diagrams of Lady Margaret, *after rebuilding.*

GWR No 13, built in 1886, was hired by the LLR from 1902 and stayed with the line until 1922. It is seen here at Looe in GWR days with guard Menhenick striking a nonchalant pose. On the footplate are driver Chaston and fireman Vincent.
AUTHOR'S COLLECTION

GWR No 13, a 4-4-0 saddle-tank dating from 1886, was a considerably larger and more powerful engine than the LLR's own and stayed on the Looe line from 1902 until 1922, being aided after absorption by 0-6-0 tanks of the GWR's '1901' and '2021' classes. During the twenties 2-6-2 side-tanks of the '44xx' and '45xx' classes took over and the latter provided motive power until steam finished on 10 September 1961.

Diesel multiple units commenced working passenger services with the new winter timetables the following day. Initially the Western Region's Gloucester-built units were used but later other types, including Swindon-built units, saw service on the line. In December 1984 a class 140 unit was on trial but in 1990 the branch was being operated by a Gloucester-built single unit. At the time of writing the branch service is maintained by units of classes 150 or 153.

Freight services, following the demise of steam, were initially handled by North British Locomotive built 1,100 h.p. diesel hydraulic locomotives of the D63xx class (later known as class 22). After the withdrawal of that class, class 25s took over but from the late 1970s the ubiquitous class 37 were in charge of clay trains, working them through to Fowey for shipment. Later they worked stone and cement traffic to Moorswater, but before this traffic ceased class 66 diesels were in use.

GOODS STOCK

The early wagon stock of the LCR is something of a mystery. No specific records have survived, if indeed there ever were any, and we have only a few clues to guide us.

In 1844 a limit of five tons per wagon was stipulated and two years later the West Briton reported 'there are several carriages now on the line, one on eight wheels of very superior construction, and heavy loads of granite have been brought down ...'[8] Bearing in mind that the directors initially had higher hopes of granite as a source of traffic than copper this reference is almost certainly to granite wagons and the mention of eight wheels would support this. One load of granite contemplated at this time was a block weighing 11 tons for the works at New Passage, Devonport, which on the flimsy trackwork of the day would need eight wheels to spread the weight. With the LCR's curves this would have to be a form of bogie vehicle, and an early example, but no more detail is available. In 1858 the minutes record that the Engineer was to obtain tenders for 'two new single granite waggons and one new double granite waggon' as further evidence of a bogie vehicle. These came from Messrs Nicholls Williams & Co's foundry at Tavistock at a total cost of £269.

The earliest reference to wagons in the minutes is the order in 1855 of two copper ore wagons from Nicholls Williams. These were quoted at £95 per ton and in the event cost £90 each thus weighing about 19 cwt apiece. The ore wagons were of the chaldron type with tapering sides and a bottom door in the floor permitting them to discharge straight into the canal barges or onto ore floors from trestles above the wharves at Moorswater.[9] The probable capacity was about two or three tons and all must have been braked, to enable them to run by gravity down the line. Very similar wagons ran on the Bodmin & Wadebridge Railway.

Possibly there were timber wagons also, and coal, although both commodities could have been accommodated in granite or ore wagons, as could the comparatively small amounts of sand and lime that went up the line. The earliest statutory returns to give the numbers of wagons, that for the year 1860, states 24 as the total. In the return for 1861 the number had shot up to 43, £1,173 having been spent on wagons, and from 1862 51 were returned. This sudden increase was a direct result of the LCR taking on the carriage of the traffic on the LLUC's railway, opened in December 1860, but there were many complaints over the years of shortages of wagons. In 1867 the number dropped to 47 (including four timber wagons) and in 1878 to 40 (eight timber wagons). A covered van was acquired in 1880 and the total goods rolling stock numbers climbed a little to 45 in 1890, this number being taken over by the LLR in 1901.

Most, if not all, of the wagons purchased in 1861 and 1862 came from James Murphy's works at Newport, where he had been established as a railway wagon manufacturer since the mid-1850s. He remained in business until at least 1885 so probably was a source of parts and spares also. A photograph survives showing a wagon bearing his axle-boxes.

Murphy's wagons were doubtless of higher standard than the earlier ones and these latter were probably rebuilt to make them fitter for locomotive haulage. Certainly during the late 1870s and until after the Receiver was appointed a policy of improvement was followed, many wagons being rebuilt utilising sound wheels, springs and ironwork. In 1884, when giving evidence to Parliament, Silvanus Jenkin took great pains to point out that the LCR had 'the best class of trucks'. Apart from purchasing ten second-hand wagons in 1906 the LLR did very little major work on the wagon stock and the inventory made at the time the GWR took over the working of the two lines shows the stock much as the LCR left it.

The GWR, on taking stock, was not greatly impressed. G. J. Churchward valued the wagons at £4 each and a valuation report stated 'the wagons are in a very low state indeed ... the brakework in all cases is very shaky'. The list of stock with the valuation provides much useful information on the 50 goods vehicles the GWR took over. All had oak frames and the majority possessed end screw brakes, four having lever brakes. The reason for screw brakes, rather than levers, was for the ease of use by brakesmen, who stood on a small platform on the buffer. Only five wagons sported spring buffers at both ends; the remainder sufficed with one end fitted with dumb buffers. Two thirds of the stock had wheels of three feet diameter, a quarter had two feet eight inches and the few others two feet ten inches. The livery in LCR days was described as the same as the carriages, which were dark reddish-brown, and the LLR probably continued with this style.

The majority of wagons, 42, were open goods of, in the main, six tons capacity. Exceptions were an ex-GWR eight-ton wagon and two Moorswater rebuildings which also had eight-ton bodies. The only real consistency was

Six ton wagon No 84 at Moorswater, 1901. It is unusual in having sprung buffers at each end but is otherwise typical of LCR wagons. The screw brakes at the right hand end apply to all four wheels, good braking being a necessity for gravity working. The axle boxes are marked 'J Murphy, Newport, Mon'. Despite the lack of paint on the woodwork, the wagon is in good condition, the ironwork is clean and the painted number new. It had been rebodied at Moorswater in 1898 using old wheels and springs.
BRITISH RAILWAYS

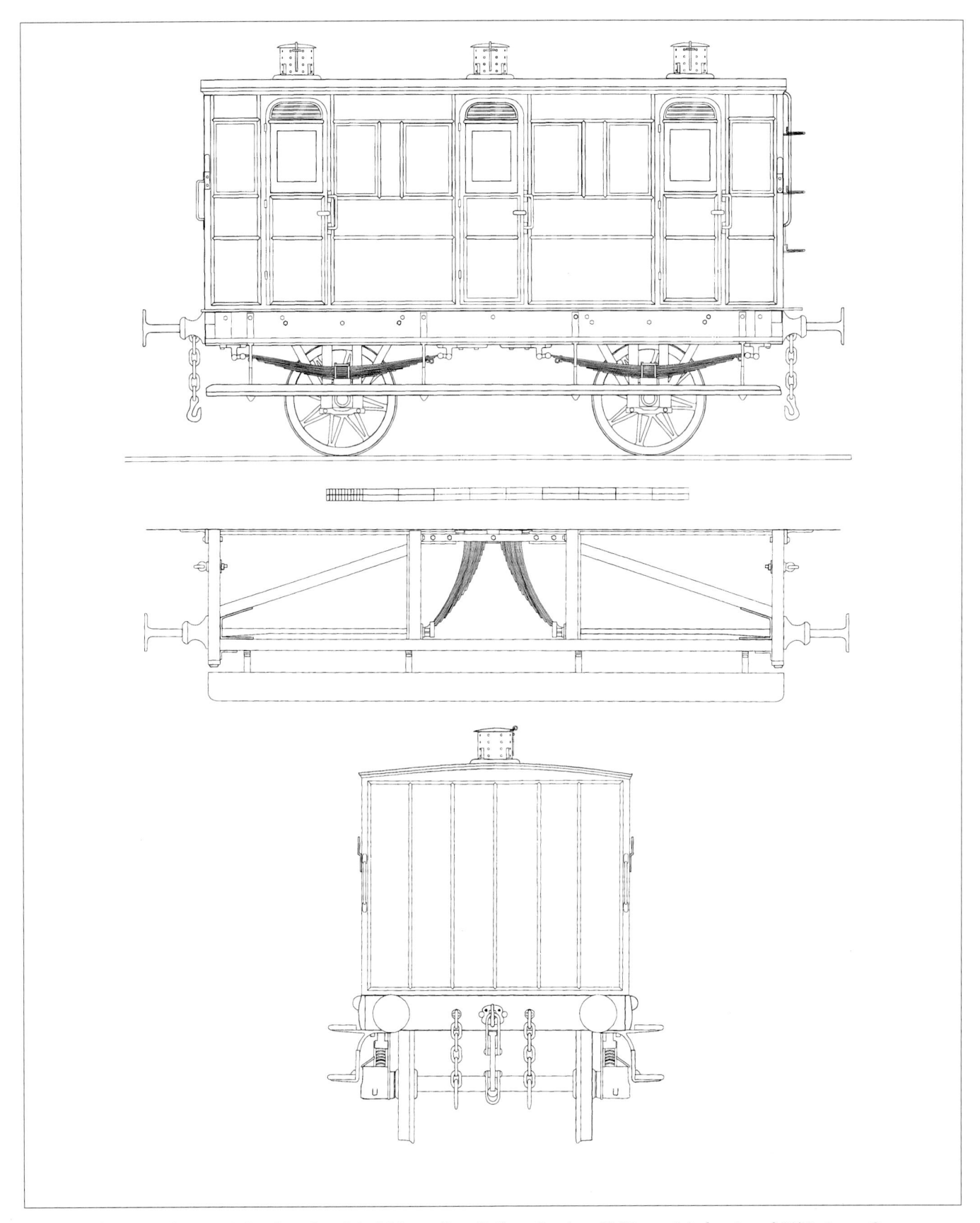

Drawing of LCR carriage No 1, based on the original Metropolitan Railway Carriage & Wagon Co's drawing of 1879. JOHN CORKETT

Almost all traces of lettering have been worn away but it is believed this is carriage No 1 of 1879. It is just possible to detect that the compartments are marked, from the left, second, first and third. This also by the GWR photographer in 1901. Note that in addition to screw couplings the carriages are also coupled by double safety chains.
BRITISH RAILWAYS

in the ten wagons bought in 1906 for £10 each from the Bute Works Supply Co whose bodies were slightly larger than the local products but were otherwise similar. They were built in 1902 and were hired at first in 1905; their purchase reflected a brief boom in mineral traffic. Of the six timber wagons four were also described as stone wagons but all had the same dimensions.

The goods van was also described as a passenger brake van and had double doors on each side and four large windows. It weighed but three tons and its condition in 1909 was 'bad, shocking and quite worthless'. The goods brake van had been bought from the GWR in 1903 for £10 and six years later the body was described as 'shaky'.

Almost none of the stock matched standard GWR fittings and in view of its condition and the major rebuilding necessary to bring it to twentieth century standards the GWR soon disposed of it.

PASSENGER STOCK

Passenger services commenced between Moorswater and Looe on 11 September 1879 to provide these two coaches and a passenger brake van were purchased from the Metropolitan Railway Carriage & Wagon Co Ltd of Birmingham. The coaches had three compartments, one first-class and two third-class, but the latter may have been changed to second-class. An additional carriage with four third-class compartments was bought the following year. The carriages were all small because of the restricted loading gauge of the bridges on the line. First-class carriages enjoyed

Third class carriage No 3, built 1879, sat 40 people. Even with a strong glass, this photograph of 1901 reveals little sign of lettering and not much paint of any sort.
BRITISH RAILWAYS

CARADON & LOOE – THE CANAL, RAILWAYS AND MINES

For the opening of the line to Liskeard in 1901 three new carriages were purchased from Hurst Nelson. No 1 had both first and second class saloons as well as a guard's compartment whilst nos 2 and 3 were third class saloons. Their end balconies and plate frame bogies were quite unlike the typical British branch line carriage.
HURST NELSON/HMRS COLLECTION T10/44 AND T10/42

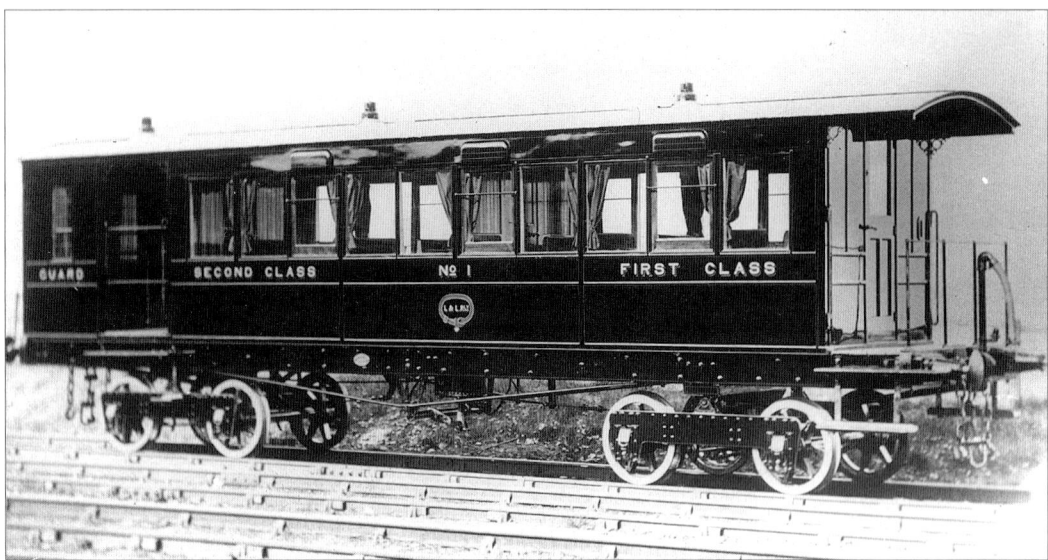

blue cloth upholstery and second-class had American leather but the third-class passenger had to manage without any upholstery. An 1899 passenger noted that 'the pleasure of the ride is marred by the incessant jolting', although this could have been due as much to the track as to the carriage's springing. All were lit by oil lamps and were fitted with vacuum brakes, at L. C. Foster's own expense on the insistence of the Board of Trade, in 1896.[10] Prior to this two carriages and a brake van had been fitted with a patent brake invented by Walter Parker Smith of Lostwithiel and fitted by him, without cost to the LCR, in 1881 as a trial. The mechanism included a screw driven from the axle via a clutch and, on being activated by a chain from the guards van, the brakes were applied.[11] This crude form of continuous brake did not meet with the approval of the Board of Trade and it was replaced eventually. The livery of these vehicles was a dark reddish-brown with gilt lettering and numbers,[12] and all survived to be acquired by the GWR in 1909 although only as scrap.

For the inauguration of the passenger service in May 1901 over the new extension to Liskeard the LLR bought three bogie carriages from Hurst Nelson & Co., of Motherwell, for £1,245. Variously described as Swiss or American style, the crimson painted coaches had end doors and balconies and the outside plate frames of the bogies were a further distinctive feature. These unusual carriages were all open saloons; a 1st/2nd-class brake composite, an all third and a brake third. They provided 124 seats in all and were a considerable improvement on the LCR stock. They were numbered from 1 to 3 but their dimensions are not recorded.

136

LADY MARGARET at Looe with a rake of three of the Ashbury built ex-Mersey Railway carriages. LPC/JOHN ALSOP COLLECTION.

They were not very successful for reasons that are unrecorded but their appearance is more of tramway coaches than railway and they may not have been substantial enough, particularly on the rough original LLR track. In 1904 they were sold to Messrs Jackson & Co. for the Lindsay Light Railway Syndicate Ltd. and were to be stored at Moorswater for six months. However, they were still there in 1906 to be collided with on 14 June by the runaway train from Liskeard. The composite merely had its windows broken but the other two were smashed. The owner was then a Mr Hogan of Messrs Hogan & Hughes who complained to little effect and the one survivor and the remains of the other two were still there in 1909.

Early in 1904 advantage was taken of the electrification of the Mersey Railway to purchase some of the surplus steam-hauled stock of that railway. Thirteen coaches were acquired in all between 1904 and 1907. All were four-wheeled, vacuum-braked and gas-lit and were built by the Ashbury Railway Carriage & Iron Co. Ltd, of Manchester, between 1885 and 1888. Quite the largest stock to run on the railway they cost the LLR anything from £20 to £70 each. They were numbered in sequence commencing at 1, so by 1904 the LLR had three carriages bearing the number 1. The livery was brown but the GWR in 1909 pointed out that some had not been painted since new and all were in a poor condition. A value of £20 each was purely

LADY MARGARET at Looe with an assortment of wagons and the ex-GWR brake van. About 1904. JOHN ALSOP COLLECTION.

Brake van No 4 was a very interesting vehicle, probably originating second-hand from the West Cornwall Railway in 1868. The photograph with guard Joseph Uren standing by the rear buffer was taken at Moorswater in 1901 and a comparison with the older photograph below, taken in the early to mid-1880s, shows some of the changes that had taken place. The left hand door now is labelled 'Parcels', instead of 'Third', so it no longer carries passengers, and another door has been fitted, to the loss of the central window. On the older view the small wheel close to the roof of the brake van is possibly connected with the patent brake fitted in 1881.
AUTHOR'S COLLECTION/ BRITISH RAILWAYS

nominal, for several were beyond repair while others sported split panels, poor roofs and bad underframes. The valuation reports

the fittings of all these coaches are of an obsolete type, the gas lamps being in a very dirty condition. The draw and buffing gear is all of the close-coupled type and a great expense would have to be incurred to replace the existing gear.

No 11 had been destroyed in the Moorswater smash of 1906 but the remaining twelve acquired GWR numbers in 1909. Six were scrapped in 1910 and in 1912 the rest were transferred to the Rhondda & Swansea Bay Railway for two years, where they are said to have worked colliers' passenger trains. The GWR finally condemned them in 1917.

The story of the vans and brake vans is even less clear than that of the other rolling stock. No 4 was a very old vehicle with horizontal planking, separate guard's and parcels' compartments and curious little windows with semi-circular tops. The parcels compartment was originally for third-class passengers but was converted about the last decade of the nineteenth century when double doors were fitted in each side. Quite possibly this is the West Cornwall Railway 'carriage suitable for a guards van' offered to Trathan in 1868. A payment of £85 was later made to the WCR which more than likely was for the carriage.

No 6 is clearly from the same stable as the Metropolitan carriages and was delivered in 1879 with the first two of these. As well as double doors on each side there were small square windows in each end. It was extremely short, only ten feet, with a wheelbase of only five feet.

A third van, believed to be No 8, appears in the photograph on page 59. Little is known about this vehicle other than what can be gleaned about its size from the photograph. There is an inference in LLR papers of another van, No 7, but even less is known of this.[13]

(Fuller details of locomotives and rolling stock are given in Appendix 4)

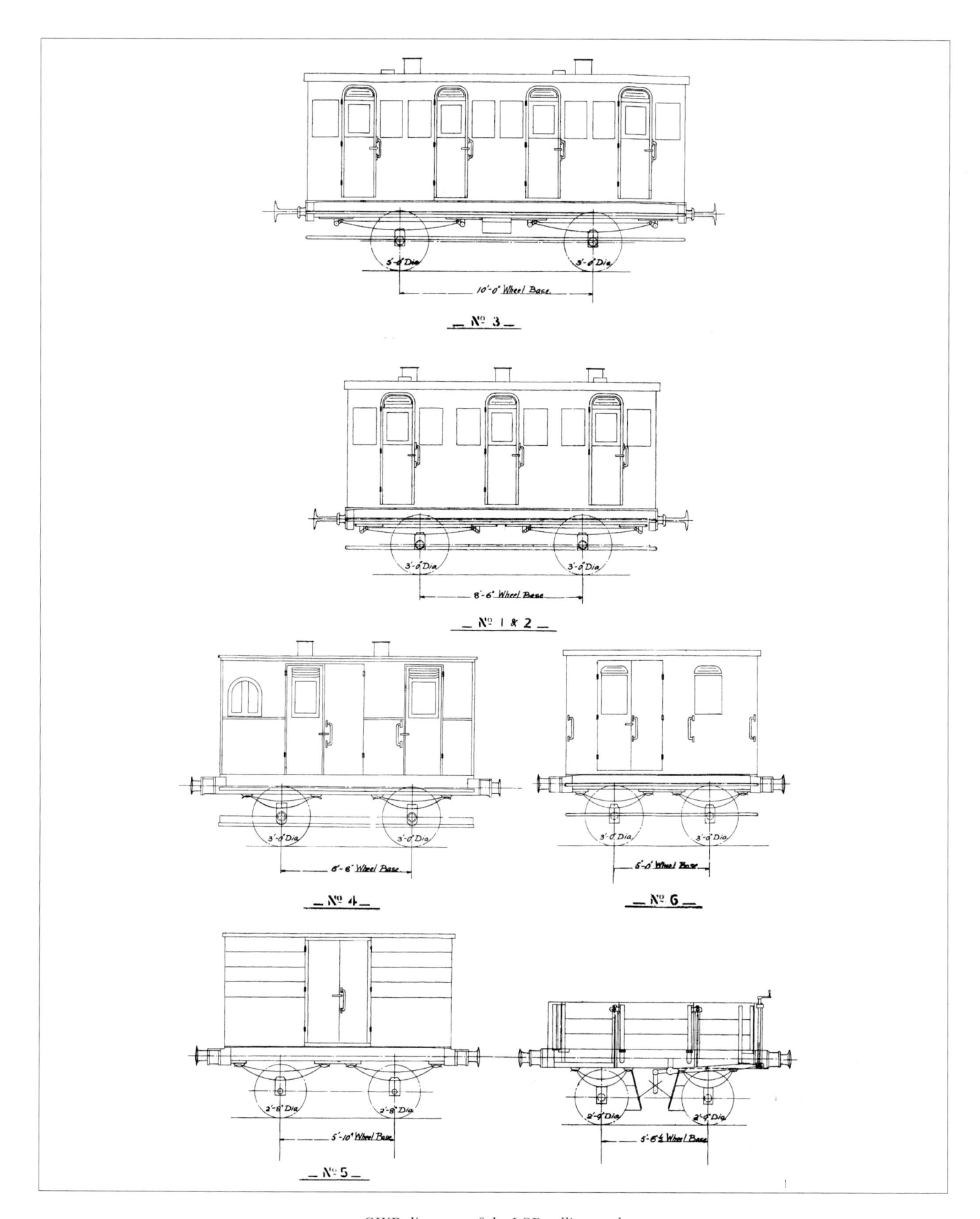

GWR diagrams of the LCR rolling stock.

Although there is no documentary proof that MRC&W built brake van No 6 the family likeness to the carriages is clear. The van had an incredibly short wheelbase and was even narrower than the carriages. Posed at Moorswater, 1901, with shedman Jonathon Symons who seems to have been in charge of placing the stock for the GWR photographer.
BRITISH RAILWAYS

The first three vehicles seen here were built by the Metropolitan Railway Carriage & Wagon Co in 1879 and 1880. From left to right they are No 6, the passenger brake van, No 3, the third class carriage and either No 1 or No 2, a first/second composite. At the far end is brake van No 4. Note the longitudinal sleepers which were used on the Looe line south of Sandplace. L&GRP

CHAPTER TEN
MEN AND MACHINES

'The Committee of Management are not composed of Men of Education but I believe of a very artful and cunning description.' JOHN BULLER 1829[1]

'The services of the Committee, so long and faithfully afforded, are entirely gratuitous as are those of the Caradon Railway Directors.' JOHN ALLEN 1856

The disparity between the two quotations above is readily apparent. John Buller was a Member of Parliament and one of the land-owning gentry whereas those who ran the canal, and later the railways, although prominent people in Liskeard and district, were latter-day yeomen; practical men. Although Buller may not have trusted them, they were trusted and respected by their fellows and as well as running the railways and canal, mines and quarries, they took a leading part in the affairs of Liskeard town and the surrounding area. Many were members of the Borough Council and became mayors of Liskeard, contributing much to the improvement of the town and its facilities during the prosperous years at the centre of the nineteenth century. Essentially they were local men and, whilst their experience of the outside world may have been limited, their main concern was to do what they could for the district. With but one exception none of the local directors of the two companies took any payment for their services throughout the companies' independent years.

The first major parts in the story of the Liskeard & Looe Union Canal were played by Robert Coad and Richard Retallick who conceived and constructed the new canal. Both were local men without experience, as far as we know, in engineering matters but who devoted all their intellect to the job. Robert Coad was born in Menheniot in 1779 and is variously described as a land surveyor or agent and, latterly, an architect. He was surveyor of the Liskeard Turnpike until he was 75. Whilst working over much of north Cornwall, he seems to have lived and worked in Liskeard all his life. The canal and, twenty years later, the LCR appear to be the only major engineering schemes he was involved in, although he did survey the proposed Delabole & Rock Railway in 1843. Richard Retallick was five years older and was a clockmaker in Liskeard. In 1825 he was specifically thanked for his 'devotion to the cause' of the LLUC. He undertook no other subsequent engineering work and stated, with pride one presumes, in 1848, 'the Liskeard Canal was a child of my own'[2]. Both died in Liskeard, in 1864 and 1854 respectively.

One of the most consistent enthusiasts for the Liskeard & Looe Canal was Edward Geach. Not a native of Liskeard, he had moved there in 1801 and practised in the legal profession as a conveyancer. He was one of the original subscribers to the Act of 1825 and served on the Committee of Management, with few breaks, from 1826 to 1876, always playing a leading part in its activities. He was also a director of the Liskeard & Caradon Railway continuously from its inception to his death in his 80th year in 1876. Mayor of Liskeard in 1842, he was also a major promoter of the Liskeard Water Company and of several local roads and turnpike roads. When he died, the *Cornish Times* described him as 'a link between the past and the present, between the time of non-improvement and public listlessness, and the era of improvement and energy …'[3]

Peter Glubb, a solicitor, was also prominent in the district. As well as being very active during the Canal Bill's passage through Parliament, he was also involved in the proposed suspension bridge across the Tamar, was Treasurer of the East Cornwall Savings Bank and Clerk to the Liskeard Poor Law Board. He married a daughter of the Lyne family, of which Benjamin Hart Lyne was prominent in the early years of the LCR.[4]

Another solicitor active on the LCR's behalf was Christopher Childs, the first Secretary of the railway company, who also had the distinction of laying the first granite pavement in Liskeard during his mayoralty in 1848. When he died in 1877 he was succeeded by his son, John Borlase Childs, as Secretary until the job ceased to exist in 1909. Thus throughout its life the LCR had but two secretaries, father and son.

Long service seems to have been a characteristic of many of those who helped run the two organisations. On the Committee of Management of the LLUC, Edward Geach's fifty years has been noted and fourteen others, including Peter Clymo, Samuel Abbott, William Nettle and John Alleyne Chambers gave over twenty years each. Several were in excess of thirty and Thomas Sargent totalled forty-four years continuously. In fact a member of the Sargent family was involved with the Looe company during almost every year of its life; Gustavus Sargent being on the original committee in 1825 and William Sargent attending the final meeting on 12 December 1922.

On the LCR board of directors Edward Geach was the longest serving director too, thirty four years, and others with more than twenty years behind them were the Reverend Norris and Peter Clymo (both with twenty eight years), Samuel Abbott, Samuel Elliott, Richard Hawke and Lewis Foster, although the last named perhaps had little choice. The repetition of names is interesting for it shows how close the two companies were, although pursuing their separate ways.

Both the Clymo brothers, Peter and James, were involved in the LCR at the outset, representing their interests in South Caradon Mine. James was more prominent until his early death in 1849, managing South Caradon from 1842. He was also purser of East Caradon at the time of his death. Peter appears then to have taken his place, becoming manager of the mine from 1852, and his management skills became highly regarded in the district. His early experience was in the mines of the St Blazey area and he later invested heavily in the lead mines of Menheniot, but Liskeard was his home and where he took a leading role in the town's affairs.

The Clymo's friend Thomas Kittow was from old farming stock but took a strong interest in mining matters. He was important in the Cornwall Great United venture and may have been instrumental in bringing the Clymos to Caradon. Possibly he provided the initial finance for South Caradon, where he was purser from 1837 to 1876. He was briefly on the Committee of the Canal and also loaned money to the LCR. He died in 1887 aged 100. His brother Richard was also a major shareholder in South Caradon Mine and was a director of the LCR.

The Reverend George Poole Norris, Rector of East Anstey in Devon, was the mineral lord of South Caradon Mine, owning the mineral rights that the miners exploited. However he was no 'absentee' lord as many of his kind were in Cornwall and Devon but he took a close interest in the mine that brought him so much wealth. He was one of the original instigators of the LCR and like Peter Clymo Junior and Edward Geach served as a director from the line's inception until his death, in 1870, after many years as an invalid. Several presentations of silver plate were made to him during his lifetime but a greater indication of the respect in which he was held is the report that 2,000 people, including 600 or 700 miners from South Caradon, attended his funeral at St Cleer.[5]

His interests were inherited by his widow and daughters although John Samuel Hawker, who married Sarah Norris soon after her father's death, appears to have exercised control over them. Educated at Jesus College, Cambridge, and a Justice of the Peace for Cornwall he joined the Board of the LCR in 1870 on the death of G. P. Norris and in 1878 had a holding of but 10 shares in his own name.

He does not seem to have played a very active part until 1878 when he and Richard Hawke took over supervision of traffic on the dismissal of James Trathan and the following year he joined the Joint Committee with the LLUC. In 1880 he became Deputy Chairman and, as well as a special vote of thanks at the A.G.M. that year, he was awarded £50 for his expenses over the previous two years. He thus became the first and only LCR director to receive any remuneration other than dividends. Eighteen months later, however, his popularity had waned drastically and it cannot be without significance that South Caradon Mine was at the same time having great difficulty in renewing its lease. At the next General Meeting, in February 1883, it was Hawker's turn to retire – two of the directors retired each year – but there were three candidates for the two vacancies including himself. He demanded a poll vote and lost it ignominiously. This was another Hawker first for this was the only election in the history of the LCR and the first of only two poll votes at General Meetings; he was responsible for the second also, nine years later. Now removed from office John Hawker contented himself with demanding repayment of overdue debentures

Richard Hawke was a major shareholder in the LCR, a director from 1868 and Chairman from 1878 until his death in 1887. Born in Helston about 1824 he came to South Caradon Mine as a mine barber but invested well, dying a wealthy man.
LISKEARD TOWN MUSEUM

held by Mrs and Miss Norris, his mother- and sister-in-law, and by his wife. The company's finances being what they were he received little satisfaction and, apart from the occasional *contretemps*, he faded from the scene.

Richard Hawke was Chairman during John Hawker's involvement and remained in the Chair until his death in 1887. He was born in Helston but early in his working life he became mine barber at South Caradon. He moved into the world of mining finance where a number of astute moves made him a wealthy man. As well as having interests in several mines and in the LCR, he was part owner of Liskeard Gas Works.[6] His last years must have been sad ones for he had seen the decline and demise of all the mines locally, including South Caradon, while the LCR, which he had been a director of since 1868 was then in Receivership. He was one of the first people in Cornwall to be cremated and his remains are interred in a monument in the grounds of his house in Liskeard, Westbourne House.

One of the longest involvements with the railway was that of Silvanus Jenkin, its engineer for nearly sixty years. He was born at Redruth in 1821 into a well-known family of mining engineers and in 1842, after training as a civil engineer, went to Liskeard as assistant to Robert Coad with whom he was employed in surveying the LCR. Sometime during the next four years he succeeded Coad as Engineer of the railway, a position he retained until after the LLR took over in 1901. In 1851 he became steward and agent to the Robartes' estates at Lanhydrock, following in the footsteps of both his father and grandfather, and he was County Surveyor of bridges and roads for east Cornwall from 1856 until his death. He was a Liskeard councillor, later alderman, and Mayor in 1877 and 1878 and amongst other interests in the town he was a magistrate and a director of the Liskeard Temperance Hotel. Other railway work was with Brunel's team surveying parts of the Cornwall Railway, work on the Helston and Lostwithiel & Fowey railways and on the Newquay & Cornwall Junction line from Burngullow. Harbour, mine and water works also ensured he had left an indelible mark on the face of Cornwall when he died in 1911. He was highly respected in Cornwall and his lengthy funeral procession was led by representatives of the fire brigade, police, town council and magistrates and the bearers were drawn from the Lanhydrock estate.[7]

James Jenkin Trathan was a relative of Silvanus Jenkin and, like him, a Quaker. He was not formally trained as a civil engineer but when family tragedy sent him looking for work he joined the team building the Liskeard & Caradon Railway, becoming traffic superintendent on the line's completion. In 1854 he was appointed superintendent, surveyor and engineer to the Looe line and he held these positions on both railways until a few months before his death. He was manager of Cheesewring Quarry from 1850 until Freemans took it over in 1863. In 1855 he and Jenkin went into partnership and together they became responsible for many railway, harbour and waterworks in Cornwall, Devon and further afield, although one suspects Silvanus Jenkin was the driving force. Jenkin's wife's nephew, William Triscott, joined the partnership in 1867 but six years later it broke up acrimoniously, for reasons not recorded. A few years later Trathan was reported as being in very poor health and, as related elsewhere, the LLUC dismissed him in 1878 and the LCR followed suit the next year. He died at Teignmouth in 1880 aged 56.

The final engineer involved in this story, Joseph Thomas, also had a long association with the district and railways. Not only were his grandfather and father employed on the construction of the Looe canal but he assisted his father in the building of the Looe railway and extensions to Looe harbour. After a career working in Hungary, the United States and the Channel Islands, he played a large part in developing London's docks. In the 1890s he returned to his childhood home of Cornwall with, as he said himself, a desire to do good for the district. After working on Mevagissey and St

Silvanus Jenkin in the latter years of his life. Born in Redruth in 1821, he moved to Liskeard in 1857, although he was involved with the LCR from about 1842. He died in 1911.
WITH KIND PERMISSION OF THE NATIONAL TRUST/ LANHYDROCK

Joseph Thomas, engineer of the Liskeard & Looe Extension Railway. It was to be his last work as he died a few months after the opening in 1901.

Lewis Foster appears to be striking a pose as he stands with one foot on the wagon door but in fact he is taking the photograph himself by means of a bulb and tube, and is probably timing the exposure with a watch. He and his friends are about to travel down the line by gravity in wagon no 56. The guard, Jonathan Symons, stands to the far left and he will brake the wagon down the Hill. Believed to be April 1898.
AUTHOR'S COLLECTION

Ives harbours he became involved in the Hannafore Estate, with Captain Spicer, and Looe pier, but the extension railway was to be his last work for he died a few months after the line was opened.[8]

Lewis Charles Foster had been appointed Treasurer of the LCR in 1879, at the age of 35, and as a partner in the East Cornwall Bank he was also the company's bank manager. Such potential conflict of interest seemed not to matter in those days and certainly did not present a problem in 1886 when he became Receiver. His longevity in office was probably not voluntary but was also seen possibly as part of his service to the local community. Foster also served a term as Mayor of Liskeard and was a magistrate for many years.

Stationmasters are first mentioned in 1865, in the LCR minutes, when John Frances and John Howard at Moorswater and Looe respectively had their salaries increased by £5 a year. John Howard had been lock keeper at Terras and in 1851 had the job of policeman to the whole line of the LLUC added to his duties. Responsible for the traffic on the canal, his wages then were 16s a week and he had a new suit each year. By 1865, when he was in his early 50s, the title had become stationmaster, a job he retained until at least 1884. Arthur Bailey succeeded him but when the new regime came in in 1901 Bailey was reduced to a porter-signalman, although the *Cornish Times* kindly referred to him as a ticket collector.

John Frances had been appointed booking constable at Moorswater, probably coming from the Cornwall Railway, in 1863 at a salary of £60 a year, but by 1871 John Henry Smythurst was stationmaster. At the age of 47, in 1878, he was promoted to Traffic Manager to replace J. J. Trathan at a salary of £100 per annum. It rose to £150 by 1886 but was reduced, along with all other salaries, to £120 on Lewis Foster's appointment. He did not last long after that, as He died in 1890 but had already been replaced; H. G. T. Hawken was described as Traffic Manager in 1888. John Symons was stationmaster about 1893.

The new regime of the turn of the century brought many changes. The new Superintendent of the Line, Horace Holbrook, still in his mid-thirties, came from the Great

Horace Holbrook in 1901 shortly after arriving from the Great Eastern Railway. After the GWR took over the LLR he stayed with them and rose to Chief Assistant Stationmaster at Paddington before leaving in 1921 to join the Light Railway Section of the Ministry of Transport. He died in 1958.

Guard Joseph Uren poses at the door of one of the Metropolitan carriages. He joined the LCR in 1860 at the age of 18 and retired in 1902.
L&GRP

Below is a studio portrait of him, taken by Thomas Searle of Liskeard about 1870.
STEPHEN ROWSON COLLECTION

Eastern Railway, where he was a relieving stationmaster, and he brought a number of his colleagues with him. Among these were the new stationmasters, Alfred Burridge and Herbert Hawes, who exchanged Theobalds Grove and Chadwell Heath for Liskeard and Looe respectively.

Septimus Bolton came from Robert Stephenson & Co's works with the locomotive *Looe* and stayed as Locomotive Inspector, and driver Smith also came from Newcastle. Several other staff came from the GWR locally but a number were taken over from the LCR. One of these was Joseph Uren who had joined the LCR in 1860 at the age of 18, having worked previously for three or four years with the Cornwall Railway. He became a very well-known local figure as guard of the LCR passenger trains but retired in 1902 to become Liskeard's poor-rate collector.[9]

In 1908 the LLR had 53 employees to operate both railways compared with 64 in 1875 between the two companies. Wages in 1901 ranged from 17s for a porter-signalman to 22s for a passenger guard, but as has been noted earlier almost none of the LCR directors or

Even a minor branch line employed a considerable number of staff in the early years of the twentieth century. Here the 53 staff of the Liskeard & Looe Railway pose in front of the wagon works doors at Moorswater in December 1908, immediately prior to the GWR takeover. They are, from left to right: (Front row) W. Hocking, cleaner; Mr W. H. Johns, cartage agent; Mr E. Hunter, goods clerk; Mr. H. Hawes, stationmaster, Looe; Mr S. Bolton, locomotive superintendent; Mr H. H. Holbrook, Superintendent of the Line; Inspector Scantlebury, permanent way; Mr A. Burridge, stationmaster, Liskeard; Mr Morgan, superintendent's clerk; A. Richards, parcels clerk; J. Prout, striker.
(Second row) J. Ough, relief carman; H. Cox, carman; H. Menhenick, passenger guard; R. Bassett, T. Bowden, porter-signalmen; J. Cole, fitter; A. Stephens, goods guard; J. Husband, porter-signalman; E. Marsh, signalman; W. H. Pengelly, porter-signalman; C. Colmer, lamp lad; R. Grant, carriage cleaner, J. Carne, blacksmith.
(Third row) M. Harris, cleaner; P. Turner, painter; W. Martin, platelayer; J. Martin, J. Sambells, gangers; W. Symons, fireman; W. Vincent, W. Chaston, drivers; H. Menhenick, fireman; R. Miller, driver; Albert Bray, fireman; J. Toms, ganger; H. Medland, linesman; W. J. Godfrey, junior, W. Godfrey, carpenters.
(Fourth row) S. Tamblin, T. H. Davey, R. Bennett, J. Hancock, J. Horrell, J. Wilton, J. Crabb, platelayers; J. Hunkin, ganger; W. Moore, W. Kennedy, J. Cannon, H. Hancock, J. Harvey, platelayers; J. Symons, shed man. AUTHOR'S COLLECTION

LLUC Committee of Management received a penny remuneration and only in 1909 did the LLR directors (as the Committee of Management had by then become) receive £25 each for their services.

After the GWR take-over some employees stayed on the line but others transferred elsewhere on the GWR system. Not all fared well under the new regime. John Husband, for example, who narrowly escaped trouble in 1906 when he let empty carriages run away from Liskeard, was cautioned in 1910 when, as signalman at Coombe Junction, he sent a Liskeard-bound train back down the line towards Looe. He was reduced to a porter-signalman at Liskeard for this misdemeanour but one wonders if it would have been noticed in LLR days, certainly not in LCR days. He resigned the following year.

ACCIDENTS

The drowning of a drunk young man in the canal in 1833 is the only human fatality recorded against the waterway. Accidents were rather more common on the two railways and reflected a rather more casual attitude to safety than was probably enforced on contemporary main line railways.

Trespassers were a problem on both lines; despite official discouragement, particularly on the Looe line, the tracks were regarded by many as public rights-of-way and some guide books

LOOE off the road at Coombe Junction. The high centre of gravity of LOOE made it vulnerable to the rough track on the way to its namesake town but here it has derailed on almost brand new trackwork.
GRAHAM ROOSE COLLECTION

actually recommended the walk up the Looe valley alongside the canal or to the moors by way of the mineral railway track. Horses, donkeys and cattle are all recorded as having been killed by trains but human deaths were fortunately few. In May 1855 William Ralph, aged 10, the son of a lead miner, was run over and killed by a wagon 'while incautiously standing on the line at Moorswater'. He was said to have been trespassing.[10] A 19-year-old Looe mason, Charles Medland, was hit by a down train at St Cleer whilst he was crossing the line in May 1878.[11] Both may well have been victims of wagons descending by gravity, in comparative silence.

This was not the case in April 1870 when a young boy, aged 4½, was killed near Lamellion. Henry Rickard Harris and an older brother had gone to the canal to fish, and the brother had just crossed the line when a train came into sight. He told Henry to stay where he was, as did the engine driver, but at the last minute he tried to cross the line to his brother and was hit by the engine. He fell across the rail and the train passed over him, cutting him in half. The coroner's jury decided it was an accidental death and, in a touching gesture, gave their fees to Henry's parents.

Sparks from the engines set light to various things over the years and one day in June 1870 saw two such fires. In the morning a wagon in a train from Looe caught fire south of Liskeard. It was laden with nitrate of soda (used for fertiliser at that time) which burnt rapidly. The *Cornish Times* reported: 'The molten mass ran out like so much molten lead, and the appearance this produced was both singular and picturesque.' That afternoon a train bound for Caradon set light to several acres of plantation near Highwood.

A number of horses and carts seem to have come into contact with trains with varying degrees of damage and small sums in compensation were paid out.

One particular practice that caused accidents was that of leaving wagons standing on the main line at various points to load or unload. Sidings were few and far between on both lines and it became a habit to leave wagons on the line and to pick them up later by propelling them in front of the locomotive. This was the only means to get coals to Looe Gas Works, St Cleer depot and Rule's Shaft coal-yard, for example.

In August 1862 two wagons that had been left to load on the Caradon line ran away and killed four horses that were waiting at Moorswater to haul empty wagons up the line.[12] On the Looe line in April 1877 a train ran into a wagon that had been left near Sandplace to load timber; neither the driver nor guard saw a signal that the line was blocked.

The deteriorating state of the Caradon line in later years was the cause of a number of incidents, mainly derailments which became embarrassingly frequent. A defective coupling caused a train to break in half at Highwood in February 1906 and some damage was done to the rolling stock when the two parts collided, although no-one was hurt.

Locomotives were not allowed on Looe Quay, and LADY MARGARET has come unstuck on one unofficial visit in the first decade of the twentieth century.
GRAHAM ROOSE COLLECTION

By chance Moorswater signal box appears in a corner of an official Great Western photograph of the newly built Moorswater Viaduct, partly obscured by the granite works chimney. This is 1881 and the box is less than a couple of years old.
THE NATIONAL ARCHIVE

Opposite page: The signalman's view of Coombe Junction. Beside the lever frame is the Tyer's electric token equipment installed in 1901. 4559 is leaving for Liskeard. July 1959.
PETER W. GRAY

The comedy of errors that resulted in the line's worst accident, on Friday 15 June 1906, when a train of six carriages ran away from Liskeard, has already been described in Chapter 6. That this resulted in no loss of life was a matter of luck and the whole incident does illustrate the relaxed approach that prevailed on the line towards regulations. This changed rapidly when the GWR took control. One surprising aspect of this is the apparent ability of the track between Coombe Junction and Moorswater to take a train travelling at, allegedly, 60 m.p.h. without throwing it off.

SIGNALLING

It is most unlikely that there was any signalling on either the Caradon or the Looe lines until passenger services commenced on the latter. On the Caradon line, before the introduction of steam locomotives, up trains ran in the morning and down trains, by gravity, in the afternoon. After locomotives were introduced this appears to have continued but each line is likely to have been worked independently on the 'one engine in steam' principle and under these conditions signals were unnecessary.

However, with the introduction of passenger trains on the Looe line, signalling became not only necessary but obligatory; equipment was bought from Stevens & Sons and installed between Colonel Rich's two reports of April and September 1879. Looe was protected by a home signal, with a distant signal 600 yards before, and also had a starting signal for up trains. At Moorswater the signal arms were mounted in pairs on two 20-feet-high posts. Up trains were controlled by a signal post just south of the viaduct; the upper arm was for mineral trains with the lower as a home signal for passengers. The other, down, signal post was opposite the station, the upper arm being the starter for passengers and the lower for down minerals. Safety, or catch, points were interlocked with the signals and a small cabin erected by Silvanus Jenkin south of the station controlled these and one set of points. The signal box was on a stone base with a pyramidical slate roof and an outside staircase ran up the north side. A distant signal also protected Moorswater from the south and the LCR undertook to work the Looe line with one engine in steam.[13] All this survived until the LLR take-over in 1901.

Saxby & Farmer of London provided the signalling equipment for the new line and also for the existing passenger line to Looe. Tyer's

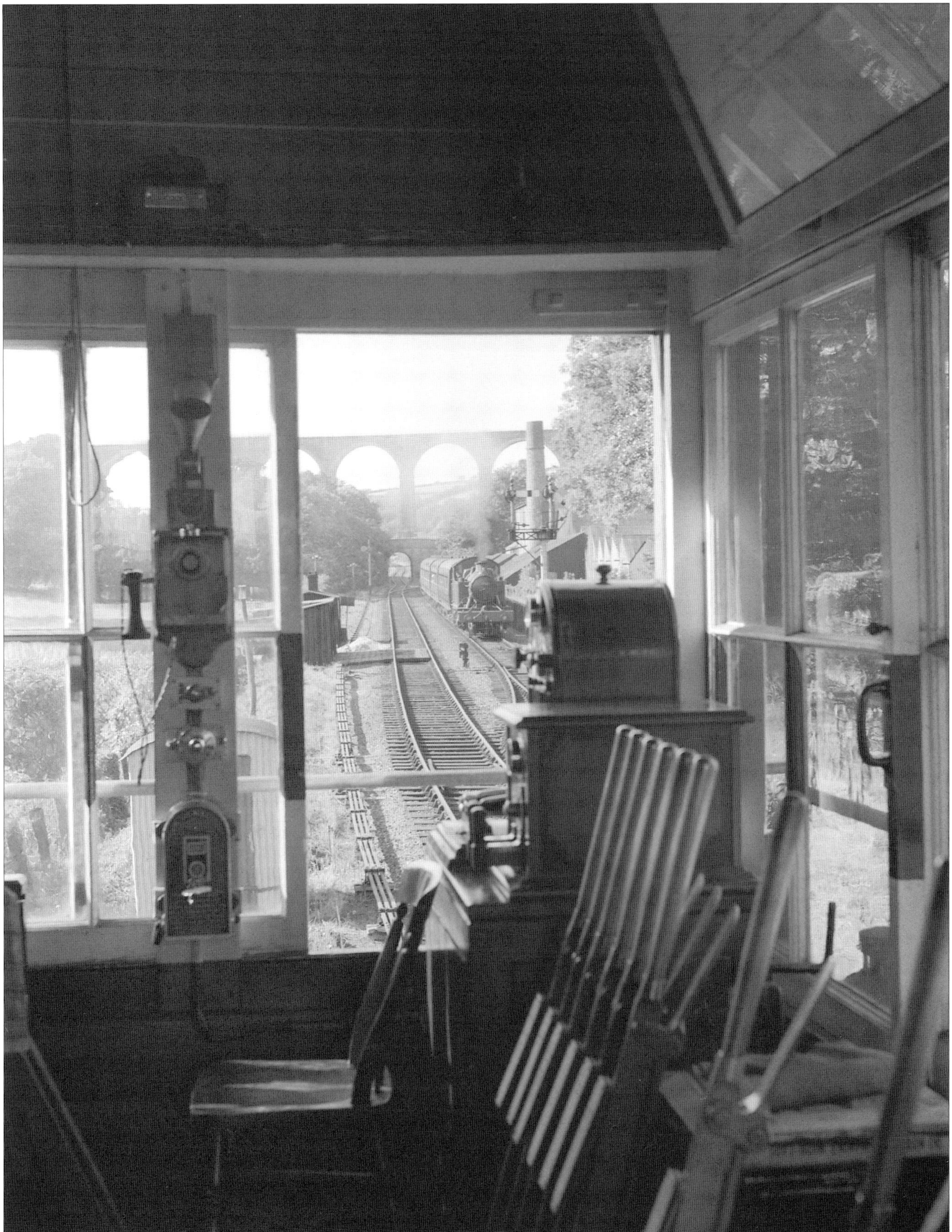

The tiny signal box at Looe housed just seven levers. 9 September 1961.
M. J. MESSENGER

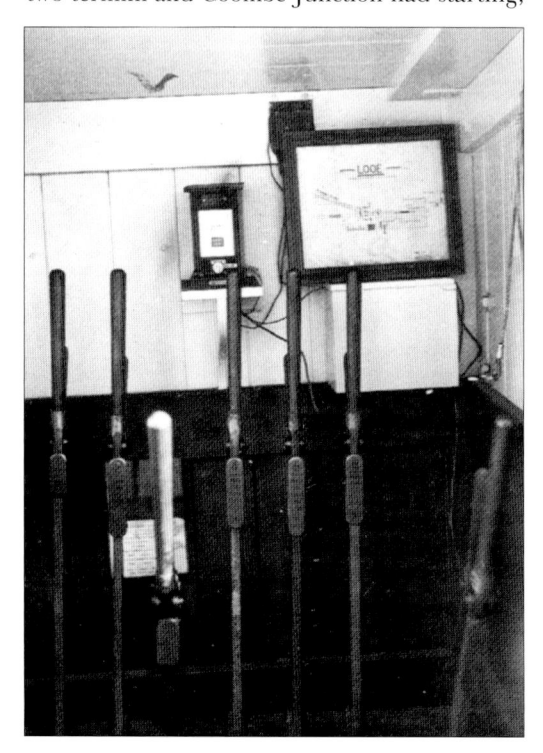

Inside the signal box at the south end of Looe platform. Behind the seven levers is the signalling instrument and the track diagram.
ROBERT TIVENDALE COLLECTION

electric tablets were used for the two sections from Liskeard to Coombe Junction and Coombe to Looe, while a wooden staff sufficed for the section from Coombe to Moorswater. Signal boxes were built at Liskeard, Coombe and Looe, with 18, 26 and 7 levers respectively, although Liskeard and Coombe only used 13 and 21 of the available levers. Very much fuller signalling was erected, although the Caradon line continued much as before – with nothing. The two termini and Coombe Junction had starting, home and distant signals installed but the only intermediate signals were at Terras Crossing, from 1902. Signals were also provided for freight trains leaving the passenger sections at Liskeard, Coombe and Looe to go to the main-line, Moorswater and Looe Harbour respectively. Coombe even boasted a three arm bracket signal to control Moorswater traffic and the approach to the platform by either the southern or the centre crossovers.[14]

The standards were much as the GWR would wish for and no amendments are recorded on their take-over but successive years brought a number of changes. In 1921 Moorswater was reduced to the status of a 'station yard' and the wooden staff withdrawn. At Terras the signalling was modified and a new ground frame installed late in 1929 and the following year all the line's distant signals were changed to yellow arms and lights. Some time between the GWR take-over and the early twenties the signal box at Looe was moved from the platform, where it was within the station buildings, to a small hut at the south end of the platform. A number of changes were made to the signalling at Coombe in 1956 and later in the fifties some signals at Looe and Coombe were replaced by discs but the biggest changes came after dieselisation. On 8 March 1964 Looe and Liskeard boxes and signalling were abolished and the electric tokens between Coombe and Looe replaced by a wooden staff. The token instrument at Liskeard was retained, but transferred to the main-line signal box, to enable clay trains to work to Coombe Junction independently of Looe passenger trains. Subsequently Terras level crossing became ungated on 1 July 1970 and the signals were removed.[15]

Coombe Junction retained much of its previous appearance, the signal box with most of the original 1901 equipment, until May 1981 when the layout was considerably simplified. The signal box was replaced by two ground frames: No 1 at the junction and No 2 south of Lamellion Bridge.

PERMANENT WAY

The original rails of the LCR were wrought iron weighing 40 lb per yard laid in small cast iron chairs on granite sleeper blocks. Although described as Vignoles rail it was a type of single-headed rail of 'T' section with a small flange on the foot, hence the need for the chairs. This was used on the original route, the Kilmar Railway and the Tokenbury and Phoenix branches; about a mile and a half survived until 1909. Some can still be found close to the line below Gonamena. Most was replaced with a heavier flat-bottomed rail spiked direct to the blocks and late in the 1860s a serious effort was made to renew with wooden sleepers. Finance as ever was a problem though and to economise several lengths below South Caradon were laid with alternate wood and granite sleepers. 1,500 surplus granite blocks were sold to Looe Harbour Commissioners in 1866. The Kilmar Junction Railway from Tokenbury to Rillaton was laid on half-round timber sleepers with flat-bottom iron rails. From 1879 steel flat-bottom rails of 95 lb per yard were obtained on a barter system of two tons of old iron rails for one ton of the new.

Stub points can be seen in a number of photographs, taken in the early 1900s. This type of point, common until recently in the north Wales slate quarries, was used on a number of early standard gauge lines in Cornwall and elsewhere and it is quite likely that the LCR and the LLR used it in their early days. Its simplicity, utilising moveable lengths of rails instead of finely tapered point blades, would doubtless appeal to the lines' engineers and it was quite suited to the relatively infrequent, slow moving trains.

The Looe line was also laid with 40 lb rails on chairs and blocks but, from Tregarland down, 56 lb bridge rail was used on longitudinal timber sleepers in broad gauge fashion. The lighter track was replaced by 1879 with 70 and 72 lb flat-bottomed rails on blocks or timber sleepers. Both the bridge rails and the granite blocks survived well into the present century, albeit in a terrible condition.

Joseph Thomas described it as unsafe for passengers in 1901 with some lengths $1^{1}/_{2}$ inches over gauge. In 1905 Holbrook reported that they were replacing the blocks with wooden sleepers but utilising the old blocks on the Caradon line. The GWR replaced the last of the granite blocks on the Looe line – three

The lever frame at Terras Crossing. 9 September 1961.
M. J. MESSENGER

A view along the track near St Cleer. The early T-section rail has been replaced with flat-bottom rail spiked direct to the granite sleeper blocks. Believed to be about 1902.
L&GRP

CARADON & LOOE – THE CANAL, RAILWAYS AND MINES

A carefully posed photograph at Causeland, with staff appearing to ballast the newly laid flat-bottom track and clean up the platform. The hut is in good condition and is likely to have been recently refurbished. The photograph probably dates from soon after the GWR takeover in 1909. The timetable is a Great Western local one but the poster advertises the Great Northern East Coast route.
AUTHOR'S COLLECTION

A view along the track at Tremabe, under the road bridge that has now been filled in. Repairs have replaced some sleeper blocks with timber cross sleepers, but in horse-drawn days the trackbed would have been level between the rails as a path for the horses.
AUTHOR'S COLLECTION

miles survived in 1905 – during or after the Great War and these must have been amongst the last in this country to carry passengers. The GWR also relaid some sections of the Caradon line. The extension to Liskeard was laid with bull-head rail in chairs in the best practice of the time.

The GWR's Motor Economic System of track maintenance, using petrol-driven platelayers' trolleys, was introduced in 1932.

The Looe branch now conforms to standard Railtrack practice with flat-bottom rail of 113 lb per yard replacing the previous 98 lb per yard. In many places wooden sleepers have given way to concrete and only the sinuous route, with its many flange greasers, now gives away the line's humble origins.

152

CHAPTER ELEVEN
THE FUTURE

When the first edition of this book was written there was no real future to consider. The canal was long gone, overgrown and forgotten, while the Caradon line made a good walk around Caradon Hill and across the moors, but lower down was overgrown and being absorbed into fields. The branch line was still active but, despite having escaped one closure proposal, it still retained the sword of Damocles that threatened most rural branch lines.

It is that very amnesia that has been the saving of the canal. Lying hidden in the undergrowth and protected by being behind railway boundaries its remains, such as they are, have survived and now a new generation is ready to discover it. Caradon District Council recognised the potential of the long-dormant canal remains and commissioned the British Waterways Board to survey them. The need to secure the remains and to make them accessible was part of an overall plan to widen tourism and to spread it further than the present over-used popular sites. Clearly it would be impractical, or impossibly expensive, to restore the canal to full working order as the construction of the railway in 1860 put a positive end to its working life. So a partial restoration was proposed to conserve certain key accessible points, providing interpretation and linking them by trails for walkers and cyclists. To support these aims the East Looe Valley Improvement Society was formed in April 2000 at a well attended meeting at St Keyne but these plans seem to have faltered.

On Caradon Hill the County Archaeological Unit has surveyed the remains of all periods – not just mines and railways – around Minions, as it has done more recently at Moorswater. The potential for leisure and tourism has at last been recognised and, fortunately, people are interested in their past, particularly when it is in beautiful surroundings. A visitor centre is now housed in the engine house of Houseman's Shaft at Minions. In 2006 the Cornwall and West Devon Mining Landscape was granted World Heritage Site status and this includes not just the mining areas of Caradon Hill but most of the route of the Liskeard & Caradon Railway from a little north of Moorswater.

No doubt the success of the Camel Trail, on the former railway trackbed between Wadebridge, Padstow and Wenford Bridge, and of the Mineral Tramways Trail in west Cornwall have been an inspiration, but a similar trail on the Liskeard & Caradon trackbed may not be a feasible proposition as its ownership is now in many different hands, particularly below Polwrath.

The branch line itself, down to Looe, is also being actively promoted, not only as easy access to the charms of Looe but for the attractions of the ride down the Looe Valley as well. Free car parking is offered at Liskeard to encourage visitors to Looe to use the train. The activities of Devon & Cornwall Rail Partnership are having beneficial results, with considerable effort to promote the line both for tourism and local people. Since 1997 the European Regional Development Fund has made monies available to promote the branch lines of the south west and in 1999 about £16,000 was spent on the Looe line. This has resulted in some excellent publicity leaflets and the helpful information displays at stations. Substantial grants have also been made by the Countryside Agency and the Regional Development Fund with beneficial results. As noted in Chapter 7, the future of the branch line is a lot less precarious than for many years although the need of its operating company to renew its franchise periodically, or even face another bidder for the right to run the branch line, means there is always uncertainty.

The Liskeard & Looe Railway's part in the local community has changed considerably in the past few decades but a service is still provided and a century and a half of this tradition has not yet ceased. With attention now being given to their charms it is to be hoped that the Liskeard & Looe Union Canal and the Liskeard & Caradon Railway will, in a somewhat different way, also return to providing a service to the community in the twenty-first century.

It is incumbent on all who read this book to take advantage of these facilities, to travel on the branch line and to visit and explore, or re-explore, the other remains. It is only use and continued public interest that will ensure their survival for the future.

Above can be seen some of the present-day signs dotted along the Looe Valley directing to the stations on the Looe line.
M. J. MESSENGER

The new shelter erected at St Keyne in 1998, at the same time as that at Sandplace.
M. J. MESSENGER

SOURCES & ACKNOWLEDGEMENTS

'Merely corroborative detail, intended to give artistic verisimilitude to an otherwise bald and unconvincing narrative.'
POOH-BAH 1885

The story of these transport systems has been sadly neglected in the past and frequently misrepresented. Some very fundamental mistakes have been made, even by that doyen of the GWR, MacDermot, and perpetuated by writers of less standing. It says much for the standing of MacDermot that errors he published in 1927, such as the opening dates of both the LCR and the LLR, should still be quoted despite clear evidence in correction.

In recent times there have been other publications which have attempted to tell the same story but which differ in some important details. One in particular, fortunately now out of print, had remarkable similarities to a chapter of the first edition of this book but its unacknowledged sources could be clearly traced to an article of mine in the *Journal of the Trevithick Society*. Alas, its author did not copy all the words, with some disastrous results. I have assembled this story almost entirely from original or contemporary sources with but rare resort to existing published works and, when making comparisons, I can only suggest that readers check that an author has had the confidence to state his sources. Sadly, despite my first putting my researches into the public realm over thirty years ago, some most extraordinary accounts are still being published; history is based on facts, not what the writer wants it to be.

The prime source for both railways and canal has been the Companies' Minute Books, preserved in The National Archives. Other items of a railway and an official nature in the same hands have added meat to the bones of the story, as has much valuable information in the records of the Duchy of Cornwall. The Buller family papers in the County Record Office at Truro and the files of the *Royal Cornwall Gazette* at the Royal Institution of Cornwall proved enormously helpful in tracing the early history of the canal. Local newspapers, *The West Briton* and *The Cornish Times*, in addition to the *Royal Cornwall Gazette*, have been a great benefit throughout the period under study although time has not, alas, been sufficient to read them completely. Much valuable information has been gleaned from Parliamentary records at the Parliamentary Archives and the British Library and from the letter books of the Looe Harbour Commissioners. *The Mining Journal*, both the files at Redruth Cornish Studies Library and in Justin Brooke's private collection, were essential reading for the mining story. Many precious 'snippets', large and small, have come from friends but the most important source for the many smaller, but equally essential, details particularly of the twentieth century has been the vast files of C. R. Clinker.

It is gratifying that no major errors or omissions came to light following the publication of the first edition. Nor have any major new sources of information surfaced, although the good work published by Norman Burrows and by the Cornwall Archaeological Unit must be acknowledged. The second and third editions have benefited from research which has added additional detail and clarified a few outstanding mysteries. A much wider range of photographs and illustrations has also become available, with obvious benefits.

As a general rule information emanating from the Minute Books and official company papers has not been specifically identified although other sources have.

My thanks expressed in the first edition have not diminished with time and I repeat them again. First and foremost my thanks must go to the late C. R. Clinker for his valuable and unstinting guidance and assistance. I am honoured to have had such a mentor. The mining story in this book would have been very much the poorer without the help of Justin Brooke and free access to his own extensive researches. It is iniquitous to have to single out a few of the many individuals who have helped but my gratitude must be given to E. Craven, Mrs Maud Crowle, the Lord Eliot, George Davies, Charles Hadfield, J. Heath, A.K. Hamilton Jenkin, R. J. Law, Stanley Opie (of the Duchy of Cornwall Library), the late W. H. Paynter, Miss Ruth M. Phillips, K. P. Plant, C.G. Skinner (of British Railways), Peter Stanier and Douglas Vosper. Perhaps I may include the rest by thanking my many friends in the Trevithick Society, the Railway & Canal Historical Society, the Plymouth Railway Circle and the Industrial Railway Society.

In addition to the staff and officers of the organisations and institutions mentioned above I must mention those of the British Association, Exeter City (now Devon) Record Office, North Devon Athenaeum and Plymouth City Library Local History Section.

One of the many good things that came about following the first edition has been the contact with descendants of some of the players in the story; Keith Retallick, Paul Roberts (Glubb, Sargent and Lang) and Cliff Trethewey. Rather sadder is the death of a number of people who helped me, some were good friends; Miss Ruth Phillips and Messrs. Clinker, Davies, Hadfield, Jenkin, Opie and Vosper are no longer with us.

Photographs are acknowledged to their source where-ever possible. Many photographs, particularly older ones, tend to circulate in various collections but I have tried to ascertain their correct origins in all cases.

Peter Stanier has been of continuous help since we first met in the Cheesewring Hotel over forty years ago, and additional help with these new editions has also come from Stephen Bartlett, Gerry Beale, Grahame Boyes, Angela Broome (Courtney Library of the Royal Cornwall Museum), Paul Burkhalter, Richard Burningham, Norman Burrows, Roger Carpenter, John Corkett, Tony Crofts, Maurice Dart, Bryan Gibson, the Library of the Institution of Civil Engineers, Dr Michael Lewis, John Mann, Dr Dan McCarthy, Middlesbrough Central Library, Neil Parkhouse, Mrs Joyce Paton, Roger Penhallurick (Royal Cornwall Museum), John Rapson, R. C. Riley, Graham Roose, Bob Spalding and Robert Tivendale. If I have omitted anybody then my humble apologies are offered. With rare exception I have been hospitably received wherever my researches have taken me and invariably my requests for assistance have been generously responded to.

BIBLIOGRAPHY

Allen, J. *History of the Borough of Liskeard* 1856
Barrie D. S. & 'Precursor' (C. R. Clinker) 'From Looe to the Cheesewring' *Railway Magazine* vol. 33 1935
Barton, D. B. *A Historical Survey of the Mines and Mineral Railways of East Cornwall and West Devon* 1964
Barton, D. B. *The Cornish Beam Engine* 1969
Barton, D. B. *Essays in Cornish Mining History, Vol 2* 1971
Beale, G. *The Liskeard and Looe Branch* 2000
Bennett, Alan *The Great Western Railway in East Cornwall* 1990
Bond, T. *Topographical & Historical Sketches of the Boroughs of East and West Looe* 1823
British Railways Board *The Reshaping of British Railways* [The Beeching Report] 1963
Burrows, N. S. 'The Rolling Stock of the Liskeard & Caradon and Liskeard & Looe Railways 1844-1923' *Historical Model Railway Society Journal* vol. 10 1980,1981
Burt, Waite & Burnley *Cornish Mines* 1987
Caunter, F. L. *Under the Surface* c1960
Childs, J. Borlase Letter to A. K. Hamilton Jenkin 5 April 1929
Chisholm, A. J. 'A Cornish Railway and its Engines' *Locomotive Magazine* v.3 1898
Collins, J. H. *London & West Country Chamber of Mines Year Book* 1907 et seq.
Collins, J. H. *Observations on the West of England Mining Region* 1912
Collins, Wilkie *Rambles beyond Railways* 1851, rep 1948
Cornwall Archaeological Unit *The Minions Area, Archaeological Survey & Management* 1989
Cornwall Archaeological Unit *Moorswater, an Archaeological Survey* 1999
Deacon, B. 'Migration and the Mining Industry in East Cornwall in the mid-19th Century' *Journal of the Royal Institution of Cornwall* 1986-7
George, Brian *James Green, Canal Builder and County Surveyor 1781-1849* 1997
Goodman, F. 'The Liskeard & Caradon Railway' *Railway Magazine* vol. 4 1899
Green, James. *Report on a Canal, Rail Road and Turnpike between Looe and Liskeard* 1823
Grigson, Geoffrey *Freedom of the Parish* 1954
Harman, Fred W. *The History and Locomotives of the Tees Engine Works* 1999
Hutchings, W. J. *Cornwall Constabulary 1857-1957*, c1957
Isham, K. *Lime Kilns and Limeburners in Cornwall* 2000
Jenkin, A. K. H. *Mines & Miners of Cornwall, Part XII* 1966
Leach, E. *A Treatise of Universal Inland Navigation* c1785
Leifchild, J. R. *Cornwall: Its Mines and Miners* 1857
Looker, S. J. *Cock-fighting and Game Fowl, from the notebooks of Herbert Atkinson* 1938
Marshall, W. *Rural Economy of the West of England* 1796
Matthews & Tuke *History of Barclays Bank Ltd* 1926
Measom, G. *Guide to the Cornwall Railway* 1864
Messenger, M. J. 'Passenger Traffic on the Liskeard & Caradon Railway' *Jno. Railway & Canal Historical Society* 1973
Messenger, M. J. 'The Liskeard & Looe Canal' *Jno. Trevithick Society* 1974
Messenger, M. J. 'The Demise of a Successful Canal' *Jno. Railway & Canal Historical Society* 1976
Messenger, M. J. 'Boatmen on the Liskeard & Looe Union Canal' *Jno. Railway & Canal Historical Society* 2010
Messenger, M. J. *The Bodmin & Wadebridge Railway 1834-1983* 2012
Messenger, M. J. 'Sources of Finance for early Cornish Railways' *Early Railways 5* 2014
Michell, J. *A History of St Neot* 1833
Mitchell, V. & Smith, K. *Branch Line to Looe* 1998
Murray's *Handbook for Devon & Cornwall* 1859, rep 1971
Polsue *A Parish History of Cornwall* 1870
Priestley *Navigable Rivers & Canals* 1831
Rowe, J. *Cornwall in the Age of the Industrial Revolution* 1953
R.C.T.S. *Locomotives of the Great Western Railway Part 3* 1956
Smyth, J. *A History of Looe* 1950
Stanier, Peter 'Granite Working in the Cheesewring District of Bodmin Moor' *Journal of the Trevithick Society* 1985
Stanier, Peter 'The Granite Quarrying Industry in Devon and Cornwall' *Industrial Archaeology Review* 1985, 1986
Stanier, Peter *The Minions Moor* 1986, 1996
Stanier, Peter 'Early Mining and Water Power in the Caradon Mining District of Eastern Cornwall' *Journal of the Trevithick Society* 1987
Stanier, Peter *South-West Granite* 1999
Thompson, Ian *Cornish Milestones* 2013
Webb & Geach *History & Progress of Mining in the Liskeard & Caradon District* 1863
Woodfin, R. J. *The Centenary of the Cornwall Railway* 1960

REFERENCES

Abbreviations:
BL   British Library
CRO   Cornwall Record Office
CT   *The Cornish Times*
DCL   Duchy of Cornwall Library
DRO   Devon Record Office
HC   House of Commons
HL   House of Lords
LHC   Looe Harbour Commissioners
MJ   *The Mining Journal*
PA   Parliamentary Archives
RCG   *Royal Cornwall Gazette*
TNA   The National Archives
WB   *West Briton*

Printed sources are identified by author, and detailed in full in the Bibliography.

Chapter 1: Beginnings
1. Allen 1856; Marshall 1796
2. Leach c1785
3. Bond 1823; RCG 23 December 1824
4. RCG 9 August 1823
5. Green 1823
6. CRO Buller papers DDBU 648
7. RCG 25 December 1824
8. PA HC Journal; CRO Rashleigh Papers DDR 5100 & 5101
9. RCG 12 March 1825
10. PA Estimate & Subscription List, Liskeard & Looe Union Canal Act 1825
11. RCG 23 July 1825
12. RCG 17 July 1826
13. CRO DDBU 648

Chapter 2: The Canal
1. Allen 1856
2. DCL Petitions, Report dated 16 November 1826 and correspondence
3. Michell 1833
4. CRO DDBU 648
5. Messenger 2010
6. TNA RAIL 367/5 LLUC Engineers' Report 30 September 1857
7. WB 7 June 1833
8. TNA RAIL 367/1 LLUC Minute Books 2 February 1836
9. LHC Letter Book; 28 October 1850 Letter to Capt. Washington RN
10. CRO DDR 3829 Letter 2 October 1847 from Richard Retallick
11. CRO DDR 3829 Letter 25 August 1854 George Taylor to Thomas Coode
12. Childs 1929
13. LHC Letter Book; 28 October 1850
14. TNA RAIL 367/5 LLUC Engineers' Report 30 September 1857
15. PA Minutes of Evidence HC Cornwall Railway Act 1846
16. RCG 4 January 1861
17. William Pease's Diaries
18. CRO DDBU 810
19. CRO DDBU 810
20. CRO DDBU 810
21. TNA RAIL 1057/563; TNA RAIL 893/6 13 June 1911 Licence, GWR to Admiral Charles H. Cross.

Chapter 3: Horses and Gravity
1. MJ 8 May 1858, 30 January 1869, 28 September 1872, 12 May 1883
2. Allen 1856; MJ 27 May 1882
3. Webb & Geach 1863
4. MJ 25 February 1844
5. DCL Memorial of John Trethewey 24 February 1843
6. MJ 11 October 1862
7. DCL LCR Prospectus, undated
8. TNA LCR Circular 19 December 1842
9. CRO PDR 10/1 LCR Deposited Plans
10. MJ 20 May 1843
11. DCL Correspondence and reports; WB 8 March 1844
12. DCL Duchy Council Minute 14 December 1844
13. WB 6 December 1844
14. WB 20 March 1846
15. Murray 1859; A similar account of gravity traffic appears in Measom 1864
16. BL Parliamentary Papers, Returns to the Board of Trade of Employees 1847-1859
17. Diary of William Pease 10 March 1843
18. DCL Correspondence and reports
19. Webb & Geach 1863; Collins 1912
20. Jenkin 1966 gives a fuller account of the smaller Caradon mines.
21. Census Returns 1851; Deacon 1987
22. Jenkin 1966
23. Hutchings 1957
24. Rowe 1953
25. MJ 4 May 1844
26. Collins 1851; [A remarkably similar, although more highly coloured, description also appears in Leifchild 1857]
27. Webb & Geach 1863
28. Allen 1856
29. RCG 3 September 1858

Chapter 4: The Steam Railways
1. CT 14 January 1860
2. Leifchild 1857
3. CT 9 August 1862
4. LHC Letter Book; CT 27 December 1862
5. LHC Letter Book 1 September 1864 Charles Tregenna to Christopher Childs
6. Collins 1907
7. Webb & Geach 1863
8. Collins 1912
9. WB 28 June 1850
10. CT 25 August 1877
11. Childs 1929
12. LHC Letter Book 29 August 1869 Charles Tregenna to J. J. Trathan
13. WB 7 May 1872
14. *Western Daily Mercury* 28 May 1868
15. RCG 30 November 1877
16. CRO DDBU 810 Buller Papers
17. TNA MT6/280/1 Board of Trade papers
18. PA Minutes of Evidence HL LCR Act 1884; CT 29 March 1884

Chapter 5: Hopes & Despair
1. MJ 24 June 1882
2. DRO Rodd papers 49/1/144/2-5 LCR prospectuses and letters
3. CT 9 December 1882
4. TNA BT286/551 South Caradon Mine Ltd
5. PA Minutes of Evidence HL & HC Liskeard & Caradon Railway Act 1884
6. PA Minutes of Evidence HL & HC Liskeard & Caradon Railway Act 1884
7. TNA RAIL 1005/185 4 July 1884 J. C. Isaac to J. B. Childs
8. *Railway & Travel Monthly* November 1910

9 Undated paper by H. L. Hopwood, courtesy G. Roose
10 CRO SR/Darite/1
11 CT 2 December 1882
12 MJ 31 October 1885
13 Liskeard & Caradon Railway Act 1887 50-l Victoria cap.cxxvi
14 Collins 1907
15 Liskeard & Caradon Railway Act 1892 55-6 Victoria cap.cliii
16 TNA MT6/767/1 Board of Trade papers
17 Goodman 1899

Chapter 6: Change of Direction
1 CT 25 May 1901
2 PA Minutes of Evidence HL Liskeard & Caradon Railway Act 1884
3 Goodman 1899
4 CT 18 May 1901
5 CRO PDR 10/18 Deposited Plans; Liskeard & Looe Junction Railway 1892
6 Agreement 2 March 1895 appended to Liskeard & Looe Railway Extension Act 1895
7 TNA 1897 Circular to LLR shareholders
8 Looe Museum, undated paper by J. A. Chambers
9 TNA 18 January 1898 Circular Special Report to LLR shareholders
10 CT 18 May 1901
11 TNA RAIL 1057/557 11 May 1901 Report by Joseph Thomas
12 A very full account of the day's proceedings appears in CT 18 May 1901
13 CT 18 May 1901
14 *The Times* 26 October 1901
15 *The Law Times* 12 December 1903
16 TNA RAIL 1057/557 August 1901 Report by Arthur Stride
17 TNA RAIL 367/6 Report 5.1.1909 by W. H. Waister, GWR Running Dept
18 TNA RAIL 10571569/1 H. H. Holbrook's Report to the LLR Directors 16 June 1906;
    CT 16 June 1906;
    Caunter 1960
19 TNA RAIL 1057/556 7 November 1907 Report by J. A. Chambers
20 Collins 1907 et seq.
21 TNA RAIL 1057/551 21 October 1908 GWR Board Minute; Looe Museum, unda ted paper by J. A. Chambers
22 TNA RAIL 1057/552 2 March 1907 Declaration of Trust J. E. P. Spicer and GWR
23 TNA RAIL 1057/551 10 June 1908 Letter GWR Solicitor to GWR Chairman;
    Matthews & Tuke 1926

Chapter 7: The Great Western and after
1 Collins 1907; Barton 1969
2 DCL Report 16 January 1934
3 s.39 of 21-22 George 5.cap.lxi
4 TNA RAIL 367/3 LLR Minute Book 21 February 1913
5 TNA RAIL 250/736 GWR *Report on Branch Lines* 1926
6 TNA RAIL 266/45 GWR Traffic dealt with at Stations
7 Barrie & 'Precursor' 1935; *GWR Magazine* September 1937; CRO PDR 25/18 Deposited Plans; GWR (Additional Powers) Railway No 2 1935
8 British Railways Board 1963;
   Western Morning News 2 July 1963
9 TNA MT 124/745
10 J. R. Barker, British Railways, Bristol.
11 I am grateful to Richard Burningham of the Devon and Cornwall Rail Partnership for information on the Looe Valley Line Working Party.
12 Office of Rail Regulation, Station usage statistics www.orr.gov.uk/statistics

Chapter 8: From the Sea to the Moor
1 Leifchild 1857. The full quotation reads: 'Hallo! here is a rough tramroad - a real rough tramroad over the moor here! Why, there must be spirits here who travel by railway, for nothing of human kind or art is here. Let us follow it.'
2 Priestley 1831
3 WB 6 June 1898
4 CT 18 May 1901
5 Stanier 1999
6 Goodman 1899
7 RCG 12 October 1855 (The advertisement which gives the details of the lime kilns is also that in which Evan Hopkins advertised for sale a coal store that belonged to the LLUC.)
8 TNA RAIL 367/6 Report on the LLR at the take-over by the GWR
9 CRO X103/5/1
10 I am grateful to S. C. Crispin for this suggestion
11 DCL Letter 19 January 1844
12 DCL Report on the Manor of Rillaton, G. Richardson 2 September 1861
13 *Western Daily Mercury* 28 May 1868

Chapter 9: Locomotives and Rolling Stock
1 TNA RAIL 367/5 LLUC Engineers' Report 5 February 1861;
   RCG 28 December 1860;
   CT 22 December 1860
2 I am grateful to Mr E. Craven for much information on the Bury locomotives of the London & Birmingham Railway.
3 Childs 1929
4 Harman 1999
5 Chisholm 1898
6 RCTS 1956 (I am grateful to this publication of the RCTS for most of the technical details of the LCR locomotives quoted and would refer the reader there for fuller information.)
7 K. P. Plant has kindly made available to me much information from the Peckett records now in the possession of himself and the Industrial Railway Society.
8 WB 20 March 1846
9 Childs 1929
10 TNA MT6/767/1
11 Patent No 434, 31 January 1880
12 Goodman 1899
13 See Burrows for a full and lucid discussion of the finer aspects of LCR and LLR rolling stock.

Chapter 10: Men and Machines
1 CRO Buller Papers 9 September 1829 Copy letter from John Buller to B. H. Lyne
2 PA Minutes of Evidence, East & West Looe Harbour Bill 1848
3 Allen 1856;
   RCG 1 April 1876;
   CT 1 April 1876
4 Allen 1856
5 CT 3 April 1869
6 Barton 1971
7 I am grateful to the late Miss R. M. Phillips for much useful information regarding her forebear, Silvanus Jenkin.
8 CT 18 May 1901
9 CT 22 November 1902
10 BL, Parliamentary Papers, Return of Railway Accidents 1855
11 CT 18 May 1878
12 CT 9 August 1862
13 TNA MT6/236/1;
    Goodman 1899
14 CT 18 May 1901
15 I am grateful to the records of C. R. Clinker for most of the details of the changes that took place during the GWR period and later.

APPENDIX ONE
CHRONOLOGY

1777	Leach's canal proposal
1795	Bentley & Bolton's canal proposal
1823	James Green's Report on Canal, Rail Road or Turnpike Road
1824	Meeting at Liskeard to revive plan
1825	Liskeard & Looe Union Canal Act
1827	Canal partially in use (Aug)
1829	Canal road built
1837	South Caradon Mine raised first copper ore
1840	West Caradon Mine commenced
1842	Meeting at Liskeard to propose Liskeard & Caradon Railway
1843	Liskeard & Caradon Railway Act
1844	LCR construction commenced (Feb)
	LCR opened Cheesewring and South Caradon to Tremabe (28 Nov)
1846	LCR opened Tremabe to Moorswater (8 Mar?)
1848	Looe Harbour Commissioners established
1852	Phoenix Mine struck copper ore
1853	Cheesewring Granite sett taken over by Tregelles & Crouch
1854	Phoenix Mine tramway built
1856	Kilmar Granite sett taken
1857	Jenkin & Trathan report on a railway to Looe
1858	Liskeard & Looe Railway Act
	Kilmar Railway opened (26 Aug)
1859	Cornwall Railway opened Plymouth to Truro (2 May)
1860	Liskeard & Caradon Railway Act
	LLUC open railway Moorswater to Looe (27 Dec)
1861	LCR Tokenbury branch opened
1862	Joint Committee formed between LLUC and LCR
1863	Peak of Caradon copper production
	Cheesewring Quarry taken over by Freeman
1864	Phoenix Mine re-equipped for tin production
1868	Bearah Quarry branch built
1869	Phoenix branch built
1870	Agreement re Kilmar Junction Railway made
1871	New Cheesewring branch built
1877	Marke Valley branch built
	Kilmar Junction Railway opened (2 Nov) and Gonamena incline abandoned
1878	LLUC leased to LCR (29 Jan)
1879	Sandplace siding built
	Moorswater - Causeland - Looe opened for passengers (11 Sept)
1881	Sandplace station opened (Sept/Oct)
	Cheesewring and Kilmar quarries stop work
1882	South Caradon give notice of abandonment (May)
	LCR Act authorising Trewint line
1884	Cheesewring Quarry recommenced
	Trewint line construction commenced
	LCR Act authorising Launceston line
	Col. Rich's inspection of LCR and suggestion of free passengers (Aug)
1885	South Caradon Mine finally abandoned (July)
1886	Lewis Foster appointed Receiver of LCR (13 Oct)
1890	Marke Valley Mine abandoned
1895	Liskeard & Looe Railway Extension Act
1896	'Free' passenger service ceased
1898	Phoenix Mine closed
1901	LLR extension opened (8 May) and LCR taken over
1902	St Keyne station opened (1 Sept)
1904	First clay traffic from Moorswater
1907	Phoenix Mine leased
	Lewis Foster calls for a Receiver of the LLR to be appointed
1908	Captain Spicer acquires LCR
1909	GWR commence working LLR and LCR (1 Jan)
	Great Western Railway, Liskeard & Looe and Liskeard & Caradon Railway Act
	LCR vested in GWR
1914	Phoenix Mine finally abandoned
1917	LCR closed 'temporarily' and rails lifted (1 Jan)
1923	LLR vested in GWR (1 Jan)
1931	LCR legally abandoned
1933	St Germans to Looe direct line proposed
1948	Nationalisation (1 Jan)
1951	Sandplace siding closed (18 June)
1963	'Beeching Report'
	Freight traffic, except clay from Moorswater, ceased (4 Nov)
1966	Ministry of Transport refused closure (20 Sept)
1968	Looe station becomes unstaffed
1996	Moorswater china clay dry ceased production
2001	Looe branch enters the twenty-first century, still running

APPENDIX TWO
TRAFFIC FIGURES AND ACCOUNTS

Date	Goods (tons)	Income £	GrossProfit £	%	Passengers	Goods (tons)	Income £	Gross Profit £	%	Notes
1847		1,772								
1848		1,996	783	39						
1849	10,252	1,887	709	38	21,713					
1850	11,244	1,986	821	41						
1851	10,705	1,988	780	39						
1852	11,191	1,953	731	37						
1853	13,152	2,404	1,095	46						
1854	20,462	3,603	1,665	46			2,025	1,421	70	
1855	24,119	4,215	1,913	45			2,311	1,687	73	
1856	26,450	4,760	2,275	48			2,461	1,734	70	
1857	26,791	4,874	2,389	49			2,419	1,753	72	
1858	28,650	5,114	2,439	48	44,505		2,290	1,706	74	
1859	32,191	5,514	2,673	48	48,193		2,525	1,892	75	
1860	32,028	5,494	2,407	44	45,555		2,303	1,540	67	
1861	37,101	6,458	2,495	39	44,272		4,833	2,379	49	
1862	43,902	7,678	1,382	18	56,855		6,216	2,440	39	1
1863	48,326	8,440	960	11	62,212		6,795	3,094	46	
1864	48,386	8,386	(41)	-	62,285		6,643	2,932	44	
1865	48,655	8,404	(698)	-	63,286		6,743	2,764	41	
1866	42,144	7,219	858	12	56,270		5,948	2,356	40	
1867	40,472	6,769	864	13	55,334		5,837	2,457	42	
1868	61,863	16,021	3,752	23			6,008	2,550	42	
1869		16,068	1,989	12			6,244	2,195	35	
1870		15,280	2,345	15			5,723	2,377	42	
1871	54,813	14,830	3,179	21			5,530	2,183	39	
1872	57,096	13,762	2,337	17			5,347	1,753	33	
1873	51,205	12,874	2,384	19			5,198	2,266	44	
1874	44,642	11,284	2,163	19			4,387	1,821	42	
1875	44,004	11,341	2,076	18			4,374	1,275	29	
1876	47,881	12,027	1,840	15			4,604	1,368	30	
1877		11,711	1,068	9			4,581	1,869	41	
1878		9,197	1,397	15						2
1879		9,079	2,079	23						
1880	45,464	9,876	2,649	27	19,932					
1881	39,837	8,286	2,703	33	19,726					
1882	40,899	8,320	375	45	21,565					
1883	39,423	8,005	3,630	45	21,733		1,460	1,321	90	
1884	35,455	7,107	2,706	38	19,667		1,395	1,270	91	
1885	33,283	6,909	2,109	31	22,767		1,401	1,274	91	
1886	24,148	4,507	857	19	25,429		1,408	1,263	90	
1887	23,822	5,037	1,748	35	25,977		1,411	1,257	89	
1888	27,002	4,729	1,318	28	19,186		1,706	1,547	91	
1889	27,806	4,929	1,039	21	21,293		1,710	1,609	94	
1890	24,664	4,638	1,136	24	24,110		1,717	1,614	94	
1891	22,429	4,280	725	17	22,852		1,712	1,610	94	
1892		4,268	735	17	23,031		1,710	1,605	94	
1893	18,833	3,645	191	5	24,789		1,715	1,614	94	
1894	21,835	4,112	699	17	24,469		1,722	1,651	96	
1895	16,401	2,997	233	8	24,827		1,721	1,615	94	
1896	17,265	3,102	324	10	23,989		1,723	1,645	95	
1897	18,080	3,167	27	1	23,654		1,723	1,651	96	

APPENDIX TWO – CONTINUED

Date	Goods (tons)	Income £	Gross £	Profit %	Passengers	Goods (tons)	Income £	Gross Profit £	%	Notes
1898	14,380	2,769	(374)		24,983		1,720	1,620	94	
1899	15,536	2,845	(382)		23,626		1,725	1,645	95	
1900	13,214	2,598	(192)		26,583		1,716	1,629	95	
1901	4,241	672	(671)		5,056 to 8 May 1901					3
from 8 May 1901					42,502	10,028	2,972	(144)	-	
1902		29	(238)		55,224	15,411	4,249	97	2	
1903		71	(10)		60,490	21,884	5,160	411	1	
1904		116	71	61	64,129	27,534	5,672	921	16	
1905		112	60	54	64,436	38,199	6,657	1,023	15	
1906		74	33	45	69,066	29,925	5,975	351	6	
1907		78	29	37	70,654	21,447	6,418	500	8	
1908		70	31	44	70,798	18,811	5,575	1,295	23	
1909							1,403	1,334	95	4
1910							1,422	1,334	94	
1911							1,264	1,181	93	
1912							1,217	1,135	93	
1913										
1914							1,282	1,178	92	
1915							1,255	1,143	91	
1916							1,272	1,164	92	
1917							1,258	1,161	92	
1918							1,266	1,153	91	
1919							1,275	1,211	95	
1920							1,320	1,225	93	
1921							1,309	1,214	93	
1922							1,307	1,222	94	5

Figures in brackets indicate a loss.

Notes:

1	1861	LLUC's canal replaced by railway and steam introduced on the LCR.
2	1878	LLUC formally leased by LCR.
3	1901	LLR gains control of its own railway and of the LCR.
4	1909	LCR vested in GWR and LLR worked by GWR
5	1923	LLR vested in GWR

APPENDIX THREE
COPPER & TIN PRODUCTION OF THE CARADON DISTRICT

Year	South Caradon	West Caradon	Marke Valley	Phoenix (Copper)	Gonamena	Craddock Moor	East Caradon	Glasgow Caradon	All Cornwall	Phoenix (Tin)	West Phoenix	South Phoenix	Marke Valley
1845	4,631	4,457	165										
1846	4,159	4,736	853										
1847	4,570	4,135	1,016										
1848	3,473	3,668	1,209	194	75								
1849	2,965	3,966	1,359	150									
1850	2,999	4,049	1,612	720	96								
1851	2,818	4,128	1,701	962	159								
1852	2,834	4,048	2,021	1,338	243								
1853	2,871	4,355	2,466	2,068	391								
1854	3,006	4,018	2,330	3,005	50					5.5			
1855	3,679	3,941	2,318	3,543					161,576	11.8			
1856	4,694	4,313	2,316	4,581	780	623			163,958	9.5			
1857	4,538	4,217	1,884	5,170	862	989			152,729	4.8			
1858	4,995	3,702	1,377	4,965	675	1,252			147,330	4.8			
1859	5,164	3,778	1,533	4,260	784	1,433			146,093	2.6			
1860	5,232	3,936	3,114	4,444	961	1,434	836		145,359	4.5			
1861	4,777	3,166	3,983	5,337	937	1,755	2,773		143,119	13.1			
1862	5,460	3,090	4,821	4,628	31	1,879	5,265		141,810	21.5			
1863	5,846	2,520	4,912	5,656		2,083	5,911		129,221	28.4			
1864	5,744	1,834	5,020	5,142	373	1,663	5,933	862	127,033	131.8			
1865	6,306	1,270	5,174	4,662	678	1,247	5,098	888	121,353	178.2			
1866	5,785	1,002	5,041	2,995	369	933	3,761	757	103,670	275.7			
1867	5,993	728	5,240	2,182	50	854	3,279	515	88,603	358.0			
1868	6,416	600	5,430	2,137	327	930	2,202	1,575	86,722	349.3			
1869	6,433	794	5,884	2,444	701	990	2,527	1,703	71,790	421.2			
1870	6,706	720	5,896	1,750	558	708	2,766	1,338	56,526	405.0			
1871	6,125	782	5,926	1,309	490	516	2,349	1,531	46,766	406.1			
1872	5,195	853	4,427	1,348	95	479	2,133	2,195	41,756	364.9	19.8		
1873	5,293	638	3,945	756		342	2,096	2,966	40,285	343.2	69.6	7.0	2.1
1874	5,467	172	4,283	420		31	1,755	2,950	40,445	312.4	85.2	5.6	1.5
1875	6,006		4,243	532			1,515	2,962	39,393	490.9	133.2	3.3	
1876	6,157		4,357	650			1,390	2,980	43,016	693.3		2.2	
1877	6,468		4,822	673	8		1,126	2,978	39,225	494.5		14.4	
1878	6,102		4,380	442			249	2,562	36,871	678.6		19.4	
1879	6,049		3,400	597			84	2,300	30,371	564.6		9.2	
1880	5,872		2,694	188			64	1,926	26,737	416.0		6.4	
1881	5,185	227	2,694	179			119	835	24,510	504.9			0.4
1882	5,485	332	2,379	229			280	979	25,641	586.0		6.3	1.3
1883	3,016	418	1,776	89			303	933	23,252	549.1		17.3	5.7
1884	4,096	277	685	118			183	481	21,541	552.1		26.8	41.6
1885	3,436	122	50	61			52	1,802	19,736	596.0			52.4
1886	162	20	4	14					7,541	611.0			12.1
1887				102					3,422	786.0			58.8
1888				52						733.3		10.7	83.0
1889										775.3		44.0	102.3
1890										648.0		61.4	27.2
1891										483.9		128.9	
1892										603.7		67.7	
1893										576.7			
1894										458.4			
1895										278.7			
1896				96						261.0			
1897										265.2			
1898										90.6			
1899													
1900													
1901													
1902													
1903													
1904													
1905													
1906													
1907										10.2			
1908										16.2			
1909										26.3			
1910										24.2			
1911										14.0			
1912										2.2			
1913										6.6			

Caradon District figures taken from Burt, Waite & Burnley *Cornish Mines* 1987
All Cornwall figures taken from Louis, H. A. *Treatise on Ore Deposits* 1896

APPENDIX FOUR
LOCOMOTIVE & ROLLING STOCK DETAILS

LOCOMOTIVES

Name	Type	Manufacturer	No	Mfgr Date	Cost	Driving Wheels	Cylinders (in inches)	Disposal
Liskeard	0-4-0ST	Bury?	?	1838/46	£600	4/5ft	13/15in dia	? 1866/71
Caradon	0-6-0ST	Gilkes Wilson & Co	138	1862	£1,460	4ft	13x24in	Scrapped 1907
Cheesewring	0-6-0ST	Gilkes Wilson & Co	195	1864	£1,900	4ft	13x24in	GWR 1311 Wdn 1919
Kilmar	0-6-0ST	Hopkins Gilkes & Co	264	1869	£1,700	4ft	13x24in	GWR 1312 Wdn 1914
–	0-6-0ST	Peckett	444	1885	Hired	3ft 6½in	14x20in	Returned 1886
Looe	0-6-0ST	Robert Stephenson	3050	1901	£1,995	3ft 6in	16x20in	Sold 1902, Scr 1951
Lady Margaret	2-4-0T	Andrew Barclay	956	1902	£1,570	4ft	14½x22in	GWR 1308 Wdn 1948
GWR No 13	4-4-0ST	GWR	1094	1886	Hired	4ft 1½in	16x21in	Scrapped 1926
GWR 45xx	2-6-2T	GWR (for comparison)				4ft 7½in	17x24	

GOODS STOCK (in 1909)

Type	Capacity	Wheelbase	Body Length	Width	Height	Number	Running Numbers
Stone wagons	4 tons	5ft 9in	11ft	6ft 6in	11in	6	44-5, 48-9, 73-4
Open wagons	6 tons	5ft 6in	10ft 6in	6ft 3in	2ft	29	46-7, 50, 55-72, 75-8, 80-1, 83-4
	8 tons	5ft 6in	12ft 6ft	6in	2ft	1	87
	8 tons	7ft	13ft 6in	7ft	2ft	1	53 ex-GWR
	8 tons	7ft	12ft 9in	6ft	2ft 3in	1	79 under construction 1909
	6 tons	5ft 6in	10ft 6in	6ft 10in	3ft 6in	10	88-97 ex Bute Works Supply Co 1906
Van		5ft 10in	11ft 9in		5ft 9in	1	5
Covered van	3 tons	6ft	11ft	7ft	6ft 6in	1	7
Brakevan	10 tons	9ft	15ft 6in	7ft 5in	5ft 8in	1	9 ex-GWR 1903

PASSENGER STOCK

No	Type	Capacity	Manufacturer	Date	Wheelbase	Body Length	Height	Width		Disposal
1	Composite	28	MRC&W	1879	8ft 6in	16ft	6ft 3in	7ft 4in		Scr 1909
2	Composite	28	MRC&W	1880	8ft 6in	16ft	6ft 3in	7ft 4in		Scr 1909
3	Third	40	MRC&W	1879	10ft	19ft 5in	6ft 3in	7ft 4in		Scr 1909
4	Brake (Third)	10 ?	? ex-WCR		6ft 8in	13ft 2in				Scr 1909
6	Brake		MRC&W	?	5ft	10ft				Scr 1909
8	Brake		?	?	7ft 6in	13ft	6ft 6in	7ft		Scr 1909
1	Brake Composite	36	Hurst Nelson	1901					Sold 1904/6	Scr 1909
2	Brake third	40	Hurst Nelson	1901					Sold 1904/6	Destroyed 1906
3	Third	48	Hurst Nelson	1901					Sold 1904/6	Destroyed 1906
1	First	32	Ashbury	1885/8	15ft 6in	27ft	7ft 4in	8ft	GWR 8144/3977	Wdn 1917
2	Third brake	30	Ashbury	1885	15ft 6in	27ft	7ft 4in	8ft	GWR 3971	Wdn 1910
3	Composite	44	Ashbury	1885	15ft 6in	27ft	7ft 4in	8ft	GWR 6212/3975	Wdn 1917
4	Third	50	Ashbury	1885/8	15ft 6in	27ft	7ft 4in	8ft	GWR 3966	Wdn 1917
5	Third brake	30	Ashbury	1885/8	15ft 6in	27ft	7ft 4in	8ft	GWR 3972	Wdn 1917
6	Third brake	30	Ashbury	1885	15ft 6in	27ft	7ft 4in	8ft	GWR 3973	Wdn 1910
7	Third brake	30	Ashbury	1885	15ft 6in	27ft	7ft 4in	8ft	GWR 3974	Wdn 1910
8	Third	50	Ashbury	1885/8	15ft 6in	27ft	7ft 4in	8ft	GWR 3967	Wdn 1917
9	Third	50	Ashbury	1885/8	15ft 6in	27ft	7ft 4in	8ft	GWR 3968	Wdn 1910
10	Composite	44	Ashbury	1885	15ft 6in	27ft	7ft 4in	8ft	GWR 6213/3976	Wdn 1917
11	Third	50	Ashbury	1885/8	15ft 6in	27ft	7ft 4in	8ft		Destroyed 1906
12	Third	50	Ashbury	1885/8	15ft 6in	27ft	7ft 4in	8ft	GWR 3969	Wdn 1910
13	Third	50	Ashbury	1885/8	15ft 6in	27ft	7ft 4in	8ft	GWR 3970	Wdn 1910

APPENDIX FIVE
EARLY BYLAWS & REGULATIONS

LISKEARD & LOOE UNION CANAL COMPANY'S BYELAWS
At a special General Meeting of the Committee of Management held at the Guildhall in Liskeard on Tuesday the 30th day of September 1828 Rev. John Jope was named and elected Chairman
Resolved
That the following Rules Orders and Bye Laws having been read and approved be agreed to and adopted

1. That no person shall draw more water by any of the paddles or sluices of the Locks of this Navigation than shall be sufficient to fill the Chamber of any Lock for the convenient carriage of any Boat through the same nor draw any water out of one Pound of this Navigation to increase the water in another Pound and that every person who shall offend in either of the said particulars shall for every such offence forfeit and pay any sum not exceeding Five pounds nor less than Forty Shillings.
2. That no Boats shall be passed through the Locks at Tarras Pill on this Navigation of less measurement than Ten Tons nor above Sandplace of less measurement than Eighteen Tons, nor pass through any of the Locks above Sandplace before four o'clock in the morning nor after nine o'clock at night between the first of March and the first of November nor before six o'clock in the morning nor after six o'clock at night between the first of November and the first of March in every year without licence in writing from the Committee of Management first obtained, and that every person who shall offend in any of the said particulars shall forfeit and pay for every such offence any sum not exceeding Five pounds nor less than twenty shillings.
3. That if any person or persons navigating on the said Canal shall use any Shaft, Pole or other Instrument except the same be of six inches in diameter at the least at the end thereof to prevent the same penetrating into the banks of the canal every such person shall forfeit and pay for every such offence the sum of Ten Shillings.
4. That no person shall load or unload any goods in or upon any of the Stops, Locks, Aqueducts or Bridges of this Navigation under the penalty of Five Pounds for every such offence.
5. That no person shall raise the Sluices of the Locks of this Navigation before closing the Gates of such Locks intended to stop the water under the penalty of Five Pounds for every such offence.
6. That every person using this Canal shall draw the water out of every Lock immediately after passing through the same to the level of the Canal below (unless where there shall be an order of the Committee of Management to the contrary and unless where any Boat shall be in the level above and about to enter such Lock) under a penalty of Forty Shillings for every offence contrary to this Order.
7. That if any Boatman or other person shall suffer the horse or other Animal used in drawing the Boats on this Canal to brouse on the plants forming the fences of the Towing Paths or tow such Boats beyond the Guide Posts every such Boatman or other person shall forfeit and pay for every such offence Twenty Shillings.
8. That if any person or persons shall break down or damage any of the Gates, Stops or fences or leave open any Gate or other stop on the Towing Path of this Navigation or on the roads of the said Company or suffer any horse or other grazing beast to go loose on such Towing Path or roads every such person so offending shall forfeit and pay Twenty Shillings for every such offence.
9. That no person save a Shareholder in this Canal or other person engaged in the navigation thereof or labouring thereon shall go upon or use the Towing Path of this Navigation without leave in writing from the Committee of Management under the penalty of Twenty Shillings.
10. That if any Boat shall be navigated on this Canal without having the owners name painted on the stern thereof and the number by which the Committee of Management shall require such Boat to be distinguished painted on each side of the stern in white letters and figures on a black ground full four inches high and of proportionate breadth the person having the command of such Boat shall forfeit and pay Forty Shillings.

Peter Glubb, Clerk

LISKEARD & CARADON RAILWAY REGULATIONS
To be observed for the use of the Railway

1. That no Carriage used on the Railway shall pass over the line at a greater average rate than Eight miles an hour; nor shall, on any portion of the Line, exceed the rate of Twelve miles an hour; nor shall any Carriage when crossing any Public Carriage Way, exceed the rate of Six miles an hour. And that every Conductor of any Carriage which shall pass over any portion of the Line contrary to the above Regulations, shall for every such offence forfeit any sum not exceeding Five Pounds, unless the permission in writing of the Directors or their duly authorized Agent for the purpose be first obtained.
2. That every Conductor, when approaching any Highway, Turn Out, Curve, or Station, shall give such signals as the Directors may from time to time order to be given; and every Conductor offending against such Order shall, for every such offence, forfeit any sum not exceeding Forty Shillings.
3. That no person shall be allowed to act as the Conductor of any Carriage, unless he has previously received the approbation of the Directors; and every such Conductor shall carry with him a certificate of such approbation, and shall wear such Badge of his office as the Directors shall from time to time order to be worn. And every such Conductor shall show forth to either of the Directors or to any of their authorized Agents, when required so to do, such Certificate of approbation; and if any Conductor shall refuse so to do, or shall be found conducting a Carriage on the Line without wearing the Badge of his appointment in the manner required by the Directors, he shall forfeit for every such offence any sum not exceeding Forty Shillings.
4. That all Carriages passing over the Line shall be subject to such Regulations, and for the times of arrival at or departure from any Station, and for the use of the Turn Outs, as the company shall from time to time issue; such Regulations to be printed and affixed in some conspicuous part of each Station. And every Conductor who shall offend against such Regulations shall, for every such offence, forfeit any sum not exceeding Forty Shillings.
5. That not more than Five Tons weight shall be carried by any one Carriage over any portion of the Line without the express permission in writing of the Directors or the duly authorized Agents first having been obtained; and that every Conductor who shall offend against this Regulation shall, for every such offence, forfeit and pay any sum not exceeding Forty Shillings.
6. That no Carriage shall be on, or pass over, the Main Line at any time between one hour after Sunset and one hour before Sunrise; but Carriages delayed on the Line may be left in a Turn Out, and must join the Main Line at the earliest possible time, not interfering with the Company's Regulations for the times of arrival at and departure from any Station. And if any Conductor of any Carriage shall allow it to remain on the Main Line contrary to such Regulations, he shall forfeit and pay for every such offence any sum not exceeding Forty Shillings.

BY ORDER OF THE DIRECTORS
CHRISTR. CHILDS, Secretary
Dated, 18th day of December, 1844

APPENDIX SIX

Copy of letter from John Borlase Childs to the late A K Hamilton Jenkin 5 April 1929, by courtesy of the latter.
[The original spelling and punctuation have been retained.]

John Borlase Childs was born about 1846 and in 1877 succeeded his father, Christopher Childs, as Secretary of the Liskeard & Caradon Railway, a position he retained until 1909 when the company was taken over by the GWR. He practised in Liskeard as a Solicitor.

The Caradon Mines

The Liskeard & Looe Union Canal Co & The Liskeard & Caradon Railway

The Canal was opened in the Year 1828, and was 6 Miles long, from Tarras Pill 1½ miles above Looe where it joins the East Looe River, to Moorswater 1¼ miles from Liskeard. There were 24 locks each rising about 6 ft. The Liskeard & Caradon Railway was made about the year 1845. It was about 8¾ miles in length viz: from Moorswater, where it linked up with the Canal, to Cheeswring – 8¼ miles & and a branch to South Caradon Mine – ½ a mile. The gradient was about 1 in 60, except at Gonamena, not far from Cheeswring, where there was an incline of 1 in 11. This was worked by a chain the full wagons coming down dragging the empty ones up. The rails were not laid on wood sleepers but on granite blocks. The trucks were drawn up by horses, but ran down by gravitation.

I remember the Canal well. I was down at Moorswater one day with my Brother Walter fishing in one of the locks with worm. A Canal Boat from Looe entered the lock & we threw our rods & lines back, & watched the Barge go through the lock. When the barge had passed, we turned round to pick up our rods to resume our fishing. Alas! we had two large fowls on – the poor animals having swallowed the worms & hooks, and they had to be "killed to save their lives".

The barges brought up Coal & Pit-props &c & took back Copper, Lead, & tin ore & granit, & lime from the Moorswater & St Keyne Lime Kilns. My Father was Secretary of the Caradon Railway Co from 1856 or before, until his death in 1877. The Directors & a few friends used to have an expedition up the line to the mines & quarries once a year or occasionally, & I was, as a boy, invited to go once or twice. We started from Moorswater in two or three open trucks which had been swept & garnished, & provided with seats for the occasion. We had several horses to drag the wagons up. About middle-day we had a nice lunch, in the open if fine. Then in the evening we got on board the wagons again & returned to Moorswater. The man in charge of the trucks had a whistle which he blew lustily when we came to any crossings.

The Liskeard & Looe Union Canal Co was turned into a Railway Co about the year 18[59] but retained its name of the Liskeard & Looe Union Canal Co. As in the case of the Caradon Railway, the lines were laid on granit blocks, except the portion from Sandplace to Looe, which was on wood balks laid longways not crossways as at present. I saw the first Engine taken on a trolley from Liskeard G.W.Ry Station (then Cornwall Ry) to Moorswater. It was a bitterly cold day & there had been a heavy fall of snow.

Going down from Dean Street to Moorswater they put a drag on the Trolley, & had two long ropes tied on at the end of the trolley, with about 20 men on each rope. To regulate the pace. The drag made a beautiful slide on the snow, and every now & again the men on one rope or the other would step on the slide & all go sprawling, to my intense delight!

However they got the Engine down safely, though they took a long time to negotiate the Corner opposite the Inn at Moorswater. I dont know that Mine Host improved the shining hour! The Engine was called "Liskeard", & only had 4 wheels & the foot-plate was bobbing up & down all the time like an agitated see-saw. I think horse-haulage was discontinued for the Caradon Line from that time.

In the Canal days the barges went into a sort of lock at Moorswater which had the lines some 6 or 8ft above it. The Trucks for Ores had sloping sides to a trap door in the middle of the bottom. The trucks were put into position over the barges & then the trap door was opened & the ore fell into the barges.

The Mines I remember that were being worked in my young days were South Caradon (Copper), West Caradon (Copper), Phoenix (tin & Copper), East Caradon (Copper) & Marke Valley (Copper), and Wheal Mary Ann in Menheniot Parish (Lead). The Ores were all taken to Looe & put on East Looe Quay. I have often seen the Quay covered with thousands of pounds-worth of Ore of different sorts, at a time. The Ores when being weighed were put into two-handed barrows & carried by two men to the weighing machine, where it was weighed by a man called Cap: Climo (but nicknamed "Cap Fust-day", as he was a Quaker). If the amount of Ore in the barrow was not quite up to weight, Climo said to one of the men "a little bit more – a little bit more – AND CARRY".

The men then took the barrow to the heap that had been weighed where a boy stood ready with a wooden hammer with a long handle. The men turned the barrow up-side-down &, exactly as it was up-side-down, the boy brought the hammer smartly down on the bottom of the barrow & shouted "1", "2" "3", &c as the no. might be & when it had got to 5, I think, he shouted "tally". At each call of the boy Climo made a white chalk mark on the post that supported the Scales, up to 4, & at "tally" put a line across the other 4 lines. When a Ship was being loaded at the Quay, the ore was taken from the weighed heaps in wheel barrows. Planks were run out over the hold of the ship & the Ore was wheeled out on the planks & tipped – a scaffolding pole being put along side of the plank to prevent the barrow from falling into the hold. Having emptied his barrow the man went to the further end of the plank & tipped his barrow with the handles perpendicular, & so the next man, until there were 4 or 5 men on the plank. They then all turned round in turn & wheeled back again for another barrowful. It was very strenuous work & the muscles of the mens arms were as hard as steel. They would allow an Amatateure to try his hand at wheeling one of the barrows, but if he spilt a bit of the Ore he was fined a 1s/-. Looe Schooners took the Ore to Swansea to be smelted and brought back Coal.

South Caradon was the richest Mine in the district. My Father, in order that he might be able to attend the Meetings of the share holders & look after the interests of "the Lord" (Mr Norris) bought one share at £300. The Shares went up to £500. Many of the old Ladies in

Liskeard invested their little all in the Undertaking, thinking at was a little gold mine. After my Fathers death I sold the Share for £20 & the man I sold it to disposed of it after, I heard, for £1. Many of the poor old Ladies were pretty well ruined. I have always understood that there is plenty of Copper still left in South Caradon, but that it is too deep down to pay to work, owing to Foreign competition. The Cheesewring granit is noted all the world over, & large quantities were supplied for Westminster Bridge, Portland Breakwater, &c. & more recently for the Thames Embankment, & the Mole at Gibraltar. A good deal of it used to be polished at Moorswater before being sent away. I have seen the polishing plant there.

About 28 years ago the Looe Railway was joined up to the G.W.Ry at Liskeard by a short line from Coombe, on the Looe line, to Liskeard Station. This was opened for Passenger traffic on the 15th May 1901.

The granit blocks were long since taken away & replaced by wooden sleepers. The rails of the Caradon Ry were taken up & sent to France during the great War & have never been replaced – to the great detriment of the local roads, as all the heavy granit traffick has to go to Liskeard & Moorswater by road.

The Directors of the Canal used to have a days fishing in the Canal about once a year. The water was let out from the Canal and men went in with two-handed nets of regulation legal mesh & scoop up the Salmon Peel. But as many of the fish were small enough to get through the legal mesh, another man went behind the big net with a shrimping net to make sure that some fish were secured for their Lordships lunch. The fish were taken to "the Bullers Arms" Hotel at Sandplace (now a private residence) & cooked for lunch. I was a guest at one or two of these lawbreaking entertainments!

APPENDIX SEVEN
PRINCIPAL MINES OF CARADON HILL

These notes give a brief summary of the major mines around and north of Caradon Hill. There are enormous gaps in our knowledge of many of the mines, and contemporary evidence is often conflicting, particularly regards engines. The route of the Liskeard & Caradon Railway, which either served or ran close to all the mines, is the ideal way to view them. Do remember that old mines can be dangerous places. Where known depths of shafts are given in fathoms, and this should also serve as a warning to keep safely away.

Caradon, East (Copper) SX 277 703
1840 trial. 1851 restarted and became profitable in 1860. Branch from LCR opened in 1861. Mining ceased 1885 with the closure of South Caradon.
Remains: Count house, some buildings, much demolished.
Shafts: William's (150), Seccombe's (110), North Engine (84).
Production: 1860-1885 54,049 tons Copper

Caradon, Glasgow (Copper) SX 282 703
Started in 1841 as Tokenbury mine, restarted in 1850 as Tokenbury & Yolland. In1860 a new company opened it as Glasgow Caradon Consols, Glasgow being the home town of many of the investors. £40,000 invested by 1870. 1885 closure. Briefly reopened 1889-1890 with South Caradon.
Remains: Count house, some walls of engine houses.
Shafts: Dunlop's (78), Elliott's (126).
Production: 1864-1885 38,018 tons Copper

Caradon, South (Copper) SX 264 699 to 274 699
Sett taken up 1833 by Clymo and Kittow families and ore struck 1836. Initial capital of £640 (worth £30,000 today) remained unchanged as all subsequent investment was paid for out of copper sold. Vast sett stretching over three-quarters of a mile east-west and a mile north-south, with eleven lodes. Initial development in Seaton valley, where LCR had siding from 1844, but extended eastwards to Rule's and Kittow's shafts. Lease surrendered 1883 but a new limited company bought the mine for £16,000. Closed 1885, due to overseas competition forcing copper prices down, and the stoppage of pumping closed the adjacent mines. On closure the mine had 13 engines of various types, ranging from 70-inch pumping to a 23-inch man-engine, and more than 3,000 fathoms of tram rails, both underground and at surface. By 1883 £1,650,000 of ore had been sold, £384,510 paid in dividends and over £90,000 in lord's (mineral) dues.
Remains: Numerous engine houses and ruins of count house and other buildings on dressing floors.
Shafts: Engine (250), Pearce's (100), Jope's (140), Clymo's (120), North Engine (230), Rule's (210), Kittow's (210, 110, 60), etc.
Production: 1845-1885 202,208 tons Copper

Caradon, West (Copper) SX 263 701
Started 1837, became profitable 1841 after expenditure of £6,000 and surpassed South Caradon for a time. Ten lodes. Connected to the LCR Cheesewring branch by a short steep incline. Ran out of steam in the mid-1860s and closed 1874. Reopened 1881-1886.
Remains: Count house
Shafts: Crouch's (104), Fox's, Marina (66), Hallet's (80+), Elliott's, Footway
Production: 1845-1886 85,012 tons Copper

Cornwall Great United Mining Association (Tin)
An 1836 attempt to work several mining setts, including Phoenix and Jenkin, by a London based concern that also controlled mines in the west. Despite spending over £50,000 they were unsuccessful and remote management appears to have been to blame. James Clymo and Thomas Kittow were involved locally.

Craddock Moor (Copper) SX 257 701
Started 1844, hoping to build on the success of its neighbours to the south, and worked intermittently until 1873. Some profits were made but it was never a great success.
Remains: Ruined engine houses
Shafts: Harris's (100), Main (100).
Production: 1856-1874 20,141 tons Copper

Gonamena (Copper) SX 253 704
Vast streamwork dating from at least 1662. Much faulting in the Seaton valley with shifted lodes made mining difficult. Several attempts were made at working the sett but they were never very successful and abandonment came in 1872.
Remains: Large tinwork, ruined engine house wall.
Production: 1848-1872 9,685 tons Copper

Jenkin, Wheal (Tin) SX 266 712
1836-37 Worked by Cornwall Great United Mining Association (CGUMA).
Re-opened 1881 by Marke Valley. Whim Shaft reopened as Bellinghams with a 70-inch engine erected in 1886. Closed 1890. Dressing floors to north, across LCR.
Remains: Engine house, dressing floors.
Principal shaft: Bellinghams (117).
Production: 1881-1890 384.8 tons Tin

Marke Valley (Copper) SX 277 717
Early workings were in 1828 (Tin) with 50-foot water wheel. Re-opened in 1837 for copper. Main period of working was from 1840. First dividend 1852. Several water wheels in use but methods of working were very behind the times. Connected to LCR 1877 but then in decline. Moved emphasis to Wheal Jenkin in 1880s.
Remains: Ruined engine houses
Shafts: Salisbury (148), Engine (112), Fawcett (100).
Production: 1845-1886 128,740 tons Copper

Phoenix (Copper & Tin) SX 255 723 to 266 723
Working with a Newcomen engine in 1730 and also 1807-1825, probably for tin.
In 1836 the Cornwall Great United Mining Association was seeking tin here and in several adjoining setts but was unsuccessful. Local shareholders took over part of the sett in 1842, renaming it Phoenix, and sought copper which was eventually found in quantity in 1852, after £12,000 had been spent. In 1861 machinery was installed to process tin, which was unusually found alongside the copper, and this became more important. Having provided much of the machinery William West acquired a controlling interest in 1868 and, using ten steam engines of various types, he concentrated on tin production from a sett a mile east-west and 500 fathoms north-south. In 1869 a branch of the LCR was brought in. The West Phoenix sett was taken over in 1870, the mine becoming a major tin producer. Falling tin prices brought liquidation in 1894 and in 1898 the mine closed, the twelve engines on the site being scrapped.
Sales: 1843-1882 £393,00 Tin, £432,000 Copper.
Remains: Account house and other offices, dressing floors.
Shafts: Polkinhorne's (70), New Engine (135), Stowe's (85), Hamilton's (48), West's (135), Old Sump (212), Seccombe's (225), etc
Production: 1848-1888 80,092 tons Copper, 1854-1898 16,658 tons Tin

Phoenix, South (Tin) SX 261 715
1830s Wheal Prosper, part of Cornwall Great United Mining Association.
1847 restarted for copper, four or five lodes, little record.
1862 reworking for copper, 1870-1875 tin, 1880-1884 intermittently for tin, 1887-1892, 1906-1910 tin
In 1853 a 50-inch pumping engine installed on Houseman's shaft. The 1887 company resank Houseman's, put a new shaft at Prosper, recut Parson's as an incline and installed the new dressing floors. In 1907 the sett was taken by Cornwall Consolidated Tin Mines.
Remains: Houseman's engine house (now visitor centre), dry, dressing floors.
Shafts: Houseman's (45), Prosper, Parson's.
Production: 1873-1892 430.6 tons Tin

Phoenix United (Tin) X 266 720
1907 Cosmopolitan Proprietary Co Ltd (Australian) took Phoenix sett.
1909 Phoenix United Mines (Cornwall) Ltd (Cornish) took over.
Capitals of £100,000 and £160,000 respectively.
Commenced new shaft 1907 and ordered a new 80-inch pumping engine from Holman's, designed by Nicholas Trestrail. Engine officially started 9 June 1909 by HRH Prince of Wales (later George V) and shaft named after him. Other shafts were cleared but little tin was produced and in 1914 the mine closed. The Duchy (mineral lords) bought the engine and retained it until 1935 when it was scrapped.
Remains: Fine engine house, winder, boiler, compressor houses.
Shafts: Prince of Wales (200), Seccombe's, Stowe's, Old Sump
Production: 1907-1913 99.7 tons Tin

INDEX

Accidents 17, 22, 37, 70, 71, 74, 76, 138, 146 et seq.
Acts & Bills 11-12, 21-2, 27, 30, 36, 48-9, 52, 54-7, 64, 66-7, 72, 81, 84
Altarnun 47, 54
Banka Mill 12, 15
Bearah Quarry branch 47, 119-21
Beeching Report 88
Boats, canal 12, 14, 17-18, 20, 24
Boscastle 55
British Association 44
Byelaws 14, 28, 29, 163
Callington 47, 56
Calstock 21, 34, 39
Camelford 55
Canal Cross 109
Causeland 10, 50, 73, 90, 93, 98, 152
Cheesewring branch 27-8, 30-1, 33, 35-6, 110, 115
Cheesewring Quarry 22, 26, 29, 31, 34, 45, 47, 49, 52, 61, 64, 72, 74, 84, 116-19
China clay 45, 72-3, 84, 86, 90, 92-3, 108
Coombe 7, 12, 71, 75, 87-8, 90-1, 93, 100-2, 149-50
Craddock Moor branch 37, 111, 113
Crylla feeder 12, 14, 20, 23, 72
Darite 58, 64, 110-11
Dividends 17-19, 31, 34, 56, 62, 67, 74, 84
Duchy of Cornwall 14, 21, 25, 28, 42, 84
East Caradon branch 37, 113
East Cornwall Bank 20, 30, 80
East Looe Valley Improvement Society 153
Employees 17, 29, 31, 38, 62, 69, 82, 83, 86, 145-6
Extension Railway 66 et seq., 101, 152
Freeman & Sons 45, 47, 49, 52, 60, 61, 84, 105, 117, 119-21
Gold Diggings Quarry 54
Gonamena 30, 31, 36, 46-8, 112-13
Gravity power 8, 26, 30, 35, 36, 63, 132
High Wood 15, 28, 108
Inclined planes, canal 10
Inclined planes, railway 16, 27, 31, 36, 67, 107, 112-13
Junction Railway 66-7, 100
Kilmar Junction Railway 47, 52, 54, 114, 151
Kilmar Railway 8, 34 et seq., 47, 52, 84, 117-21, 150
Kilmar Tor 34, 120-1
Lamellion 19, 20, 104
Landlooe 12, 52, 98
Launceston 47, 54, 56, 57
Launceston Railway 64, 79
Lerryn 19
Light railway 8, 49
Lime kilns and trade 9, 14, 16, 17, 19, 56, 96-7, 99, 104, 106-7
Liskeard 9, 23, 25, 36, 66, 70, 75, 80, 81, 86, 88-92, 103-5, 150
Litigation 14, 20, 23, 71, 74
Locks 10, 13, 18, 21, 98, 101, 104
Locomotives 23, 37, 122 et seq., 162
   Liskeard 37, 122-3

   Caradon 37, 71, 76, 82, 108, 123-4, 127, 152
   Cheesewring 37, 59, 60, 62, 65, 124-7
   Kilmar 45, 53, 62, 70, 75, 125-7
   Peckett 444 62, 128
   Looe 70, 71, 73, 128-30, 147
   Lady Margaret 73, 129-131, 148
   GWR No 13 73, 82, 129, 132
   Sharon 90
   Diesel power 88, 92-3, 102, 132
Looe 6, 14, 17, 19, 22, 23, 33, 34, 37-9, 45, 46, 48-50, 53, 55, 58, 63-5, 67, 70, 79, 80, 85-6, 88-91, 94-5, 140, 148, 150, 153
Looe Harbour Commissioners 20, 22, 34, 38 et seq., 45, 94, 151
Looe Valley Line Working Party 91, 153
Lostwithiel 11, 12
Marke Valley branch 47, 114
Menheniot 67
Mine finance 25, 42
Mine machinery 32, 42, 55
Miners 32, 45, 53, 61
Mines:
   Caradon, East 25, 35, 37, 39, 42, 45, 47, 55, 61, 63, 72, 113-4, 142, 161, 165
   Caradon, Glasgow 35, 47, 55, 61, 63, 161, 165
   Caradon, South 25, 26, 28, 31, 33, 35, 40-42, 44-5, 47-8, 53, 55, 57, 61, 63, 111, 142-3, 161, 165
   Caradon, West 25, 26, 28, 31, 33, 35, 37, 39, 42, 45, 48, 53, 55, 58, 61, 63, 110-11, 113, 161, 165
   Cornwall Great United 18, 25, 31, 42, 165
   Craddock Moor 32, 37, 39, 113, 161, 165
   Drakewalls 14, 17
   Jenkin 114, 165
   Marke Valley 31, 35, 39, 42, 45-7, 52, 55, 63, 114, 119, 161, 165
   Mary Ann 38
   Phoenix 31, 39, 42 et seq., 52, 55, 62, 63, 76-8, 83 et seq., 115, 119, 161, 165
   Phoenix, South 76-7, 115, 119, 161, 165
   Minor mines 17, 32
Minions (see also Rillaton) 28, 35, 62, 115-6, 118, 153
Moorswater 8, 11, 12, 15-17, 19-21, 23, 27, 29-31, 45, 49, 50-2, 56-8, 60-1, 65-6, 72, 75, 85-6, 88, 90-1, 104-8, 148
Nicholls Williams & Co 132
Northern Extension 54, 56, 61, 62, 64, 79, 82, 119
North Kilmar branch 113, 121
Passenger traffic 44, 49, 50, 47-9, 64, 73-5, 82, 86, 135, 159-60
Permanent way 8, 22, 35, 49, 58, 69, 76, 79, 82, 84, 150-2
Phoenix tramway and branch 31, 35, 54, 72, 84, 118-9, 150
Polwrath 27, 57, 58, 110
Railways (other than LCR and LLR):
   Bodmin & Wadebridge 29, 47, 56, 73, 113
   British Railways 88 et seq.
   Cornwall & Devon Central 19, 47

167

INDEX

Cornwall Railway 19, 21, 22, 27, 30, 36, 47, 48, 64, 66, 103, 120, 143
Great Eastern 69, 74, 144
Great Western 47, 56, 64, 67, 79, 81, 82 et seq., 133, 145
Launceston, Bodmin & Wadebridge 44
Lindsay Light Railway Syndicate Ltd 137
London & Birmingham 122
London & South Western 44, 47, 52, 55, 56, 61, 79-81
Mersey 73, 137
North Cornwall 54, 55, 57, 61, 79
Pentewan 29
Rhondda & Swansea Bay 138
Temple Mineral 73
Wales & West 93
West Cornwall 138
Rillaton 58, 62, 79, 114-5, 118-9
Roads 12, 15, 19, 26, 141
Rolling stock 22, 29, 34, 36, 59, 64, 69, 70, 73, 75, 132 et seq., 162
St Blazey 90, 93
St Cleer 82-3, 109-10, 147
St Germans 9, 17, 19, 21, 48, 86
St Germans Direct line 86
St Keyne 73, 99
St Neot Clay Co. 72
Sandplace 10, 11, 14, 17, 20, 23, 24, 49, 50, 58, 64, 73, 88, 97, 147, 153
Saxby & Farmer 148
Sea-sand 17
Sharptor 84, 119
Signalling 64, 88, 104, 148-50
Stow's Hill (see also Cheesewring Quarry) 18, 25
Tees Engine Works 123
Terras 11, 12, 14, 17, 20, 22, 23, 24, 47, 89, 90, 96, 150-1
Tickets 54, 90
Timetables 51, 61, 64, 84, 87
Tokenbury branch 26, 27, 29, 35-7, 46, 47, 58, 84, 112-14, 150
Tolls 14, 17-19, 27, 30, 36, 37, 45, 48, 61
Traffic working 29-30, 34, 64, 72, 74, 86
Tregarland 17, 22, 98
Tremabe 27-8, 109-10, 152
Trewint 52, 54-7, 61, 120
Treworgey 78, 109
Turnpike, Liskeard 9, 15, 28, 141
Woodhill 45, 109

People:
Abbott, Samuel 27, 141
Allen, John 27, 141
Bentley, George 10-11
Bolton, Thomas 10
Bowden, John 17, 19
Buller, John 11-14, 17-18, 21, 34, 141
Buller, John Francis 21, 23-4, 49, 96
Castle, Barbara 88
Caunter, Henry 55
Chambers, J. A. 69, 141
Charlesworth, Arthur 80

Childs, Christopher 28, 141
Childs, John Borlase 57, 61, 63, 141, 163
Clogg, John 27, 31
Clymo, James 18, 25, 27, 42, 141-2
Clymo, Peter 18, 22, 25, 27, 42, 141-2
Coad, Robert 10-12, 15, 26-9, 31, 141, 143
Collins, Wilkie 33, 112
Crouch, E. A. 27, 31
Edgcumbe, John 12
Eliot, Lord 10-13
Esterbrook, Thomas 12
Foster, Lewis Charles 55, 62-4, 67, 71, 79-81. 100, 142, 144
Fox, Francis 54
Galbraith, W. R. 57
Geach, Edward 20, 27, 141-2
Gilbert, Davies 12
Glencross, William 17
Glubb, Peter 10-13, 18, 141
Green, James 10-11, 14
Hawke, Richard 63, 142-3
Hawker, John S. 42, 53, 55, 58, 142-3
Hodge, William 16, 17
Holbrook, H. H. 69, 71, 74, 82, 126, 144
Hopkins, Evan 20
Howard, John 18, 144
Isaac, J. C. 58
Jenkins, Silvanus W. 21, 27, 28, 31, 36, 44, 47, 57, 58, 66, 69, 73, 82, 98, 122, 143, 148
Kittow, Richard 27, 42, 142
Kittow, Thomas 27, 42, 142
Lang, T. & Son 69
Leach, Edmund 9
Lyne, B. H. 12, 27, 31, 141
Marsh, Edward 75-6,
Moorsom, W. S. 27
Murphy, James 22, 37, 122, 133
Norris, G. P. 26, 27, 36, 42, 53, 142
Pease, William 23
Pringle, Sir William 12, 13
Rean, Robert 12
Retallick, Richard 11-12, 18, 20, 27, 141
Rice, Henry 28
Rich, Col. J. H. 49, 57
Sansom, John 103
Seccombe, Samuel 31, 42
Smith, W. P. 136, 138
Smythurst, J. H. 49, 56, 144
Spicer, Capt. J. E. P. 68, 74, 79, 81, 129, 144
Thomas, Joseph 67-8, 71, 95, 128, 143-4
Trathan, J. J. 21, 28, 31, 47, 49, 128, 143-4
Tregelles, Nathaniel 31
Tregenna, Charles 17, 38, 45
Trethewey, John 25, 29, 31, 117
Uren, Joseph 138, 145
West, William 39, 42, 55, 63